International Human Resource Management

International Human Resource Management offers a contemporary and multilayered introduction to international and comparative human resource management for university study. It critically analyses the core issues and emerging trends in the field, with a consistent emphasis on real-world scenarios and concerns.

At the macro level, the book examines how IHRM fits within and adapts to the ever-changing environment of international relations and global development. At the firm level, it elucidates the strategic goals served by IHRM, and the processes used to achieve them. At the individual level, the analysis extends beyond the traditional focus on expatriates to encompass the various IHRM actors and their motivations.

With contributors drawn from universities across four continents, this book presents a genuinely international perspective on IHRM. Each chapter features a case study, tutorial activities and discussion questions. The book concludes with three extended case studies, each based on a specific region, to help students consolidate their understanding.

Comprehensive online resources, including an instructor's manual and review material for students, are available at www.cambridge.edu.au/academic/IHRM.

Mustafa F. Özbilgin holds professorships at Brunel Business School, Brunel University in London, Université Paris-Dauphine and Koç University in Istanbul.

Dimitria Groutsis is Senior Lecturer in Work and Organisational Studies, University of Sydney.

William S. Harvey is Senior Lecturer at the University of Exeter Business School and Associate Fellow in the Centre for Corporate Reputation at the University of Oxford.

International Human Resource Management

Edited by

MUSTAFA F. ÖZBILGIN
DIMITRIA GROUTSIS
AND
WILLIAM S. HARVEY

CAMBRIDGE
UNIVERSITY PRESS

CAMBRIDGE
UNIVERSITY PRESS

477 Williamstown Road, Port Melbourne, VIC 3207, Australia

Published in the United States of America by Cambridge University Press, New York

Cambridge University Press is part of the University of Cambridge.

It furthers the University's mission by disseminating knowledge in the pursuit of education, learning, and research at the highest international levels of excellence.

www.cambridge.org
Information on this title: www.cambridge.org/9781107669543

© Cambridge University Press 2014

First published 2014
Reprinted 2016

Cover designed by Kerry Cooke, eggplant communications
Typeset by Integra Software Services Pvt. Ltd
Printed in Singapore by C.O.S Printers Pte Ltd

A catalogue record for this publication is available from the British Library

A Cataloguing-in-Publication entry is available from the catalogue of the National Library of Australia at www.nla.gov.au

ISBN 978-1-107-66954-3 Paperback

Additional resources for this publication at www.cambridge.edu.au/academic/IHRM

We would like to dedicate this book to all those who live or dream of living a life elsewhere. And to some special friends who have shaped our lives.

To Ayala Malach Pines, a boundless source of inspiration as a colleague, friend and confidante.

To George Groutsis, the eternal storyteller. Remembered always, never forgotten.

To the Harveys: Ruth, Robert, Pippa and George, the rocks of my life.

Contents

Contributors   *viii*
Acknowledgements   *x*

Introduction: a multilevel approach to international human resource management   1
Mustafa F. Özbilgin, Dimitria Groutsis and William S. Harvey

1   Global trends in international human resource management   6
Yasin Rofcanin, H. Pinar Imer and Matthew Zingoni

2   Cross-cultural and diversity management intersections: lessons for attracting and retaining international assignees   23
Dimitria Groutsis, Eddy S. Ng and Mustafa Bilgehan Ozturk

3   Key players in international human resource management   47
Graham Hollinshead, Cynthia Forson, Natalia Rocha-Lawton and Moira Calveley

4   Recruitment and selection in the international context   67
Kristina Potočnik, Maria Felisa Latorre Navarro, Beliz Dereli and Blanka Tacer

5   Cross-cultural training and development for overseas assignments   93
Aykut Berber, Yasin Rofcanin and Yitzhak Fried

6   International reward   108
Glenville Jenkins

7   Employee retention   128
Maria Balta

8   International labour relations   148
Mustafa F. Özbilgin

9   Reputation in the international context   165
William S. Harvey

10   Expatriation and repatriation in the Asia–Pacific region   179
Valerie Caven, Susan Kirk and Cindy Wang-Cowham

11   Balancing inflows and outflows in the European context   194
Joana Vassilopoulou, Barbara Samaluk and Cathrine Seierstad

12   Self-initiated expatriation: case study lessons from Africa and the United States   214
Ahu Tatli, Daphne Berry, Gulce Ipek and Kurt April
Conclusion   236
Mustafa F. Özbilgin, Dimitria Groutsis and William S. Harvey

Index   *244*

■ Contributors

Kurt April is Sainsbury Fellow and Professor of Leadership, Diversity and Inclusion at the Graduate School of Business of the University of Cape Town, an Associate Fellow of Said Business School, University of Oxford, Research Fellow of Ashridge Business School, Faculty Member of Duke Corporate Education, Duke University, USA, and Visiting Professor at Rotterdam School of Management, Erasmus University, the Netherlands.

Maria Balta is Lecturer in Strategy and Work Placement Director at Brunel Business School.

Aykut Berber is Associate Professor at Istanbul University.

Daphne Berry is Assistant Professor of Management at the Barney School of Business, University of Hartford.

Moira Calveley is Principal Lecturer in Human Resource Management and a member of the Work and Employment Research Unit at Hertfordshire Business School, University of Hertfordshire.

Valerie Caven is Senior Lecturer in Human Resource Management at Nottingham Business School.

Beliz Dereli is Associate Professor in the Faculty of Commercial Sciences at the Istanbul Commerce University.

Cynthia Forson is Head of the Department of Management Leadership and Organisation at the Hertfordshire Business School, University of Hertfordshire.

Yitzhak Fried is Professor of Management, Whitman School of Management, Syracuse University.

Dimitria Groutsis is Senior Lecturer in Work and Organisational Studies, School of Business, University of Sydney.

William S. Harvey is Senior Lecturer at the University of Exeter Business School and an Associate Fellow in the Centre for Corporate Reputation at the University of Oxford.

Graham Hollinshead is Reader in International and Comparative Human Resource Management at the Hertfordshire Business School, University of Hertfordshire.

H. Pinar Imer works at Department of Business Administration, Kadir Has University in Istanbul, Turkey.

Gulce Ipek is a PhD student in the School of Business and Management at Queen Mary University of London.

Glenville Jenkins is Head of Postgraduate Research at Swansea Business School, University of Wales Trinity St David. He is also the CIPD's Chief Examiner in Employee Reward and a CIPD External Moderator.

Susan Jane Kirk is Senior Lecturer in Organisational Behaviour, Organisation Theory and Human Resource Management at Nottingham Trent University.

Maria Felisa Latorre Navarro is Associate Professor at ITAM University of Mexico and a researcher at IDOCAL Institute, University of Valencia.

Eddy S. Ng is Associate Professor at Dalhousie University, Canada.

Mustafa F. Özbilgin is Professor of Organisational Behaviour and Human Resource Management at Brunel University in London. He also holds chairs at Université Paris-Dauphine and Koç University in Istanbul.

Mustafa Bilgehan Ozturk is Senior Lecturer at Middlesex University Business School.

Kristina Potočnik is Lecturer in Human Resource Management at the University of Edinburgh Business School.

Natalia Rocha-Lawton is Lecturer in Human Resource Management and a member of the Work and Employment Research Unit at Hertfordshire Business School, University of Hertfordshire.

Yasin Rofcanin is a PhD student in Organization and HRM at the Warwick Business School, University of Warwick.

Barbara Samaluk is a PhD researcher at the Centre for Research in Equality and Diversity (BUSMAN) at Queen Mary University of London.

Cathrine Seierstad is Lecturer in International Human Resource Management at the School of Business, Management and Economics, University of Sussex.

Blanka Tacer is research assistant in the Department of Entrepreneurship at the University of Primorska, Slovenia.

Ahu Tatli is is Senior Lecturer at Queen Mary University of London.

Joana Vassilopoulou is Lecturer in Organisational Behaviour and Human Resource Management at the School of Business, Management and Economics, University of Sussex.

Cindy Wang-Cowham is Senior Lecturer in Human Resource Management at the Nottingham Business School, Nottingham Trent University.

Matthew Zingoni is Assistant Professor of Human Resources at the University of New Orleans.

▪ Acknowledgements

We are deeply grateful to the many authors of this book, spread throughout the world, who came together to create this unique text about international human resource management. We thank you all for your hard work, dedication, patience and good humour throughout the development of the book. We are extremely indebted to David Jackson, Jessica Pearce and Bridget Ell at Cambridge University Press for their tireless encouragement and support throughout. Bridget was key in initiating and proposing the text, and David and Jessica have been particularly important in helping us to develop and complete the manuscript. We are grateful for their efforts, without which the book would have taken much longer to develop. We would also like to thank Katy McDevitt AE for her outstanding copyediting and suggestions for this book. Finally, we sincerely thank the unnamed reviewers from academia and the human resource profession who commented on early drafts and who provided support and constructive suggestions, which have helped enrich the quality of the book.

Introduction: a multilevel approach to international human resource management

Mustafa F. Özbilgin,
Dimitria Groutsis
and William S. Harvey

International human resource management (IHRM) is a set of management interventions and activities crafted for the effective practice of recruitment, retention, deployment, development and use of human resources in an international context. The study of IHRM requires attention to the relationships that shape the dynamics of inputs, processes and outputs of human resource management (HRM) among a set of actors at international, national, sectoral, organisational, team and individual levels. The multiplicity of key actors and complexity of relationships often complicate our understanding of how IHRM policy and practice develop. To overcome this complexity, we offer a multilevel and multidimensional approach to the study of IHRM.

■ Towards a multilevel approach to IHRM

In this book, we present a novel multilevel approach to the study of IHRM, incorporating in each chapter the macro-, meso- and micro-levels at which IHRM policy is shaped, negotiated, refined and practised.

■ *Macro-level concerns*

At the macro-level, we explore four central concerns. First, we examine the context of global and international relations for IHRM, guided by the stage of a company's internationalisation and the type of business concern it represents. We incorporate definitions and explanations of the simple import–export relationship, joint ventures, mergers and acquisitions as well as expansion into foreign markets such as offshoring and outsourcing, in exploring how macro-level drivers are operationalised in meso-level organisational policy and practice. We also examine globalisation and provide an in-depth assessment of what the increased mobility of financial capital, goods, services and people means for IHRM in practice. Second, we outline the relations between foreign markets and governments as well as between key stakeholders in multiple business entities. Third, we assess the workings of international labour standards, laws, policies and processes in play between host, home and third countries. Fourth, we present a substantive debate on ethical issues and dilemmas, guided by debates on localisation versus standardisation and global convergence or divergence.

■ *Meso-level concerns*

At the meso-level, chapters focus on implications and concerns of organisational infrastructure, primarily examining them across two dimensions: first, we study organisational resources (financial, human, social and cultural) by examining short, medium and long-term agendas and strategic versus reactive approaches. Second, we scrutinise IHRM processes, including recruitment and selection, from the perspective of the host-country national (HCN), the parent-country national (PCN) and the third-country national (TCN) as well as the high-skilled migrant. We take into account workforce planning; training and development; cross-cultural training; cross-cultural awareness; diversity management; performance management; remuneration; repatriation, international labour relations (ILR), corporate social responsibility, corporate reputation and international laws and standards.

■ Micro-level concerns

Our micro-level assessment of IHRM concerns focuses on the international assignee from three dimensions. First, we examine different types of expatriate (also known as PCNs), HCNs, TCNs, business travellers and self-identified migrants. Second, we account for increased demand for skills internationally (global 'war for talent'). Third, we identify the demographic 'faultlines' that international managers must consider in the recruitment and selection process; the management of international talent; and the expectations both of management and international assignees themselves.

■ Interplay between levels

Our novel multilevel and multidimensional approach enables a focus on the interplay between the three levels of macro, meso and micro concerns. Recognising this, we explore a number of demographic shifts, including changes in generational patterns, gender dynamics, work–life arrangements and migration repertoires, as well as social, economic and political transformations around demographic change. We illustrate how organisational policies interpret such macro-level demographic changes and change them for individual employees.

The multilevel approach to IHRM is useful in bringing together three levels of consideration, previously treated separately in the literature: first, international links between the home and host country; second, the organisational expectations and requirements of the home and host countries; and third, the individual expectations, requirements and characteristics of the international assignees.

Our multilevel framework offers a comprehensive understanding of the role of human resource (HR) managers in the international context. In providing this understanding, we bridge the gap between two IHRM literatures that have been polarised between a bird's-eye view of IHRM drivers in the global context and a more limited view of IHRM as merely a set of issues for expatriate management. We do so by exploring the interplay between organisational, team and individual-level considerations, in the context of international and national drivers, rules and regulatory pressures.

■ How is this book innovative?

This book seeks to innovate in several ways. First, we extend the literature beyond the traditional focus on understanding HRM processes in the international context. Second, we examine the role of HCNs and TCNs as well as changing immigration policies, which enable the international mobility of skilled migrants (SMs), such as 'self-initiated expatriates' (SIEs), who have been little-scrutinised to date. Here, we also provide insights into the definition of expatriates by disaggregating them along multiple identity lines. Third, we transcend the limited focus of cross-cultural management by considering the importance of diversity management techniques and strategies, in the context of IHRM responsibilities within and between different spatial contexts. Fourth, we depict regional trends, including details on labour mobility, activity in multinational companies (MNCs) and IHRM processes in practice in multiple geographic contexts. Fifth, we provide students with a useful source book, linking them to the latest data and information from a variety of sources. Finally, we engage students with the business media, as we link chapters to current public events reported in the high-quality business media as a way of encouraging students to interact critically with contemporary debates in the press.

Accessibility

While this text is pitched at undergraduate students, it is also intended to be accessible to postgraduates, practitioners and scholars new to the field. Key concepts from the IHRM literature are clearly defined, helping readers to grasp core ideas and practices from the field. We have drawn our contributor team from a wide range of countries across four continents, illustrating our commitment to making the book truly international. The authors are also a diverse group of people, whether in terms of gender, ethnicity, age, discipline or other categories. International authorship and examples ensure that the text is highly accessible to readers from a range of backgrounds.

Structure of the book

The text comprises 12 chapters, planned to suit a standard one-semester course. Each chapter is packed with pedagogical and interactive features that engage readers and encourage directed and independent study, including concise introductions and summaries; quick 'take-home messages'; current, real-world case studies; questions for discussion; and extensive recommendations for further reading. Each of the chapters is summarised here.

Chapter 1: Global trends in international human resource management (Rofcanin, Imer and Zingoni). The chapter discusses shifts in the global context in terms of demographic changes, institutional arrangements and individual values and attitudes.

Chapter 2: Cross-cultural and diversity management intersections: lessons for attracting and retaining international assignees (Groutsis, Ng and Ozturk). The authors bring a fresh perspective to the cross-cultural management field by exploring how organisations need to transcend a monolithic understanding of cultures and to move beyond prescriptive approaches towards locally tailored solutions.

Chapter 3: Key players in international human resource management (Hollinshead, Forson, Rocha-Lawton and Calveley). This chapter shows that international players in the IHRM domain are changing, rendering the old world order defunct. The authors explain how IHRM policy and practice should capture the dynamism in shifts of power, resistance and contestation among new and old actors in the field.

Chapter 4: Recruitment and selection in the international context (Potočnik, Latorre, Dereli and Tacer). This chapter explains how recruitment and selection practices can be improved with better job analyses. The authors present a range of considerations and activities for international organisations to improve their recruitment and selection processes.

Chapter 5: Cross-cultural training and development for overseas assignments (Berber, Rofcanin and Fried). The authors explore shifts in the career strategies of workers as well as career management approaches of organisations in the international context.

Chapter 6: International reward (Jenkins). This chapter provides a review of the changing context, approaches and repertoires of reward in the international context.

Chapter 7: Employee retention (Balta). Balta reviews strategies for planning, choosing and implementing effective retention strategies in international organisations.

Chapter 8: International labour relations (Özbilgin). Özbilgin reviews ILR and international labour standards (ILS), exploring a number of different approaches and contemporary changes.

Chapter 9: Reputation in the international context (Harvey). Harvey focuses on how individual, group and organisational reputation is viewed, assessed and managed in the international context.

Chapter 10: Expatriation and repatriation in the Asia–Pacific region (Caven, Kirk and Wang-Cowham). The authors introduce the drivers for international mobility of talent and focus in the case of the Asia–Pacific region.

Chapter 11: Balancing inflows and outflows in the European context (Vassilopoulou, Samaluk and Seierstad). This chapter reviews inflows and outflows of labour and highlights relevant practice for IHRM through a focus on the European context.

Chapter 12: Self-initiated expatriation: case study lessons from Africa and the United States (Tatli, Berry, Ipek and April). The authors discuss how, why and under what circumstances individuals manage their own migration, with reference to North American and African cases.

Finally, in a conclusion by the book's editors (Özbilgin, Groutsis and Harvey), we summarise the book and highlight the major contributions of each chapter.

1 Global trends in international human resource management

Yasin Rofcanin, H. Pinar Imer and Matthew Zingoni

■ Learning objectives

- To identify global trends in international human resource management (IHRM).
- To offer a critical perspective on IHRM practices and trends.
- To integrate conceptual arguments with practical implications.

■ Learning outcomes

After reading this chapter, students will be able to:
- understand the strategic role of human resource practices in a dynamic and complex global business environment
- acknowledge issues that arise in human resource management when firms internationalise
- understand how firms develop and adapt their HRM strategies and policies in response to internationalised business operations
- appreciate the multinational and cross-cultural context of HRM
- understand the rising importance of human capital in an international work environment.

▪ Introduction

Human resource management (HRM) is a management function that covers the processes of selecting, training, appraising and compensating employees, with respect to regulations in areas including health and safety, labour relations and equal employment opportunity (Zheng, 2013). When companies globalise their operations, they go through certain phases (Mathews, 2006), moving from domestic to **international**, **multinational** and global stages (Farndale & Paauwe, 2007).

Most companies that become global begin their operations (such as production, marketing and distribution) in a domestic context. International companies are able to expand their presence and extend sales and marketing strategies while retaining ethnocentric structures. At the multinational stage, companies adapt various elements of the marketing mix (e.g. price, place, product and promotion) in overseas markets. Here, firms start to decentralise production and related decisions to their host-country subsidiaries, and combine, coordinate and adapt their overall global operations. The risks and returns increase as companies move closer to globalised activities. Finally, the **globalisation** stage is characterised by the realisation of similarities and differences between countries around the world, and here companies benefit from economies of scale to achieve worldwide presence.

international company An importer and/or exporter that does not have investments outside its home country.

multinational company A company that is registered in more than one country or that has operations in more than one country.

globalisation A process of worldwide business integration, designed to enable a company to reach new overseas markets.

A globalising company faces diverse challenges in managing its overseas activities (Espinoza, Ukleja & Rusch, 2010). The company has to employ management systems appropriate to managerial control systems, banking relationships and HRM systems all over the world. Thus, IHRM involves combining and coordinating **strategic HRM** practices – including selection, recruitment, training, development and performance management – in response to the challenges of internationalising in **home country**, **host country** and **third countries**. It is also important to coordinate and manage corporate strategy (e.g. De Cieri, Cox & Fenwick, 2007).

home country The country of origin of self-initiated expatriates, also known as the parent country.

host country The receiving country of self-initiated expatriates.

third country The destination country of self-initiated expatriates, which is neither the expatriate's home nor host country.

strategic human resource management The integration of key HRM processes with business strategy and the corporate culture, driven by long-term vision.

There are noteworthy differences between domestic and international HRM when it comes to their policies and practices (Edwards, 2004; De Cieri, Cox & Fenwick, 2007). One such difference, in terms of sourcing, development, rewarding, performance management and HR planning, is that domestic HRM is only involved with domestic employees, while IHRM takes a broader perspective and deals with parent, host and third countries. In the IHRM process, three aspects are especially important:

- human capital: how it is procured, allocated and utilised
- employee types: **parent-country nationals** (PCNs), **host-country nationals** (HCNs) and **third-country nationals** (TCNs)
- country types: home (or parent), host and third countries.

parent-country nationals Employees who are citizens of the country where the headquarters is located.

host-country nationals Employees who are citizens of the country where the MNC's subsidiary is located.

third-country nationals Employees who are citizens of any country other than the parent and host countries.

focal firm A firm that initiates an international transaction with the aim of producing goods or services for end customers.

ethnocentrism A strategic assumption in the MNC that tried-and-tested approaches to management can be extended from the country of origin to operating sites in other countries. Underlying this is a wish to retain power in the country of origin.

polycentrism A strategic assumption in MNCs that local managers and employees are best placed to formulate policies that reflect local needs, with a preference for decentralisation and autonomy at operating sites.

regiocentrism Customisation of human resource practices to the needs of specific regions such as European Union, North American Free Trade Agreement and the Association of South East Asian Nations.

geocentrism The idealised status of the truly global concern, combining local and international strengths. Managers are able to take a global view of the organisation, both responding flexibly to local needs and transcending them, in the pursuit of corporate goals and values at international level.

Context, firm, local unit specificities and IHRM practices shape the IHRM process (Cascio & Aguinis, 2005). The defining characteristics of the context are: cultural and institutional context; availability of staff; and the type of industry in which the company operates. The structure and strategy of a multinational company (MNC), its corporate governance and organisational culture and the **focal firm's** level of international experience, define company specificities. The specificities of the local unit include the method by which the subsidiary has been established in the host country; the strategic role and importance of the subsidiary; the need for local control; and the degree of autonomy in local decision-making.

Selection, training and development, compensation and career management related to HR practices shape the IHRM process; importantly, so does the company's **ethnocentric, polycentric, regiocentric** or **geocentric** orientation. This chapter sets out a general framework for recent issues in IHRM processes, and emphasises some of the key trends that influence IHRM.

■ Trends in economic and financial environments

The interdependence of economies around the world and the increased globalisation of today's business environment provide opportunities for domestic companies to extend their sales, manufacturing and other operations into new markets (Farndale & Paauwe, 2007). Companies expand their operations and go global for several reasons, including a drive to access new markets and to reduce labour and other operational costs (Edwards, 2004). The number of cross-border intercompany arrangements – in the form of **licensing**, **franchising**, **joint ventures**, manufacturing, marketing, research and development and **subcontracting** – has increased dramatically in recent decades (Ivancevic, 2010).

Global financial storms have become an integral part of today's work settings and affect almost all types of company across the globe (Veeran, 2009). The two major financial crises of the past 20 years, in 2001 and 2008, have had an immediate effect on international HR practices, mostly in the areas of compensation and international assignee decisions (Hudson Survey Report, 2009). When a host country experiences a crisis, employers of expatriates may seek to reduce their commitment to covering cost-of-living differentials (the difference between an employee's living costs in their home and host countries) through modified benefits and remuneration (Veeran, 2009). International companies may also opt to squeeze budgets allocated to employee training and development during financial hard times. Cost cutbacks, salary freezes and layoffs are common practice in many companies during global market crises (Schen & D'Netto, 2011).

licensing A form of international arrangement that includes franchising and subcontracting within a certain time period in exchange for a royalty fee.

franchising The practice of utilising another firm's business model within a certain time period in exchange for a royalty fee.

joint venture A form of equity-based strategic partnership that firms utilise when they internationalise their operations.

subcontracting The practice of assigning some tasks and responsibilities to another party under a contract.

■ The growth of internationalised companies

Recent decades have witnessed the growth not only of MNCs but also of **global companies**, **transnational companies** (TNCs) and **dragon companies** (Mathews, 2006; Alon & McIntyre, 2008; Zheng, 2013). MNCs make investments in countries outside their home country and yet do not have coordinated product offerings in those countries. Global companies make investments in more than one country and market their products through coordinated elements of the marketing mix. TNCs also operate in more than one country, but they are different from multinational and global companies because they decentralise to local subsidiaries their decision-making, research and development and other relevant operations (Mathews, 2006). Dragon companies are firms that have successfully internationalised out of home countries in the Asia–Pacific region; they have become prominent in certain industries, including (but not limited to) the production of building materials and contract manufacturing.

global company A company that is present in more than one country. Unlike multinational and transnational companies, global companies market their products and/or services through coordinated branding across all markets.

transnational company A company that does business in more than one country. Transnational companies do not have a national home in any single country.

dragon company An MNC that has emerged from a home country in the Asia–Pacific region and successfully extended its operations internationally.

The emergence and predominance of different types of international company are closely associated with **foreign direct investment** (FDI) flows (Mathews, 2006; Johanson & Vahlne, 1977). FDI represents a company or person's investment in production or business conducted in enterprises operating outside the investor's own country (Levitt, 1983). Emerging multinational companies (EMNCs) lead the global FDI flows and help strengthen the global economy and

foreign direct investment Investment in a company or entity by a company or entity based in another country.

emerging multinational company A global company that emerges outside traditional developed markets (e.g. Europe, United States and the Far East).

businesses (UNCTAD, 2010). Despite the rapid growth of EMNCs and their presence in the global arena, few studies have investigated how these enterprises manage their global workforce (Warner & Zhu, 2010). As a result, knowledge about the opportunities and challenges of the global workforce is limited, although it is clear that various types of international company do not make sufficient effort to utilise their global human capital to the full. The strategic IHRM framework usually applied in MNCs needs to be adapted for use in EMNCs, in response to the context of company operations.

■ Staffing the international organisation

In today's dynamic, complex and changeable business environment, global companies face recruitment and staffing challenges. Most employ a combination of locals (citizens of the country in which they work), expatriates (non-citizens of the country in which they work), PCNs (citizens of the countries in which the company is headquartered) and TCNs (citizens of neither home nor host country) depending on the management's mindset, which may be **ethnocentric**, **polycentric**, **regiocentric** or **geocentric** (Wind, Douglas & Perlmutter, 1973), in line with the company's corporate strategy. Ethnocentric companies focus on a centralised decision-making process at their headquarters; expatriates from the home country coordinate an ethnocentric company's subsidiaries most of the time. Companies with a polycentric approach treat their subsidiaries as distinct and unique decision-making entities; here, locals usually manage subsidiaries. Regiocentric companies emphasise the geographical strategy and structure of the related MNCs; employees might be assigned to specific tasks only within their regions. Geocentric companies see the world as an integrated market in which the workforce's competencies are more significant than its nationality.

ethnocentric staffing A company policy to fill key positions with PCNs.

polycentric staffing A company policy to staff the home office with home-country nationals and foreign subsidiaries with HCNs.

regiocentric staffing A company policy to permit the best personnel for key management positions to move within a specific geographic region, enjoying regional autonomy.

geocentric staffing A company policy to select the best people for key management jobs, regardless of their country of origin.

Competition for scarce international talent has increased as the number of companies and locations has grown, resulting in more **expatriation**. According to a report published by Mercer (2013), the number of international positions offered to expatriates has increased by 55 per cent between 2012 and 2013. Employing expatriates poses several challenges for MNCs, including the need for the employees to culturally adapt and for the employer to provide country-specific training; language barriers; housing provision; and spousal and family support. Other options for expatriate employment include self-initiated expatriation, short-term assignments and offshoring. Each of these forms of international assignment involves different career goals, work responsibilities and performance expectations (Bjorkman, 2005). In addition, the IHRM procedures related to selection and training tend to be rather ad hoc.

Self-initiated expatriates (SIEs) migrate to another country when they find a position there by their own efforts (Bjorkman, 2005). SIEs are different from other international assignees in terms of their contract, job security, compensation and most importantly initiation support; they do not work for a specified time period and do not receive specific training or a compensation package from the company before they start an international assignment. In short-term or temporary employment, an employee works for an MNC in another country for between one and 12 months. Unlike traditional expatriates or SIEs, a **short-term assignee's** family does not accompany him or her while they are working abroad. **Offshoring** refers to the process of exporting jobs from developed countries to developing countries, where labour costs are lower, thus enabling the company to reduce costs. In most cases, such positions include (but are not limited to) labour-intensive manufacturing and telecommunications technologies (e.g. call-centre operations and textile production). According to a Society for Human Resource Management report (2004), India is the most attractive country for offshoring certain operations, in terms of reducing costs.

expatriation The process of assigning employees to international, cross-border and cross-cultural jobs.

self-initiated expatriate A person who moves abroad for work on their own initiative.

short-term assignee An employee appointed to an international post for a short period, usually less than one year.

offshoring Relocation of business activities (generally, manufacturing or operational) from one country to another.

■ Cultural values, changing demographics and workforce diversity

Cultures and people's values vary from country to country and can be markedly different. The most cited study of cross-cultural dimensions is that by Hofstede (1980), who initially set out four cultural dimensions, to which a fifth and sixth were subsequently added. These are discussed in chapter 2. Such cultural values are conceived as having a strong influence on workplace policies and practices (Hofstede, 1980), including HRM aspects (Tosi & Greckhamer, 2004; Weech, 2001).

Research and current trends suggest that workforce demographics are changing gradually but significantly (Tarique & Schuler, 2008), with a resulting increase in **workforce diversity**. The size of the population in developed countries is expected to stay stable or shrink in some regions. On the other hand, the populations of developing and emerging countries are increasing and average ages decreasing (Strack, Baier & Fahlander, 2008). Research reveals that employees born in the early 1980s are more willing to look for international positions where they see the opportunity to benefit from global experience and advancement opportunities (Farndale & Paauwe, 2007; Faust, 2008). Thus, international HR managers are challenged to balance the

workforce diversity Diversity among employees, in terms of their age, gender, physical abilities and disabilities, ethnicity, religion, sex, sexual orientation, cultural and educational background.

Generation X Generation X, popularly known as 'Gen X', were born between the late 1960s and late 1970s.

Generation Y Generation Y, popularly known as 'Gen Y', were born in the 1980s and 1990s.

composition of their workforce in terms of planning the need for older and younger employees – commonly referred to as **Generation X** and **Generation Y** employees (Faust, 2008) – to work in a dynamic, global business environment, in addition to attracting, selecting, developing and retaining that workforce. Under these circumstances, HR professionals and practitioners are also challenged to develop and implement HR policies and practices to meet the needs of employees from different generations (Marjorie, 2008; Terjesen, Vinnicombe & Freeman, 2007).

The cross-cultural and cross-border expansion of companies has resulted in the emergence of a new class of people, who hold global attitudes, exhibit global behaviours and have global networks of relations (Roberson, 2006; Day & Greene, 2008). In this context, the workforce is characterised by diversity, in terms of ability and disability, age, cultural and educational background, ethnicity, gender, religion, sex or sexual orientation (Harding & Peel, 2007). Diversity not only affects how people perceive themselves but also how they perceive others. As these perceptions influence and shape the interactions at workplace level, HR professionals have to manage effectively the inclusion, adaptations, interactions and needs of the diverse workforce (Tatli & Özbilgin, 2009). Accordingly, companies operating globally must be ready to allocate resources to achieving a diverse workforce (Tatli & Özbilgin, 2009).

■ Technological improvements

Improvements in technology have changed our approach to almost everything we do. Smart phones and mobile devices have become integral parts of our lives, helping us to plan, work and communicate. Technology is also used in many HR practices, such as job applications, recruitment and even training. In this respect, there has been a shift from traditional HRM practices (Caldwell, 2010) to the use of unconventional HR technologies (Hendrickson, 2003). For instance, companies have started using social media as a means of recruiting new talent in the international context (Panayotopoulou, Vakola & Galanaki, 2007). Online tools (such as the professional networking site LinkedIn) have made it easier for MNCs to access talented people with distinct competencies around the world.

Technology has also helped MNCs to enhance their work flows and IHRM processes by using video conferencing, virtual teamwork, online interviews and testing in the selection process, virtual training, and even virtual performance appraisals (Schramm, 2008). The use of internet technologies for selection, interviews and training has reduced various costs for MNCs. E-learning technologies continue to develop and are integrated into the international HR practices of companies around the world (Panayotopoulou, Vakola & Galanaki, 2007). Therefore, MNC access to and coordination of competent global talent has become not only easier but also more effective.

Labour relations

In addition to diversity, companies with subsidiaries abroad may encounter national and regional differences in labour laws and labour relations practices. There are many structural differences in unions as well, as their influence on a company's operations varies between countries. Mexican employers, for instance, focus much less on the details of the written contracts of employees than do employers in the United States; in the same way, Mexican employees tend to rely more on informal agreements with their employers than do American employees (Greer & Stephens, 1996). In South Korea, the nature of labour relations in giant conglomerates called *chaebols* is set in line with a philosophy of controlling each aspect of workers' lives. In Singapore, a National Wages Council closely guides annual wage adjustments and legislation regulates working conditions (Wan & Ong, 2002). Co-determination, which gives employees a legal right to take part in setting company policies, is legally guaranteed in Germany, allowing workers to elect their representatives to the supervisory board of their employers, depending on the issue in question (Poutsma, Ligthart & Veersma, 2006). Thus, an IHRM professional should investigate the national and regional labour relations climate before a company begins to operate in a particular country or region. As companies move through the stages of internationalisation, the risks and investments associated with expansion into another country change. For instance, international and global companies are required to comply differently with overall labour relations regulations in a host country. A global company has to directly adapt to the local labour regulations and laws of the host country, since it invests directly in the country, most likely by establishing autonomous subsidiaries.

The changing nature of careers in the international context

With the predominance of international careers, individuals move between jobs and companies and are not expected to commit to a single company or a job for life (Veeran, 2009). The boundaryless career, which is independent from the organisational career arrangements and transcends physical and psychological boundaries, has increased the uncertainty (or, conversely, the flexibility) of today's work settings (Bjorkman, 2005). In other words, companies can no longer promise lifelong employment to their employees, and employees no longer demand lifelong job security from their employers. The defining tenets of a boundaryless career are the accumulation of transferable knowledge; a larger number of alternative potential employers; and the degree of personal investment an employee makes in pursuing a boundaryless career. Due to hypercompetition, integrated world markets and the unpredictable business

repatriation Voluntary and self-directed efforts of employees to develop careers abroad. Repatriation, unlike expatriation, is initiated without official support from the focal company.

environment, MNCs have become increasingly dependent on expatriates. Expatriates who complete international assignments gain personal development and career enhancement opportunities, although these may not directly benefit the MNC. Therefore, if the MNC fails to provide a **repatriation** opportunity, the expatriate who benefits from personal development or career enhancement opportunities during the expatriate assignment will still be likely to perceive them as valuable assets. Whether the MNC holds an ethnocentric, polycentric, regiocentric or geocentric mindset, it is important for IHRM professionals to align their approach to boundaryless careers with overall company strategy, taking into account recent trends in career development.

■ The changing nature of jobs and work design

Globalisation, competition and technological advances have changed the way jobs and works are designed (Morgeson & Humphrey, 2006). Gradually, the nature of jobs has shifted to include interaction with and feedback from co-workers and others, and new job categories (such as knowledge and technology-driven jobs) have emerged (Grant, 2007). Similarly, work designs have become more flexible to allow people to do their jobs outside the office and from abroad (Grant, 2007). Work arrangements such as telecommuting and job-sharing have become more common as alternatives to traditional work arrangements, depending on the needs of both the company and the employee. For IHRM professionals, these trends imply an increased reliance on knowledge workers and therefore require a greater emphasis on human capital. Moreover, employees seek to have jobs that enable them to communicate, interact with others and receive feedback. Successful IHRM professionals acknowledge the importance of **relational** elements in designing jobs and work tasks and providing employees with more flexibility than traditional assignments.

relational job design Emergent forms of job and work designs that emphasise relational elements such as feedback seeking from others, interpersonal communication and constant feedback-seeking behaviours.

■ Proactive employee practices and the changing nature of employment contracts

Proactive employee practices enable workers to shape themselves and their environments (Grant & Ashford, 2008). In workplaces, employee proactivity is more than simply a necessity in today's global, diverse, modern and dynamic organisations (Cascio & Aguinis, 2005; Den Hartog & Belschak, 2010). Unexpected and adverse circumstances, such as budget cuts, technological break-downs and layoffs, constantly threaten the progress of organisations (Finkelstein & Hambrick, 1996; Friedman, 2005). When employees engage in proactive efforts, they defend themselves against such issues. Employees who are able to adapt globally, and who realise that they do not always need to plan in advance, usually succeed in these dynamic work environments (Grant & Ashford, 2008). Some of the most observed **proactive** employee work prac-tices across organisations are job crafting (Wrzesniewski & Dutton, 2001); **idiosyncratic deals** or i-deals (Rousseau, 2001); personal initiative (Frese et al., 1997); voicing (Van Dyne, Ang & Botero, 2003); and taking charge (Morrison & Phelps, 1999).

> **proactive employee efforts** Employee behaviours that proactively attempt to change the work setting and working conditions (e.g. crafting jobs and making individualised agreements).
>
> **idiosyncratic deals ('i-deals')** Mutually beneficial, non-written and personalised individual agreements between an employee and their supervisor.

Emerging trends at macro and organisational levels may have significant influence on the configuration of the new employment relationships. One increasingly common practice is the negotiation of i-deals: unique employment agreements between a worker and their supervisor about working conditions, which differentiate the employee from their colleagues (Frank & Cook, 1995). For example, a valued engineer in Microsoft might take a year of training in an area of personal interest (e.g. underwater photog-raphy) instead of quitting his or her job (Wrzesniewski & Dutton, 2001); an employee of Walmart might visit Japan to learn how to manage a plant Japanese-style. I-deals are now widespread across countries and organisations because of the need to innovate and a dependence on high-tech jobs, knowledge work and human capital in response to change and complexity in the business environment. Employees' higher levels of educa-tional attainment, and their concerns about training and development, make custom-isation of various aspects of employment more visible and acceptable than ever before on the employer's side (Lawler & Finegold, 2000). Negotiations of some types of i-deals may be limited in countries where labour markets are controlled and strict regulations exist. Also, assertive negotiations of working conditions may be less appropriate in countries where norms and culture lean towards compliance with rules (e.g. China, Thailand).

Although such employee practices certainly seem relevant to domestic HR profes-sionals, they are actually most often seen in an international context, especially in expatriate assignments. An expatriate who negotiates for extra training or asks for additional compensation to cover the expenses of his or her children in the host country is effectively arranging an i-deal. Thus, IHRM professionals may be better able to reach agreements if they take contextual factors into account when negotiating.

■ Conclusion

Most of the pressing global challenges companies now face relate to adding global HR practices to their existing operations. IHRM professionals and practitioners have started to acknowledge the challenges and act to retain their best talent, in the context of demanding international competition. Technological advances, changing demographics and financial and economic hard times all affect different types of companies in the global arena (e.g. MNCs, TNCs). A greater appreciation of diverse workforce and labour relations is one of the most significant external trends, encouraging companies to develop and implement their global HR practices in line with their corporate strategies. In an effort to adapt themselves to the unpredictable dynamics of the business environment, employees engage in proactive efforts to shape themselves and their work settings (including job crafting, i-deals, personal initiative and voicing), especially in expatriate arrangements. In an era when almost all types of company experience the challenges of internationalising, HR practices must be managed on a global scale and must respond to the particular needs of competent global talent.

■ Take-home messages

- Key global trends that influence businesses in the international context include movements in the economic and financial environments, the existence of various types of international companies at different stages of internationalisation, the cultural context, labour-related regulations in different countries, technological advancements and the diversity of the workforce.
- Due to integrated markets and the globalisation of business, IHRM professionals are exposed to different types of international assignments.
- IHRM professionals and managers face challenges due to the highly globalised nature of businesses; alternative staffing options; technological improvements; changes in the demographics of workforce; the emergence of different types of global companies; the changing nature of works and jobs; and greater acknowledgment of the diversity of the workforce and labour relations.
- Today's employers should take all the necessary steps to compete in the global context. Most importantly, employers, acting in a coordinated manner, should develop career paths for individualised needs of more diverse, global, multicultural and multinational employees.
- Considering the gradual but meaningful changes, employers should initiate more collaborative and participative HR practices that will keep talented global competencies with them.
- In today's fierce competitive environment, companies should develop and implement HR practices that will be globally relevant but crafted to particular contexts and specific to the needs of employees with diverse backgrounds.

■ Closing the learning loop

1. After reading this chapter, you will be aware that organisations are utilising a more diverse workforce as they decide to go global. Part of this diversity comes in the form of age diversity, since individuals are working for longer time

periods. So, a manager needs to work with a wider range of age groups than before. Further, this chapter has highlighted that organisations are increasingly using technology. What challenges does advances in technology and a more age diverse workforce present? What can HR managers do to overcome these challenges?

2. This chapter has discussed both the increase in regulations around the world and the expansion of multinational companies. The combination of these two factors has created unique challenges that impact many areas of HR. Discuss the impact this may have on IHRM practices, including training and development, employee selection, employee recruitment and employee compensation.

CASE STUDY 1.1   KREWE MARKETING

Krewe Marketing, a think tank focusing on corporate branding strategies, was established by Isaac Jackson in 2005 in New Orleans, USA. The company specialises in assisting start-up companies to develop their own brands and established companies to re-evaluate their existing brands when entering new markets. Over the past eight years, Krewe Marketing has experienced growth in its business potential. The number of company clients has increased from seven in the southeast United States to 46 across the United States. Recently, Isaac has agreed to the acquisition of Krewe Marketing by Image First Marketing, a large multinational marketing firm headquartered in Zurich, Switzerland. One of the requirements for the acquisition is that Isaac stays on the board of directors and becomes the vice president, being responsible for both the North and South American client relationships. Personally, Isaac is very happy with this development but he does have some concerns. In particular, many of his existing employees are not happy with the idea of working for a large MNC and many may choose to leave after the acquisition. Further, Isaac has always been

a hands-on manager, and he is not sure if he can continue to be an effective manager in such a large market. Isaac currently oversees 24 employees in one country but will now manage 72 employees in four countries. In addition, he will oversee employees from different countries, many of which he has never visited. Overall, Isaac feels this acquisition is the right thing to do in the long-term, yet he is worried about the short-term transition phase.

Case study questions

1. What can Isaac do to remotely manage a large number of employees with diverse backgrounds?
2. What steps can Isaac take to address his concerns about managing employees from a number of different countries?
3. Before the acquisition is finalised, is there anything Isaac can ask Image First Marketing to help ensure the success of the acquisition?
4. Given Isaac's concerns and the stiff market competition in the business setting, is this acquisition a good idea?

» ACTIVITY

Student role-play

Overview

Break into groups, with one student playing the role of an HR manager in a MNC and the remaining students playing the role of employees. The students compete for a position that involves high cultural adaptability skills (the job is briefly described below). Based on the background information provided, the HR manager conducts initial job interviews and tries to evaluate whether each candidate fits the vacant position.

Objective

The objective of this role-play is to demonstrate the challenges of conducting initial job interviews with employees who will fit in different cultural contexts. Therefore, the activity will demonstrate how the need for cultural diversity affects initial job interviews.

Directions

Break into groups of four. Assign one student to the role of HR manager and the others to the employee roles described below. After each student reads the following background information, have the manager talk to each employee separately to conduct an initial job interview about his or her employment relationship. The job interview will be related to the job responsibilities, the match of the candidate with the vacancy, future work arrangements or any other aspect of the employment relationship that the manager and employee deem relevant. After the manager completes the initial job interview with each employee, he or she will make a decision on that candidate. In the end, ensure that each student has shared their experiences with the others and have the HR manager explain his or her criteria for the employment decision.

Background

Company information: The manager and employees work for R and Z Consulting, a leading global HRM consulting firm. R and Z Consulting has been in business for 13 years and has clients in 14 countries across North America, Europe and Asia. R and Z Consulting has two main offices, one in Boston, USA and the other in Istanbul, Turkey. R and Z's employees fall into two broad categories: support staff and field consultants. Most support staff are located in the two main offices. Their job requires long working hours and has an unpredictable work schedule, as these employees support the field consultants who are working internationally. Although a support employee might travel with a consultant on a large project, their international visits are minimal (less than 20%). Field consultants live in locations around the world and spend the majority of their time (80%) travelling.

The consultant role also requires long working hours and has a very inconsistent schedule.

Position description: The vacant position is the account management position for an MNC. The employee in this job will have to make frequent visits to the client's site, and he or she will be expected to adapt easily to different cultural contexts.

Manager (Terry): Terry has been with R and Z Consulting since its inception 13 years ago. Terry started as a field consultant in the Boston office right out of graduate school and was promoted to a manager after six years. He currently works in the Istanbul office. Due to this long tenure with the organisation, Terry is familiar with the demands of all the positions at R and Z Consulting.

Employee 1 (John): John is a field consultant working outside the Istanbul office. John has been with R and Z Consulting for almost nine years and has worked as an HR consultant for almost 25 years. John has travelled extensively as a consultant and has been one of the most effective consultants at R and Z Consulting. Recently, John's first grandchild was born but John currently lives just outside of Istanbul.

Employee 2 (Anne): Anne is in the final steps of negotiating the details of her contract to join R and Z Consulting. She completed a graduate degree in Boston five years ago and worked as a consultant for R and Z's main competitor for the past three years. Anne is considered as a rising star in the field and she is focused on her career and building further reputation.

Employee 3 (Mark): Mark is a leading support staff member who has been with R and Z Consulting for five years. He is the most effective support staff member, with exclusive responsibility for supporting R and Z consulting's most challenging customers. Due to his effectiveness in this role, Mark has worked more hours and has travelled more than he initially expected when he joined the organisation.

Discussion questions

1. After the HR manager has shared his or her recruitment decision with the other group members, does each employee feel the decision is fair? Why or why not?
2. What was the strongest factor in the manager's decision about the suitability of each employee for the role? Was this factor the same for each employee or did it vary from one employee to another?
3. What differences in initial job interviews were found across groups, and were there any differences between the interview of an existing employee (John) and a new employee (Anne)?

▧ Online resources

- For instructors: answers to activities; long media article with questions.
- For students: further reading; answers to case study; IHRM in practice.

▧ References

Alon, I. and McIntyre, J. R. (eds) (2008). *Globalization of Chinese enterprises*. London: Palgrave Macmillan.

Bjorkman, I. (2005). International human resource management research and institutional theory. In Bjorkman, I. and Stahl, G. (eds), *Handbook of research into international HRM*. London: Edward Elgar.

Caldwell, R. (2010). Are HR business partner competency models effective?, *Applied HRM Research*, 12(1): 40–58.

Cascio, W. E. and Aguinis, H. (2005). *Applied psychology in human resource management*. Upper Saddle River, NJ: Pearson Prentice-Hall.

Day, N. E. and Greene, P. G. (2008). A case for sexual orientation diversity in small and large organizations, *Human Resource Management*, 47(3): 637–54.

De Cieri, H., Cox, J. W. and Fenwick, M. (2007). A review of international HRM: Integration, interrogation, imitation, *International Journal of Management Reviews*, 9 (4): 281–302.

Den Hartog, D. and Belschak, F. (2010). Personal initiative, commitment and affect at work, *Journal of Occupational and Organizational Psychology*, 80(4): 601–22.

Edwards, T. (2004). The transfer of employment practices across borders in multinational companies. In Harzing, A. W. and van Ruysseveldt, J. (eds), *International human resource management*, 2nd edition, 389–410. London: Sage.

Espinoza, C., Ukleja, M. and Rusch, C. (2010). *Managing the millennials: Discover the core competencies for managing today's workforce*. Hoboken, NJ: Wiley.

Farndale, E. and Paauwe, J. (2007). Uncovering competitive and institutional drivers of HRM practices in multinational corporations, *Human Resource Management Journal*, 17(4): 355–75.

Faust, C. (2008). State of the global talent nation report 2013: Organizations struggle to ready workforces to meet growth demands, www.softscape.com. Retrieved 16 May 2013.

Finkelstein, S. and Hambrick, D. C. (1996). *Strategic leadership: Top executives and their effects on organizations*. New York: West.

Frank, R. H. and Cook, P. J. (1995). *Winner take all: How more and more Americans compete for fewer and bigger prizes, encouraging economic waste, income inequality and an impoverished cultural life*. New York: Free Press.

Frese, M. et al. (1997). The concept of personal initiative: Operationalization, reliability and validity in two German samples, *Journal of Occupational and Organizational Psychology*, 70: 139–61.

Friedman. T. L. (2005). *The world is flat: A brief history of the twenty-first century*. New York: Picador.

Grant, A. (2007). Relational job design and the motivation to make a prosocial difference, *Academy of Management Review*, 32(2): 393–417.

Grant, A. M. and Ashford, S. J. (2008). The dynamics of proactivity at work, *Research in Organizational Behavior*, 28: 3–34.

Greer, C. R. and Stephens, G. K. (1996). Employee relations issues for US companies in Mexico, *California Management Review*, 38(3): 121–45.

Harding, R. and Peel, E. (2007). Heterosexism at work: Diversity training, discrimination law and the limits of liberal individualism. In Clarke, V. and Peel, E. (eds), *Out in psychology: Lesbian, gay, bisexual, trans and queer perspectives*, 241–71. New York: Wiley.

Hendrickson, A. R. (2003). Human resource information systems: Backbone technology of contemporary human resources, *Journal of Labor Research*, 24(3): 381–94.

Hofstede, G. (1980). *Culture's consequences: International differences in work-related values*. Beverly Hills, CA: Sage.

Hudson Survey Report (2009). Tacking the economic crisis: Has HR learned from the past? http://eu.hudson.com/documents/EU_HR_survey_report.pdf.

Ivancevic, J. M. (2010). *Human resource management*, 11th international edition. New York: McGraw-Hill/Irwin.

Johanson, J.and J.-E. Vahlne (1977). The internationalisation process of the firm: A model of knowledge development and increasing foreign market Commitment, *Journal of International Business Studies*, 8(1): 23–32.

Lawler, E. E. and Finegold, D. (2000). Individualizing the organization: Past, present and future, *Organizational Dynamics*, 29(4): 1–15.

Levitt, T. (1983). Globalization of markets, *Harvard Business Review*, 1983 (May/June): 92–102.

Marjorie, A. (2008). Organizational practices and the post-retirement employment experience of older workers, *Human Resource Management Journal*, 18: 36–53.

Mathews, J. A. (2006). Dragon multinationals: New players in 21st century globalization, *Asia Pacific Journal of Management*, 23: 5–27.

Mercer, D. G. (2013). *Global compensation report*, www.imercer.com/products/2013/global-comp-planning.aspx.

Morgeson, F. and Humphrey, S. (2006). The work design questionnaire (WDQ): Developing and validating a comprehensive measure for assessing job design and the nature of work, *Journal of Applied Psychology*, 91(6): 1321–39.

Morrison, E. W. and Phelps, C. C. (1999). Taking charge at work: Extrarole efforts to initiate workplace change, *Academy of Management Journal*, 42: 403–19.

Panayotopoulou, L., Vakola, M. and Galanaki, E. (2007). E-HR adoption and the role of HRM: Evidence from Greece, *Personnel Review*, 36(2): 277–94.

Poutsma, E., Ligthart, P. E. M. and Veersma, U. (2006). The diffusion of calculative and collaborative HRM practices in European firms, *Industrial Relations*, 45(4): 513–46.

Roberson, Q. (2006). Disentangling the meanings of diversity and inclusion in organizations, *Group and Organization Management*, 31(2): 212–36.

Rousseau, D. M. (2001). Idiosyncratic deals: Flexibility versus fairness?, *Organization Dynamics*, 29: 260–71.

Schen, J. and D'Netto, B. (2011). Impact of the 2007–09 global economic crises on human resource management among Chinese export-oriented enterprises, *Asia Pacific Business Review*, 18(1): 15–21.

Schramm, J. (2008). HR technology competencies: New roles for HR professionals, *HR Magazine*, http://findarticles.com/p/articles/mi_m3495/is_4_51/ai_n26840916. Retrieved 8 June 2011.

Society for Human Resources Management (2004). *Benefits Survey Report: A study by the Society of Human Resources Management and the SRHM Foundation*. Society for Human Resources Management, USA.

Strack, R., Baier, J. and Fahlander, A. (2008). Managing demographic risk, *Harvard Business Review*, February: 2–11.

Tarique, I. and Schuler, R. (2008). Emerging issues and challenges in global staffing: A North American perspective, *International Journal of Human Resource Management*, 19: 1397–415.

Tatli, A. and Özbilgin, M. F. (2009). Understanding diversity managers' role in organizational change: Towards a conceptual framework, *Canadian Journal of Administrative Sciences*, 26(3): 244–58.

Terjesen, S., Vinnicombe, S. and Freeman, C. (2007). Attracting generation Y graduates, *Career Development International*, 12: 504–22.

Tosi, H. L. and Greckhamer, T. (2004). Culture and CEO compensation, *Organization Science*, 15(6): 657–70.

United Nations Conference on Trade and Development (UNCTAD) (2010). *World investment report 2010: Investing in low-carbon economy*. New York: United Nations.

Van Dyne. L, Ang, S. and Botero, I. C. (2003). Conceptualizing employee silence and employee voice as multidimensional constructs, *Journal of Management Studies*, 40: 1359–92.

Veeran, K. (2009). Impact of global economic crisis on HR strategies: Challenges and issues, *Political Economy Journal of India*: 18(2): 1–14.

Wan, D. and Ong, C. H. (2002). Compensation systems in Singapore, *Compensation and Benefits Review*, 34(4): 23–33.

Warner, M. and Zhu, Y. (2010). Labour and management in the People's Republic of China: Seeking the 'harmonious' society, *Asia Pacific Business Review*, 16(3): 285–98.

Weech, W. (2001). Training across cultures: What to expect, *Training and Development*, 12(1): 62–4.

Wind, Y., Douglas, P. S. and Perlmutter, V. H. (1973). Guidelines for developing international marketing strategies, *Journal of Marketing*, 37: 14–23.

Wrzesniewski, A. and Dutton, J. E. (2001). Crafting a job: Revisioning employees as active crafters of their work, *Academy of Management Review*, 26(2): 179–201.

Zheng, C. (2013). Critiques and extension of strategic international human resource management framework for dragon multinationals, *Asia Pacific Business Review*, 19(1): 1–15.

Cross-cultural and diversity management intersections: lessons for attracting and retaining international assignees

*Dimitria Groutsis, Eddy S. Ng
and Mustafa Bilgehan Ozturk*

■ Learning objectives

- To explain talent mobility in a culturally diverse global context, including issues such as attraction, retention and post-settlement adjustment.
- To describe the layers of culture and delineate their workplace implications.
- To explain cross-cultural management by focusing on cultural dimensions.
- To explain cultural diversity at individual and organisational levels.
- To demonstrate the value of employing a multilevel approach to explaining cross-cultural management and diversity management.

■ Learning outcomes

After reading this chapter, students will be able to:
- understand diversity management more broadly than has been presented in the literature to date
- understand cross-cultural dimensions beyond the macro-level measures presented in the dominant literature
- apply the insights gained from three levels of analysis: the macro (national culture), meso (organisation) and micro (individual and inter- and intragroup)
- address the implications of cross-cultural issues and workplaces staffed by people from diverse backgrounds around the globe
- understand how cross-cultural management and diversity management shape staffing, post-settlement adjustment and retention rates.

▨ Introduction

Within the context of globalisation, the pursuit of new markets and increasing labour mobility are together driving greater diversity within and between companies, and within and between diverse groups of workers. As such, firms conducting business internationally must be sensitive to, and accommodate, cross-cultural issues arising from cultural and linguistic differences (Lloyd & Hartel, 2010). A primary responsibility for international HR managers is managing cross-cultural relations among diverse employee groups. In this chapter, we explore some of the issues confronting HR managers from a cross-cultural perspective, with an emphasis on ethno-cultural and linguistic differences. Combined, these considerations are important for managers operating in a global context who seek to attract the best and the brightest talent from around the world. There are both short- and long-term incentives to ensure effective **cross-cultural management** of diverse employees, and the goal is to retain and develop a workforce with a **global mindset** (Gupta & Govidarajan, 2002; Levy et al., 2007).

cross-cultural management A group of strategies and policies designed to minimise the challenges of coordination and cooperation emergent in work environments where staff members embody a multiplicity of (sometimes competing) behavioural norms and interpersonal expectations.

global mindset The ability to live and work in and across cultures, and to negotiate cross-cultural differences. An individual with a global mindset has an understanding and appreciation of local cross-cultural differences while maintaining the identity of their organisation and a global view.

The *Workforce 2000* report (Johnston & Packer, 1987), which heralded the growing diversity of the American workforce, provided the impetus to the importance of managing diversity as a means to achieve a competitive advantage (Thomas & Ely, 1996: 79; Nkomo & Cox, 1996: 88; Edelman, Fuller & Mara-Drita, 2001: 1612). Since then, interest in the opportunities surrounding, and concerns about, greater cultural and linguistic diversity has occupied scholars and practitioners alike. An Economist Intelligence Unit report (2010: 5), based on 479 survey responses and 16 interviews with senior executives, captured the importance of understanding and managing diversity to suit the dynamic contours of workplaces in a global context now and into the future:

> Workers will come from a greater range of backgrounds; those with local knowledge of an emerging market, a global outlook and an intuitive sense of the corporate culture will be particularly valued... To build on this, many companies will send employees overseas more frequently, often for short periods, on project-based assignments or to take part in training.

While the IHRM literature focuses on the importance of cross-cultural management and cross-cultural awareness in enhancing performance and productivity (Shay & Baack, 2006; Kim & Slocum, 2008), this chapter focuses on post-settlement adjustment (that is, adjustments a worker must make on arrival in a host country) and **retention** of skilled workers as key reasons it is important to manage cross-cultural relations at work. This chapter provides a nuanced approach to understanding the implications of cross-cultural issues and the management of ethno-culturally and linguistically diverse groups of workers. This is important because insights from scholars on such issues inform and guide our approach to organisational policy and staffing arrangements.

retention The process of managing and developing organisational talent and expertise to encourage loyalty to the organisation and commitment to its preferred goals.

To date, the approach to understanding cross-cultural and intercultural relations in assisting with and facilitating post-settlement adjustment has focused on reducing people's uncertainty in the new environment (Black, Mendenhall & Oddou, 1991). Some authors argue that uncertain conditions and the loss of control over one's context that being in a foreign environment triggers exert a significant impact on post-settlement adjustment. Most notably, in studies of traditional expatriate adjustment, it has been found that cultural adjustment is key to success, which includes completion of the assignment and retention in the organisation (Bhaskar-Shrinivas et al., 2005). Retention is defined as the process of managing and developing organisational talent and expertise to encourage loyalty to the organisation and commitment to its preferred goals (Bender & Fish, 2000; Stroh, 1995). This concept can also be applied to an emerging group of workers, that of self-initiated expatriates and skilled migrants (see discussion below).

A key facet of adjustment is the 'cultural distance' from, or sameness to, one's own cultural construct in the host country location (Black & Gregersen, 1991). Cao, Hirschi and Deller (2012: 167) define cultural distance as the '... basic differences between cultures, such as value systems, beliefs, customs and rituals in addition to legal, political and economic systems'. Managing this process with an understanding of cross-cultural relations is the first step in overcoming uncertainty and its consequences (Tung & Verbeke, 2010). To this end, this chapter provides a descriptive and critical evaluation of the guiding principles for understanding cross-cultural dynamics and explores the implications of such dynamics on attracting and retaining a culturally diverse talent pool. It is outside the scope of the chapter to construct a guide on cross-cultural competence, but we see such skills as evolving over time, given exposure to different situations and encounters. Here, we lay the foundations for navigating this long-term and ongoing process of understanding cross-cultural relations and the management of workers from diverse backgrounds.

We begin with a brief examination of labour hypermobility in what is described as a super-competitive era for sourcing talent (Chambers et al., 1998; Michaels, Handfield-Jones & Axelrod, 2001; Beechler & Woodward, 2009). We then outline how the process of attracting and, more importantly, retaining skilled employees has changed in recent years. To illustrate the impact of labour mobility and talent shortages as a precursor to understanding how to effectively manage and retain the talent pool, we present evidence of skills shortages and attrition rates drawn from national and corporate data. In doing so, we lay the foundation for considering cross-cultural diversity awareness as an important tool to manage a more culturally and linguistically diverse workforce and, relatedly, to retain and develop talented employees.

We then turn to a brief description of culture before examining the main typologies informing IHR practice on cross-cultural management. We also critically examine and document the limitations of the typologies in common use, and consider the importance of understanding and managing cultural and linguistic diversity. Finally, we synthesise the arguments and suggest questions for consideration.

■ The business case for managing diversity

The landscape of international business and relatedly IHRM has fundamentally changed with the expansion of interfirm mobility (the traditional expatriate), host-country nationals (HCNs) and third-country nationals (TCNs) as the main options to staff multinational companies (MNCs). These groups are now joined by skilled and qualified individuals who are immigrating for work purposes in their own right (Brewster & Scullion, 2007; Jokinen, Brewster & Suutari, 2008; Cerdin & Pargneux, 2010). Despite the scarcity of reliable data, there seems to be a marked trend towards increased mobility among skilled workers (Wickramasekara, 2003). To describe this mobile stock of self-initiated labour we use the terms 'self-initiated expatriate' (SIE) and 'skilled migrant' (SM) interchangeably (for discussion on the differences between SMs and SIEs refer to Al Ariss et al., 2012: 94; Doherty, 2013; Howe-Walsh & Schyns, 2010). National government policies that encourage temporary and long-term immigration lure SIEs and SMs, who are in demand in regions where the 'war for talent' has generated significant competition to address key skills shortages (Burke & Ng, 2006; ManpowerGroup, 2012a and 2012b). In this regard, managing intranational diversity among SIEs is not dissimilar to managing cross-national diversity among expatriates in the host country (Tung, 1993). In addition to this (and in common with traditional expatriates), firms, occupations and industries also demand SIEs, who may be enticed by the prospect of higher wages, career opportunities and the excitement of a different cultural experience (Al Ariss et al., 2012; Harvey & Groutsis, 2012; Groutsis & Arnold, 2012).

self-initiated expatriate A person who moves abroad for work on their own initiative.
skilled migrant A well-educated individual who moves from a developing to a developed country for work.

Skilled workers are thus encouraged to relocate for work purposes, and this extends beyond those who travel for work purposes within the confines of interfirm transfers. As Cecilia Malmström (2012), the EU Minister for Migration, recently noted: 'In order for us to remain economically competitive, we need to attract workers, in particular high-skilled workers, from third countries.' With a message from policymakers to look to SMs to address skills gaps, and as a way of building cross-cultural and intercultural skills and know how, employers are finding themselves competing in a shrinking market for in-demand skills. The reason for the lack of available local skills is simply that there is unmatched supply fuelled by a demand-driven need for skilled workers (Al Ariss & Özbilgin, 2010; Cerna, 2010; Chaloff & Lemaitre, 2009; Harvey & Groutsis, 2012; Groutsis & Arnold, 2012; Beechler & Woodward, 2009;

Martin, 2003; Wickramasekara, 2003). In findings released by ManpowerGroup, from a large-scale survey based on 38 000 phone interviews across 41 different countries and territories, more than one in three employers 'encounter difficulties in filling skilled positions, with employers in the Asia–Pacific region cited as experiencing the greatest skills shortfall when compared with the Americas and Europe, the Middle East and Africa' (ManpowerGroup, 2012a: 4).

Skills shortages in particular sectors and industries are defining the developed and, increasingly, developing economies. As such, it is becoming increasingly competitive to attract and retain skilled workers where they are needed. In this regard, having the right national and organisational policies may serve to attract prospective SMs. For example, Australia and Canada espouse an official multiculturalism policy that welcomes immigrants (Ng & Metz, 2013). At the organisational level, employers who have a **diversity management** policy also attract more diverse and better qualified job applicants (Ng & Burke, 2005). However, while attracting SMs is critical in the 'war for talent', retaining them post-arrival is also becoming a challenge facing many host countries. For example, a recent study (Finch et al., 2009: 3) examining immigrant retention rates in the UK notes that since 1975:

> [A]t least 61 000 immigrants have left the UK each year with numbers rising steadily in the last decade to a peak of 194 000 in 2006, a population the size of the city of Portsmouth. This peak is likely to have been exceeded in 2008 with re-migration topping 200 000.

diversity management The strategic alignment of workforce heterogeneity to include and value each employee equally on the basis of their diverse characteristics, and to leverage organisational diversity to enhance organisational justice and achieve better business outcomes.

The study found that those who have left the UK include young, skilled and qualified immigrants, who had previously formed a growing pool of incoming immigrants (Finch et al., 2009: 4–5; see also Oishi, 2012; Wickramasekara, 2003). In Australia and Canada, for example, highly skilled migrants were prone to leave soon after arrival, due to adjustment difficulties (Brenner et al., 2010; Hugo, Rudd & Harris, 2003; Productivity Commission, 2006). The Australian Department of Immigration and Citizenship notes that between 2006 and 2008, 40 per cent of the professionals departing Australia permanently were born overseas, a trend that is set to continue (Department of Immigration and Citizenship, 2008–2009: 31). Ironically, for host-country labour markets, the issue of retention is particularly pressing given severe skills shortages in certain sectors, predicted to worsen in the coming years. Thus, host countries must work to ensure that SMs receive proper assistance on arrival to ensure that they adjust and will stay to contribute to the host-country organisation and, more broadly, to the economy.

Cross-cultural awareness is therefore important in guiding managers in the selection, post-settlement preparation and adjustment of personnel for multinational organisations. A lack of cross-cultural awareness may have a direct or indirect impact on the post-settlement effectiveness, performance, assignment completion and retention of talented personnel. At a time of global talent shortages, it makes good business sense to ensure that staff adjust well in the post-arrival phase. We will investigate these issues in the next section.

■ Beyond cross-cultural management: a multilevel approach

■ Defining culture

There is no universally accepted definition of the term 'culture', but it is possible to draw out some common threads. One of the earliest definitions saw culture as 'that complex whole which includes knowledge, belief, art, morals, law, custom and any other capabilities and habits acquired by man as a member of society' (Tylor, 1871: 1). More recently, Hofstede (1984: 51), considered the 'father' of cultural dimensions in international business, has defined culture as 'the collective programming of the mind which distinguishes the members of one category of people from another'. Kroeber and Kluckhohn (1952: 181) captured both sets of definitions, and incorporated the collective notion of visible and invisible dimensions of culture, stating that:

> Culture consists of patterns, explicit and implicit, of and for behavior acquired and transmitted by symbols, constituting the distinctive achievements of human groups, including their embodiments in artifacts; the essential core of culture consists of traditional (i.e. historically derived and selected) ideas and especially their attached values; culture systems may, on the one hand, be considered as products of action, and on the other, as conditioning elements of further action.

In short, to understand culture we should observe the dynamics between two or more people. Culture is socially constructed and historically infused and includes both visible and invisible facets. The visible components of culture include behaviours, language and artefacts, and the invisible components of culture comprise norms, values, basic assumptions and beliefs.

In business, national and corporate cultures influence management in areas such as leadership, decision-making and motivation; approaches to recruitment, selection, training and development and retention; and approaches to managing diversity. It is therefore safe to assume that working across cultures also influences HR systems, since these systems cannot be easily transferred from one country to another. Consequently, it is crucial to establish how cultural differences can affect the social relations between work groups in organisations and how to coordinate processes in organisations, such as recruiting and retaining workers, to leverage the potential gains from cross-cultural diversity. A position paper by the Australian Government emphasises the importance of facilitating cultural exchanges and building cultural knowledge through capital and labour mobility: 'Cultural connections across a range of areas can be powerful forces for bringing people together. Exchanges in culture build greater understanding, foster cultural appreciation and offer commercial opportunities' (Australian Government, 2012: 257).

■ *The multilevel view of cross-cultural diversity management*

Our multilevel critical examination of cross-cultural diversity management seeks to understand culture in national, organisational and employee (group) contexts. Klarsfeld, Ng and Tatli (2012) have documented the role of the national context, as well as voluntary and coercive pressures from regulators (the government), competitive pressures (the firm) and unions (employee groups) in diversity management. For example, in France, unions and employee groups are predominant in driving diversity management in firms, while in Canada and the UK, both government pressures and competitive pressures motivate firms to pursue a diverse workforce (Cox & Blake, 1991; Ng & Tung, 1998). In the examples from France, Canada and the UK, there is a **business case for diversity**. The examples suggest that diversity management approaches are not converging but instead require different approaches based on the national, organisational and individual worker contexts. Thus, a multilevel approach is essential to understand effective cross-cultural management. Further, the examples from France, Canada and the UK suggest that diversity management practices are not converging but, instead, require different approaches based on national, organisational and employee contexts.

> **business case for diversity** An approach based on the principle that a properly managed diverse workforce can lead to greater financial profits and market share, with an enhanced ability to attract and retain the best human talents, greater creativity and innovation and improved marketing efforts.

■ *Macro-level dimensions*

Cross-cultural management is concerned with issues that arise in the context of relationships between individuals, groups and organisations from differing cultural backgrounds (Adler, 1983; Holden, 2002). Accordingly, we must recognise the potential for misunderstandings among different groups in the workplace and across business subsidiaries, due to their different ethno-cultural and linguistic characteristics. It is important to understand cross-cultural relations because this allows us to identify the characteristics of particular cultures and make comparisons between them based on identifiable characteristics.

Cross-cultural models fall into two broad categories (Tatli & Özbilgin, 2012). In **etic model**s, behaviour is universal. That is, behaviour must be understood in the context of behaviour in other cultures. For example, there are often differences between Western and East Asian cultures, and those differences are assessed on the basis of Western cultural norms. In **emic model**s, behaviour is culture-specific. That is, behaviour must be understood in the context of a particular culture. Using the same example from East Asian cultures, a Western perspective may view Japanese, Chinese and South Korean cultures as similar (perhaps because of their shared collectivism, high-power distance and high uncertainty avoidance), but the same cultures are clearly distinct when viewed from within an East Asian subculture.

> **etic model** A cross-cultural model that seeks to understand behaviour in one culture in the context of other cultures.
>
> **emic model** A cross-cultural model that seeks to understand behaviour in the context of a particular culture.

■ Cultural dimensions

A number of scholars have attempted to define and devise categories for cultural dimensions as a method of understanding cross-cultural management (Kluckhohn & Strodtbeck, 1961; Hofstede, 1980, 2001; Trompenaars, 1993; Brake Walker & Walker, 1995; House et al., 2004). Just as there is no universal measure or definition of culture, there is little agreement among cross-cultural researchers regarding 'what constitutes culture (that is, its key dimensions), how culture should be measured and what culture implies for managerial practice' (Tung & Verbeke, 2010: 1260). What do these research projects tell us? In brief, they derive national cultural dimension scores with the aim of providing scholars and practitioners with a means of comparing cultural differences between nations.

Hofstede's six cultural dimensions

Hofstede's work has been, and continues to be, the most cited and influential on cross-cultural research (Triandis, 2004: 89; Tung & Verbeke, 2010: 1259). In 1968 and 1972, Hofstede examined employees at IBM across more than 40 countries and some 116 000 employees completed survey questionnaires; later, in 1991 and 2001, he extended his research to include 50 countries and three regions. The survey examined employees' personal values, norms and approach to communication in relation to their work situation, in each of the countries involved. Notably, Hofstede did not embark on a study of cultural dimensions. Even so, the information gathered produced five cultural dimensions from which to index similarities and differences between cultures (power distance index, individualism, masculinity, uncertainty avoidance index and long-term orientation – see box 2.1), and in 2010 a sixth dimension was added to include a measure of indulgence versus restraint (Hofstede et al. 2010; see box 2.1). Figures 2.1 and 2.2 compare four countries' scores across the first five dimensions, while table 2.1 demonstrates how a number of countries scored across all six dimensions.

Box 2.1 HOFSTEDE'S SIX CULTURAL DIMENSIONS

power distance index (PDI) The degree of inequality of influence and power considered acceptable. This dimension allows us to compare high-power distance (greater inequality) with low-power distance (less inequality) cultures. Low-power distance cultures do not tolerate unequal distribution in power.

individualism (IDV) The extent to which people indicate a preference for individual pursuits rather than acting as members of a group. This dimension allows us to compare individualistic and collective cultures. More collectivist cultures prefer group rewards and prioritise in-group over out-group members.

masculinity (MAS) The extent to which traditionally masculine values such as assertiveness, dominance and achievement predominate within a culture compared with traditionally feminine values. This dimension allows us to compare those cultures that display more masculine than feminine characteristics. More feminine cultures tend to have greater overlap in gender roles.

uncertainty avoidance index (UAI) The extent to which individuals strive for certainty and favour structured over unstructured conditions and situations. This dimension allows us to compare risk-taking and risk-averse cultures. High-uncertainty avoidance cultures use rules, technology and religion to create uncertainty for themselves.

long-term orientation (LTO) The extent to which people display a long-term as compared with a short-term outlook on things such as work, life and other elements of society. Societies with longer-term orientations tend to save (thrift) and invest, and emphasise virtues over the truth.

indulgence orientation (IO) The extent to which a society enables the pursuit of satisfaction (as opposed to restraint), with respect to various human pleasures such as leisure, sex and consumption activity. Societies with higher indulgence scores facilitate the pursuit of pleasurable activities and experiences, while societies with higher restraint scores have more restrictive normative codes, which curtail instant gratification.

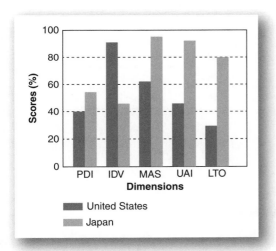

Figure 2.1 The five dimensions of culture – comparison between Japan and the United States
(adapted from www.geert-hofstede.com)

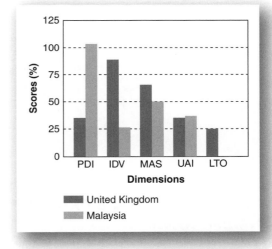

Figure 2.2 The five dimensions of culture – comparison between the United Kingdom and Malaysia
(adapted from www.geert-hofstede.com)

The GLOBE Project's nine dimensions

The GLOBE Project (House et al., 2004) is based on a survey collected from more than 17 000 middle managers, in 951 organisations, across three industries, in 62 countries or regions. The study identifies nine national cultural dimensions from which scores are derived (see box 2.2, page 32):

- power distance
- uncertainty avoidance
- institutional collectivism
- in-group collectivism

Table 2.1 The ranking of national cultures (adapted from Hofstede et al., 2010)

Country	Cultural dimensions ranking					
	PDI	IDV	MAS	UAI	LTO	IO
Australia	36	90	61	51	21	71
Canada	39	80	52	48	36	68
China	80	20	66	30	87	24
France	68	71	43	86	63	48
Germany	35	67	66	65	83	40
Hong Kong	68	25	57	29	61	17
India	77	48	56	40	51	26
Indonesia	78	14	46	48	62	48
Japan	54	46	95	92	88	42
Netherlands	38	80	14	53	67	68
Russia	93	39	36	95	81	20
South Korea	60	18	39	85	100	29
United States	40	91	62	46	26	68
West Africa	77	20	46	54	9	78

Box 2.2 *THE GLOBE PROJECT'S NINE CULTURAL DIMENSIONS*

power distance A perceived inequity in the distribution of power.

uncertainty avoidance The extent of group reliance on established social norms as a means to avoid uncertainty, including reliance on rules, structures and laws.

institutional collectivism The degree of collective action compared with individual action.

in-group collectivism The degree to which people show cohesiveness in groups.

gender egalitarianism Levels of difference between gender roles in society.

assertiveness The degree to which a culture determines behaviour in social relationships.

future orientation The degree to which planning and investing in the future is considered important.

performance orientation Value or reward attached to performance.

humane orientation Value attached to fairness, altruism and generosity.

Table 2.2 GLOBE Project country clusters (adapted from House et al., 2004)

Cluster	Countries	Attributes
Anglo	Canada, USA, Australia, Ireland, England, South Africa, New Zealand	Competitive and results-oriented; places less emphasis on family and close kinship ties.
Confucian Asia	Singapore, Hong Kong, China, Taiwan, South Korea, Japan	Results driven and focused on groups working together, with strong loyalty to family bonds.
Eastern Europe	Greece, Hungary Albania, Slovenia, Poland, Russia, Georgia, Kazakhstan	Low on performance orientation, with strong support for co-worker and gender equality.
Germanic Europe	Austria, Netherlands, Switzerland (German-speaking), Germany	Values competition; more results-oriented than people-oriented; plans and invests in the future, being considered individualistic in this respect.
Latin America	Ecuador, El Salvador, Columbia, Bolivia, Brazil, Guatemala, Argentina, Costa Rica, Venezuela, Mexico	Loyal and devoted to family, but less focused on performance and institutions.
Latin Europe	Israel, Italy, Switzerland, (French-speaking), Spain, Portugal, France	Values individual autonomy and places less emphasis on societal goals.
Middle East	Turkey, Kuwait, Egypt, Morocco, Qatar	Places emphasis on family ties; women and ethnic minority groups often hold lower status.
Nordic Europe	Denmark, Finland, Sweden	Emphasises the future; focuses on gender equality and institutional and societal collectiveness rather than family; cooperation and voice are central.
Southern Asia	Philippines, Indonesia, Malaysia, India, Thailand, Iran	Focuses on humane orientation and collectivism, with low levels of stress and policy structures; emphasises the present rather than the future.
Sub-Saharan Africa	Zimbabwe, Namibia, Zambia, Nigeria and South Africa	Devoted to a human orientation and sensitive to others and their families.

- gender egalitarianism
- assertiveness
- future orientation
- performance orientation
- humane orientation.

Unlike Hofstede's work, the GLOBE Project sets out to measure and evaluate national cultural dimensions. These dimensions are divided into two segments for the different national settings. One segment provides measures of actual societal practices ('As Is' scores) and the other segment measures the corresponding societal values ('Should Be' scores). As such, there are 18 national culture dimension scores. In addition to this, House et al. (2004) provide country cluster categories. Table 2.2 lists the countries in each cluster, and describes the attributes of that cluster.

Hofstede and the GLOBE Project: cautionary markers

While both the Hofstede and the GLOBE typologies offer useful ways to determine cultural differences, we should consider several points of caution. First, they assume that cultures are stable, which raises questions about the insights they grant to scholars and practitioners over time. Bond and Smith (1996) and Triandis (1994) have written in support of Hofstede's study and its cultural stability over time; while McSweeney (2002) and Tung (2008) are among those who have raised criticisms of such an approach.

Second, the typologies correlate cultural dimensions at the national level and apply them to derive an understanding of 'culture' and 'nations'. They also use these terms interchangeably, which raises serious concerns about external validity. This is particularly so given that, in practice, many national boundaries do not equate to clear cultural borders between one country and another. Consider the case where national borders (and the derivation of cultural dimensions) reflect colonial ties, which correspond more to the logic of colonial politics than to complex cultural realities.

Third, they assume that their cultural scores are applicable to, and valid for, an evaluation and understanding at the micro-level; that is, at the level of differences between individuals (Tung, 2008). Such generalisations are unjustified and ignore the subtleties and contradictions in many cultures. Importantly, the macro-level dimensions set out in these typologies cannot be used to make predictive statements about the behaviour of individuals.

Fourth, they argue that domestic cultures are homogeneous and universal. The flow-on effect of this is that subcultural and inter- and intragroup dynamics and differences are overlooked (Tung, 2008). It is important to consider differences in employees' race, religious affiliation, socioeconomic status, educational level and languages spoken. Indeed, differences between two countries might also be found between subcultures within a country. For example, 'Canadian culture' comprises both Anglophone and Francophone Canadians. Francophone Canadians are said to be more formal, hierarchical, moderately relationship-focused and more emotionally expressive than their Anglophone counterparts (Hofstede Centre, n.d.).

Finally, in the case of Hofstede's typology, his study has been criticised for drawing generalised conclusions from a survey limited in scope to one MNC; the MNC has also been seen as overwhelmingly espousing Western cultural values (Ailon, 2008; Javidan et al., 2006). The gaps scholars have identified in response to the cross-cultural theorists have proven fertile ground for the development of a framework that includes consideration of the meso- and micro-levels of analysis. On this basis, we now turn to consider meso- and micro-level dimensions that arise from different corporate structures and cultures, and implications for managing and working in a culturally and linguistically diverse setting.

■ Meso- and micro-level dimensions

Organisational theorists, like cross-cultural theorists, have noted the multiple layers that comprise organisational entities, describing them as 'cultural units that have within them powerful subcultures based on occupations and common histories', with visible and invisible layers (Schein, 2009: 3, 27, 39). While an organisation's culture is the sum of its members' interactions, it is also influenced by interactions within and between subcultural groupings and the external environment (that is, the broader society). Hofstede and colleagues (1990: 286) expanded on this point to define 'the organisational/corporate culture construct' as indicative of a range of features including

'1) holistic, 2) historically determined, 3) related to anthropological concepts, 4) socially constructed, 5) soft, and 6) difficult to change'.

While these facets describe the essential components of an organisation's culture, it is important to note that, in an international business setting, the organisational culture is affected and shaped by the type of its business arrangement. We must consider the nature of the arrangement – for example, whether it is a wholly owned subsidiary, a joint venture, a merger or an acquisition – since these structural forms help to shape the organisation's culture. Structures also inform the processes and policies employed in the staffing and management of the international venture, which in turn shape the organisational culture. An MNC has access to home-, host- and third-country nationals and, increasingly, to SIEs who hold multiple professional identities and cultural values located in a different country or company cultural setting. As such, while an organisation's culture is constructed over time and slow to change, the international setting makes for a more complex and dynamic entity, which is by nature subject to change. In this regard, we should also consider the management of workers from diverse backgrounds.

The need for greater awareness and accommodation in managing culturally and linguistically diverse workers is becoming increasingly clear for managers in both domestic and international contexts. Some factors driving this are:

- increasing skill shortages – in the United Arab Emirates, for example, expatriate labour is said to comprise more than 70 per cent of the working population
- demographic shifts – for example, an ageing population, changes in fertility rates and standards of and access to education and training (Al Ariss et al., 2012: 93)
- the need for organisations to attend to the diverse needs of workers in order to attract and retain their stock of talents.

The issue of cultural and linguistic diversity has been largely ignored in the IHRM literature (Bell et al., 2010; Tatli, 2011), as a result of imposing macro-level cultural dimensions on the meso- and micro-level dynamics of the workplace. When we fail to take stock of the importance of organisational and inter- and intragroup dynamics, we also fail to account for managing groups from diverse backgrounds. While this chapter focuses on diverse ethno-cultural and linguistic groups, we must also acknowledge that ethnically and linguistically diverse employees may differ further, in the dimensions of gender, age, sexual orientation and disability, among others (Brook & Lucas, 2012; Holvino, 2010).

A diverse group of employees works in MNCs, which complicates the cross-cultural issues involved. In addition to the challenge of managing a diverse workforce, MNCs are simultaneously operating in multiple foreign settings and under varying national norms and regulations, which may be at odds with an inclusive diversity management ethos. Even foreign firms with ostensibly equality-focused diversity agendas do not necessarily provide strong safeguards against discrimination of various kinds. For instance, in the Turkish context such policies are compromised once they are left to be implemented at the local level (Ozturk, 2011). MNCs often do not send expatriates who identify as lesbian, gay, bisexual, transgender or queer on international assignments to regions deemed to have challenging local norms (Gedro, 2010), which can in turn reduce the effectiveness of diversity management strategies in sustaining diverse work teams globally. While not all countries or organisations approach diversity management in the same way, it is important that HR managers make a coherent effort across their entire organisational network to monitor and manage diversity. In particular, they should focus on cultural and linguistic diversity and the inter- and intragroup dynamics that may evolve as a result of individual differences.

Diversity management is a process that is located at the workplace level and requires managers' awareness and response to individual workers (Nkomo & Cox, 1996; Dick & Cassel, 2002). As we have seen, diversity management can be understood as the strategic alignment of workforce heterogeneity where each employee is equally included and valued on the basis of their diverse characteristics. It is a process that ensures organisational diversity is leveraged to support both greater organisational justice and better business outcomes (Sanchez & Brock, 1996; Lorbiecki & Jack, 2000). Managing diversity emphasises inclusion at its core, with a view towards 'valuing each person for his or her unique combination of skill, competencies, attributes, knowledge [and] personality traits' (Heery & Noon 2001: 15) and various other demographic and social characteristics. These demographic characteristics, in combination, can shape group inclusion and exclusion; that is, inter- and intragroup dynamics and the workplace social relations that emerge as a result of them (Taksa & Groutsis, 2012). Accordingly, to manage culturally and linguistically diverse workers, we need to pay attention to the composition and distribution of particular groups; to the management of intercultural interactions; and to issues of equity and employee voice, irrespective of demographic characteristics. This requires a case-by-case assessment, given that cultural distance may play a significant part in the post-settlement adjustment phase. A person's cultural distance from the host country's culture may be influenced to a greater or lesser extent not only by the host country but also, increasingly, by the assignee's cultural background. For example, perceptions of fairness and voice vary among different cultural groups, based on the dimensions of individualism and collectivism and power distance (Au, Hui & Leung, 2001; Hui & Au, 2001; Thomas, Au & Ravlin, 2003).

■ Lessons from the multilevel approach: cross-cultural adjustment and retention

In an era characterised by increasing globalisation and worker mobility, it is important to manage across and within cultures and between cultural groups. Our multilevel approach suggests both a top-down and a bottom-up approach, where each level of analysis (the macro, meso and micro) informs the others. We have explored the established macro-level approach to explaining and understanding differences across cultures to date, which offers little insight into the meso- and micro-levels of analysis and is therefore of little use in distinguishing between or within cultures. Given what has overwhelmingly been a single-level approach to understanding cultural differences, it is not surprising that we are incapable of managing the multiple levels that constitute cultural adjustment, especially in conditions that are culturally distant from the worker's home country. In an era that is defined by the 'war for talent', we must consider managing adjustment and cultural differences from a multilevel perspective.

Conclusion

Observing cultural similarities between people from particular cultures or backgrounds may assist us in developing insights into how another person's cultural values and assumptions differ from our own. If our insights are correct, they may help us to bridge the cultural distance between ourselves and individuals from different cultures and to lay the foundation for effective management and work in another culture. However, if we make shorthand assumptions about values we think are typical of people from a particular cultural background, we may incorrectly categorise individuals who have different values. Homogenising cultural difference and arriving at inappropriate cultural stereotypes may be counterproductive and distract from understanding cross-cultural dynamics and the management of workers from diverse backgrounds.

Take-home messages

- We need to understand cross-cultural differences to attract and retain people from different ethno-cultural and linguistic backgrounds, and to manage business effectively working with people from other cultures.
- Practices and processes that are effective within one cultural setting (i.e. a national and corporate setting) may not necessarily work within another cultural setting. While macro-level cultural dimensions may provide us with some interesting insights, we must avoid the temptation to make assumptions about the values and intentions of individuals or groups based on this knowledge alone.
- Cultural insights are at best a starting point in establishing and understanding cross-cultural dynamics and managing diverse groups in different corporate and national cultural settings.
- We need to progress beyond the common approach to cross-cultural management, which is shorthand and partial and in which national (macro-level) cultural dimensions are applied to organisational level (meso-level) and individual (micro-level) interactions. Such cultural insights may misguide our understanding of organisational dynamics in an international setting.

Closing the learning loop

1. What is the difference between cross-cultural management and diversity management? Discuss with reference to the importance of diversity management insights for IHRM.
2. What are the characteristics of a global mindset?
3. What is the importance of practical insights from cross-cultural management and diversity management for the attraction and retention of global talent, and why is this so? Explain by drawing on the examples cited in the chapter.

4. What is the difference between the etic and emic models of cross-cultural behaviour?
5. What insights does cross-cultural theory provide, and what are the strengths and weaknesses of the categories they offer us? Refer particularly to Hofstede's cultural dimensions and the GLOBE Project.
6. Why is multilevel analysis useful in understanding cross-cultural management in the context of IHRM?

CASE STUDIES 2.1 AND 2.2   EXPATRIATE ADJUSTMENT IN INDIA

Rana Haq, Laurentian University

Talent mobility is a reality in today's globalised world, where organisations are competing to attract and retain skilled employees who are moving from their home countries and crossing continents to take part in higher education and to accept lucrative employment opportunities. This mobility necessitates increasing cross-cultural interactions in the workplace. Therefore, the management of diverse cultures plays a critical role in a global employment context.

India is an important emerging market that attracts many MNCs; however, it ranks as one of the most challenging countries for expatriate assignments and on the 'ease of doing business' index (Kim & Tung, 2013). In case study 2.1, we explore an example of an employee who moved from South Korea to India. South Korean MNCs, such as Hyundai Motors, Samsung Electronics and LG Electronics, all entered the Indian market in 1997, with manufacturing investments in three major Indian cities of Chennai, Mumbai and Delhi. While there is a strong South Korean presence in India, the two cultures are extremely different, particularly as India is very diverse (including in

terms of its people's ethnicity, religion and language) and South Korea relatively homogeneous (Kim & Tung, 2013). In case study 2.2, we consider the issues involved in relocating a female senior manager from Canada to India.

Hofstede's (2001) comparative index of India, South Korea and Canada is presented earlier in this chapter (see table 2.1), while the GLOBE Project (House et al., 2004) places South Korea in the Confucian cluster, India in the South Asian bloc and Canada in the Anglo group (see table 2.2). Given these cultural differences, consider the following case study scenarios.

Case study 2.1   From South Korea to South Delhi

Yeong-jin Lee, an operations manager in a South Korean MNC, was offered a promotion in the form of an expatriate assignment as a senior operations manager in the company's Indian office, which opened in 2000. He willingly accepted the three-year offer and moved to Delhi with his young family. His wife, Soo Kyong, quit her teaching job in Seoul and they moved to Delhi with their two children, a daughter aged 10 and a son aged 13. Yeong-jin was surprised by the various unanticipated challenges he faced in India, both on family and work fronts, and wondered what he and his home office in South Korea, as well as his host office in India, could have done better to prepare him and his family for the overseas assignment.

On the family front, both Yeong-jin Lee and Soo Kyong were concerned about their children's academic and social adjustment in their new school. Although there was no problem with admission to a good school, since the local education system had a significant foreigner's quota, the children were certain to experience cultural adjustment issues at school. In terms of the quality of education, Yeong-jin Lee and Soo Kyong had full confidence in the Indian education system, but were worried about whether their children would be able to adjust to the new school curriculum and make new friends. They were also concerned about how the children's time away would affect their educational opportunities on repatriation to South Korea at the end of the three-year assignment.

Confucian philosophy makes a clear distinction between the roles of the husband and wife, where the former provides financial support to the family and the latter focuses on bringing up and educating children. Soo Kyong had no regrets on quitting her teaching job in South Korea and accompanying her family to India. She found comfort in the fact that she would be a stay-at-home mother in India and would be able to spend more time with the children during this period. However, she was slightly nervous about her own personal adjustment in terms of being away from work and feeling isolated in this new country without any family or friends. In addition, she was overwhelmed by the many changes in her new environment, especially the language and food challenges. She also knew that she could not depend on Yeong-jin to help her or the children with many of these changes because he would be occupied with many pressures at work. This was consistent with the Confucian emphasis on sacrifice and the collectivist South Korean value of loyalty to the organisation over individual family needs (Kim & Tung, 2013).

On the work front, Yeong-jin was quite satisfied with the increased responsibilities associated with his elevated job title and managerial status in India. However, his home office still considered him a mid-level manager and expected him to implement centralised directives from headquarters; an expectation that he thought was unrealistic in the Indian context and that caused him significant stress. In addition, having only worked with South Korean nationals in his prior roles, Yeong-jin was ill-prepared to work with colleagues from different cultural and linguistic backgrounds and with diverse religious affinities.

In India, Yeong-jin was concerned with preventing misunderstandings and unintentionally offending the HCNs, especially his lack of knowledge regarding the nuances of the various social, religious and cultural customs in India. Further, he felt that he could not negotiate the division of labour on joint projects as effectively as he did with colleagues back at home and, as a result, he felt that some projects were bound to suffer from execution and completion problems. An example of this fear was his frustration with Indian cultural and professional attitudes towards expectations of commitment to time and project deadlines although, on the surface, everything seemed agreeable for the moment.

Case study 2.2   From Montreal to South Delhi

Kathleen Simon, a senior marketing manager in the Montreal office of a Canadian MNC, agreed to relocate to South Delhi, India for a two-year assignment. The MNC opened its Indian operations in 2002. Kathleen was single and had no dependants. As such, she felt that it was a good career opportunity. She thought that getting some international management experience would help her secure a promotion upon her return from this expatriate assignment. However, when she arrived, she found that she was not prepared for the many challenges she faced and wondered how best to deal with them, given that her company's home and host offices had not assisted her significantly during the transition process.

As an expatriate woman relocating by herself, Kathleen was quite concerned about her personal safety in India. She knew that, as part of her contract, there would be no problem with housing security since her company would provide her with a comfortable home in one of the safest and upscale neighbourhoods in South Delhi. However, she worried about how she should dress at work and during leisure time, and especially how others (including her expatriate and local colleagues) might perceive her. She was also concerned about her social life, leisure activities and making new friends in India.

In the professional context, Kathleen felt that the business culture was highly gendered, and communication was difficult when working with subordinates and other managers, most of whom were men. Some of Kathleen's colleagues and external clients saw her workplace behaviour as fastidious and demanding, while she saw it as assertive and competent. So, Kathleen had to try hard to navigate what sometimes seemed like a cultural minefield, to ensure that she interacted seamlessly with local colleagues and clients.

Case study questions

1. What are some of the cultural differences between India and South Korea, according to Hofstede and the GLOBE Project? Refer to tables 2.1 and 2.2 in this chapter.

2. What are some of the cultural differences between India and Canada, according to Hofstede and the GLOBE Project? Refer to tables 2.1 and 2.2 in this chapter.

3. What challenges may South Korean expatriates face in India, as in the case of Yeong-jin Lee?

4. What challenges may Canadian expatriates face in India, as in the case of Kathleen Simon?

5. To what extent did issues of gender influence the experiences and challenges that the two expatriate managers encountered on their assignments?

6. What insights about India should expatriates from other countries and regions (e.g. Australia, Europe, Mexico, the United Kingdom) consider when offered an expatriate assignment?

7. What can MNCs do to ensure successful selection, training, adjustment and completion of expatriate assignments in the Indian context?

8. What potential career opportunities are available to MNC managers who accept expatriate assignments to developing countries that may be considered 'more exotic' or 'less preferred'?

> **» ACTIVITIES**

Debate

Present arguments for and against this proposition:

The study of cross-cultural management has historically relied on grand theories, limiting its validity across and within different cultural contexts and countries. We need to consider multiple theories and perspectives, all of which can be partially legitimate and workable. Given that these are only points of view, there is no objective version of cross-cultural management.

Small group discussion

Break up into small groups and consider the following questions.

1. What would a United Kingdom – based organisation that wished to expand into Japan, Malaysia and the United States need to consider in terms of cross-cultural management? Discuss with reference to Hofstede's cultural dimensions.
2. How useful is Hofstede's cultural dimensions model as a guide for practitioners?

Online resources

- For instructors: answers to activities; long media article with questions.
- For students: further reading; answers to case studies; IHRM in practice.

References

Adler, N. J. (1983). Cross-cultural management research: The ostrich and the trend, *Academy of Management Review*, 8(2), 226–32.

Ailon, G. (2008). Mirror, mirror on the wall: 'Culture's consequences' in a value test of its own design, *Academy of Management Review*, 33(4): 885–904.

Al Ariss, A. and Özbilgin, M. (2010). Understanding self-initiated expatriates: Career experiences of Lebanese self-initiated expatriates in France, *Thunderbird International Business Review*, 52(4): 275–85.

Al Ariss, A., Koall, I., Özbilgin, M. and Suutari, V. (2012). Careers of skilled migrants: Towards a theoretical and methodological expansion, *Journal of Management Development*, 31(2): 92–101.

Au, K., Hui, M. K. and Leung, K. (2001). Who should be responsible? Effects of voice and compensation on responsibility attribution, perceived justice and post-complaint behaviours across cultures, *International Journal of Conflict Management*, 12(4): 350–64.

Australian Government (2012). *Australia in the Asian century: White paper*. Department of the Prime Minister and Cabinet, Canberra.

Beechler, S. and Woodward, I. C. (2009). The global 'war for talent', *Journal of International Management*, 15(3): 273–85.

Bell, M. P., Kwesiga, E. N. and Berry, D. P. (2010). Immigrants: The new 'invisible men and women' in diversity research, *Journal of Managerial Psychology*, 25(2): 177–88.

Bender, S. and Fish, A. (2000). The transfer of knowledge and the retention of expertise: The continuing need for global assignments, *Journal of Knowledge Management*, 4(2): 125–37.

Bhaskar-Shrinivas, P., Harrison, D. A., Shaffer, M. A. and Luk, D. M. (2005). Input-based and time-based models of international adjustment: meta-analytic evidence and theoretical extensions, *Academy of Management Journal*, 48(2): 257–81.

Black, J. S. and Gregersen, H. B. (1991). Antecedents to cross-cultural adjustment for expatriates in Pacific Rim assignments, *Human Relations*, 44(5): 497–515.

Black, J. S., Mendenhall, M. and Oddou, G. (1991). Toward a comprehensive model of international adjustment: An integration of multiple theoretical perspectives, *Academy of Management Review*, 16(2): 219–317.

Bond, M. H. and Smith, P. B. (1996). Cross-cultural social and organisational psychology, *Annual Review of Psychology*, 47: 205–35.

Brake, T., Walker, D. and Walker, T. (1995). *Doing business internationally: The guide to cross-cultural success*, Burr Ridge, IL: Irwin Professional.

Brenner, G., Menzies, T., Dionne, L. and Filion, L. (2010). How location and ethnicity affect ethnic entrepreneurs in three Canadian cities, *Thunderbird International Business Review*, 52(2): 153–71.

Brewster, C. and Scullion, H. (2007). A review and agenda for expatriate HRM, *Human Resource Management Journal*, 7(3): 32–41.

Brook, P. and Lucas, R. (eds) (2012). Special issue: Equality and diversity in employment relations, *Equality, Diversity and Inclusion An International Journal*, 31(4): 323–90.

Burke, R. and Ng, E. (2006). The changing nature of work and organizations: Implications for human resource management, *Human Resource Management Review*, 16(2): 86–94.

Cao, L., Hirschi, A. and Deller, J. (2012). Self-initiated expatriates and their career success, *Journal of Management Development*, 31(2): 159–72.

Cerdin, J. L. and Pargneux, M. L. (2010). Career anchors: A comparison between organization-assigned and self-initiated expatriates, *Thunderbird International Business Review*, 52(4): 287–99.

Cerna, L. (2010). *Policies and practices of highly skilled migration in times of the economic crisis*. Geneva: International Labour Organization.

Chaloff, J. and Lemaitre, G. (2009). *Managing highly-skilled labour migration: A comparative analysis of migration policies and challenges in OECD countries*. Paris: OECD.

Chambers, E. G., Foulon, M., Handfield-Jones, H., Hankin, S. M. and Michaels, E. G. (1998). The war for talent, *McKinsey Quarterly*, 1(3): 44–57.

Cox Jr, Taylor H. and Blake, S. (1991). Managing cultural diversity: Implications for organizational competitiveness, *Academy of Management Executive*, 5(3): 45–56.

Department of Immigration and Citizenship (2008–2009). *Immigration update*, www.immi.gov.au/media/publications/statistics/immigration-update/update-jun09.pdf.

Dick, P. and Cassel, C. (2002). Barriers to managing diversity in a UK constabulary: The role of discourse, *Journal of Management Studies*, 39(7): 953–76.

Doherty, N. (2013). Understanding the self-initiated expatriate: A review and directions for future research, *International Journal of Management Reviews*, 15(4): 447–69.

Economist Intelligence Unit (2010). *Global firms in 2020: The next decade of change for organisations and workers. A report from the Economist Intelligence Unit*, http://www. managementthinking.eiu.com/sites/default/files/SHM_globalfirms_finalfinal.pdf.

Edelman, L. B., Fuller, S. R. and Mara-Drita, I. (2001). Diversity rhetoric and the managerialization of law, *American Journal of Sociology*, 106(6): 1589–641.

Finch, T., Latorre, M., Pollard, N. and Rutter, J. (2009). *Shall we stay or shall we go? Re-migration trends among Britain's immigrants*. London: Institute for Public Policy Research.

Gedro, J. (2010). The lavender ceiling atop the global closet: Human resource development and lesbian expatriates, *Human Resource Development Review*, 9(4): 385–404.

Groutsis, D. and Arnold, P. C. (2012). Tracking the career decisions and experience of migrant elites: The case of South African–trained medical professionals in the Australian labour market, *Health Sociology Review*, 21(3): 332–42.

Gupta, A. K. and Govindarajan, V. (2002). Cultivating a global mindset, *Academy of Management Executive*, 16(1): 116–26.

Harvey, W. S. and Groutsis, D. (2012). Skilled migrants in the Middle East: Definitions, mobility and integration, *International Journal of Business and Globalisation*, 8(4): 438–53.

Heery, E. and Noon, M. (2001). *Dictionary of human resource management*. Oxford: Oxford University Press.

Hofstede, G. (1980). *Culture's consequences: International differences in work-related values*. Beverly Hills, CA: Sage.

Hofstede, G. (1984). *Culture's consequences: International differences in work-related values*, abridged edition. Newbury Park, CA: Sage.

Hofstede, G. (2001). *Culture's consequences: Comparing values, behaviors, institutions and organizations across nations*, 2nd edition. Thousand Oaks, CA: Sage.

Hofstede, G., Hofstede, G. J. and Minkov, M. (2010) *Cultures and organizations: Software of the mind*, 3rd edition. N.p.: McGraw-Hill.

Hofstede, G., Neuijen, B., Daval Ohayv, D. and Sanders, G. (1990). Measuring organizational cultures: A qualitative and quantitative study across twenty cases, *Administrative Science Quarterly*, 35(2): 286–316.

Hofstede Centre (n.d.). *What about Canada?* http://geert-hofstede.com/canada.html.

Holden, N. (2002). *Cross-cultural management: A knowledge management perspective*. N.p: Pearson Education.

Holvino, E. (2010) Intersections: The simultaneity of race, gender and class in organization studies, *Gender, Work and Organization*, 17(3): 248–77.

House, R. J., Hanges, P. J., Javidan, M., Dorfman, P. W. and Gupta, V. (2004). *Culture, leadership and organizations: The GLOBE Study of 62 societies*. Thousand Oaks, CA: Sage.

Howe-Walsh, L. and Schyns, B. (2010). Self-initiated expatriation: implications for HRM, *International Journal of Human Resource Management*, 21(2): 260–73.

Hugo, G., Rudd, D. and Harris, K. (2003). *Australia's diaspora: Its size, nature and policy implications*. Melbourne: Committee for Economic Development of Australia.

Hui, M. K. and Au, K. (2001). Justice perceptions of complaint-handling: A cross-cultural comparison between PRC and Canadian customers, *Journal of Business Research*, 52(2): 161–73.

Javidan, M., House, R. J., Dorfman, P. W., Hanges, P. J. and Sully de Luque, M. (2006). Conceptualizing and measuring cultures and their consequences: A comparative review of GLOBE's and Hofstede's approaches, *Journal of International Business Studies*, 37(6): 897–914.

Jokinen, T., Brewster, C. and Suutari, V. (2008). Career capital during international work experiences: Contrasting self-initiated expatriate experiences and assigned expatriation, *International Journal of Human Resource Management*, 19(6): 979–98.

Kim, H.-D. and Tung, R. (2013). Opportunities and challenges for expatriates in emerging markets: An exploratory study of Korean expatriates in India, *International Journal of Human Resource Management*, 21(5): 1029–50.

Kim, K. and Slocum, J. W. (2008). Individual differences and expatriate assignment effectiveness: The case of US-based Korean expatriates, *Journal of World Business*, 43(1): 109–26.

Klarsfeld, A., Ng, E. S. and Tatli, A. (2012). Social regulation and diversity management: A comparative study of France, Canada and the UK, *European Journal of Industrial Relations*, 18(4): 309–27.

Kluckhohn, F. R. and Strodtbeck, F. L. (1961). *Variations in value orientations*. Evanston, IL: Row, Peterson.

Kroeber, A. L. and Kluckhohn, C. (1952). *Culture: A critical review of concepts and definitions*. Harvard University Peabody Museum of American Archeology and Ethnology Papers, 47.

Johnston, W. and Packer, A. (1987). *Workforce 2000*. Indianapolis: Hudson Institute.

Levy, O., Beechler, S., Taylor, S. and Boyacigiller, N. A. (2007). What we talk about when we talk about 'global mindset': Managerial cognition in multinational corporations, *Journal of International Business Studies*, 38(2): 231–58.

Lloyd, S. and Hartel, C. (2010). Intercultural competencies for culturally diverse work teams, *Journal of Managerial Psychology*, 25(8): 845–75.

Lorbiecki, A. and Jack, G. (2000). Critical turns in the evolution of diversity management, *British Journal of Management*, 11(s1): S17–31.

McSweeney, B. (2002). Hofstede's model of national cultural differences and their consequences: A triumph of faith; a failure of analysis, *Human Relations*, 55(1): 89–118.

Malmström, C. (2012). Employment: Commissioners Malmström and Andor welcome the new OECD report on international migration trends. Reference: MEMO/12/495, event date 27 June 2012.

ManpowerGroup (2012a). *Leveraging talent through training: A ManpowerGroup Research Report*, www.manpower.com.au/documents/White-Papers/2012_LeveragingTalentThrough TrainingResearchPaper_2012_Global.pdf.

ManpowerGroup (2012b). *How to navigate the human age: Increasing demand for better skills assessment and match for better results*, www.manpower.com.au/documents/ White-Papers/2012_How_to_Navigate_the_Human_Age_Manpower.pdf.

Martin, P. L. (2003). *Highly skilled labor migration: Sharing the benefits*. Geneva: International Labour Organization.

Michaels, E., Handfield-Jones, H. and Axelrod, B. (2001). *The war for talent*. Boston: Harvard Business School Press.

Ng, E. S. W. and Burke, R. J. (2005). Person–organization fit and the war for talent: Does diversity management make a difference?, *International Journal of Human Resource Management*, 16(7): 1195–210.

Ng, E. S. and Metz, I. (2013). Multiculturalism as a strategy for national competitiveness: The case for Canada and Australia. Paper presented at the 6th Equality, Diversity and Inclusion Conference, Athens, Greece.

Ng, E. S. and Tung, R. L. (1998). Ethno-cultural diversity and organizational effectiveness: A field study, *International Journal of Human Resource Management*, 9(6): 980–95.

Nkomo, S. and Taylor Cox, M. (1996). Diverse identities in organizations. In Clegg, S. R., Hardy, C. and Nord, W. R. (eds), *Handbook of organization studies*, 338–56. London: Sage.

Oishi, N. (2012). The limits of immigration policies: The challenges of highly skilled migration in Japan, *American Behavioral Scientist*, 56, 1080–100.

Ozturk, M. B. (2011). Sexual orientation discrimination: Exploring the experiences of lesbian, gay and bisexual employees in Turkey, *Human Relations*, 64(8): 1099–118.

Productivity Commission (2006). *Economic impacts of migration and population growth*. Melbourne: Productivity Commission.

Sanchez, J. I. and Brock, P. (1996). Outcomes of perceived discrimination among Hispanic employees: is diversity management a luxury or a necessity? *Academy of Management Journal*, 39(3): 704–19.

Schein, E. (2009). *The corporate culture survival guide*. San Francisco, CA: John Wiley and Sons.

Shay, J. P, and Baack, S. (2006). An empirical investigation of the relationships between modes and degree of expatriate adjustment and multiple measures of performance, *International Journal of Cross Cultural Management*, 6(3): 275–94.

Stroh, L. K. (1995). Predicting turnover among repatriates: Can organizations affect retention rates?, *International Journal of Human Resource Management*, 6(2): 443–56.

Taksa, L. and Groutsis, D. (2012). Managing cultural diversity: Problems and prospects for ethnicity and gender at work. In Mills, A. J. and Durepos, G. (eds), *Case study methods in business research*, 247–66. London: Sage.

Tatli, A. (2011). A multi-layered exploration of the diversity management field: Diversity discourses, practices and practitioners in the UK, *British Journal of Management*, 22(2): 238–53.

Tatli, A. and Özbilgin, M. F. (2012). An emic approach to intersectional study of diversity at work: a Bourdieuan framing, *International Journal of Management Reviews*, 14(2): 180–200.

Thomas, D. and Ely, R. (1996). Making differences matter: A new paradigm for managing diversity, *Harvard Business Review*, 74(5): 79–90.

Thomas, D. C., Au, K. and Ravlin, E. C. (2003). Cultural variation and the psychological contract, *Journal of Organizational Behavior*, 24(5): 451–71.

Triandis, H. C. (1994). *Culture and social behavior*. New York: McGraw-Hill.

Triandis, H. C. (2004). Forward. In House, R. J., Hanges, P. J., Javidan, M., Dorfman, P. W. and Gupta, V. (eds), *Culture, leadership and organizations: The GLOBE Study of 62 societies*, 15–19. Thousand Oaks, CA: Sage.

Trompenaars, F. (1993). *Riding the waves of culture: Understanding cultural diversity in business*. London: Nicholas Brealey Publishing.

Tung, R. L. (1993). Managing cross-national and intra-national diversity, *Human Resource Management*, 32(4): 461–77.

Tung, R. L. (2008). The cross-cultural research imperative: The need to balance cross-national and intra-national diversity, *Journal of International Business Studies*, 39(1): 41–6.

Tung, R. L. and Verbeke, A. (2010). Beyond Hofstede and GLOBE: Improving the quality of cross-cultural research, *Journal of International Business Studies*, 41(8): 1259–74.

Tylor, E. B. (1871). *Primitive culture*. Vol. 2. New York: Harper.

Wickramasekara, P. (2003). Policy responses to skilled migration: Retention, return and circulation. In *Perspectives on labour migration*, 5th edition. Geneva: International Labour Office.

3

Key players in international human resource management

Graham Hollinshead, Cynthia Forson, Natalia Rocha-Lawton and Moira Calveley

■ Learning objectives

- To offer a broad and nuanced view of international assignments, drawing on principles of diversity.
- To challenge questions about traditional concepts in international business organisation (notably the familiar parent/subsidiary paradigm) and an exploration of complex international organisational configurations as a determinant of modern international staffing.
- To demonstrate the complexities of international staffing in an ethnically diverse organisational context, through an in-depth, original case study.

■ Learning outcomes

After reading this chapter, students will be able to:
- understand the contextual determinants for international staffing
- examine the rationale for the use of expatriates, third-country nationals, host-country nationals, biculturals and other international assignees
- comprehend the strategic rationale for multinational companies devolving managerial authority to the 'subsidiary'
- examine the significance of diversity in international staffing
- appreciate novel forms of international organisation, drawing on the concepts of the international division of labour and global value chains.

▓ Introduction

It is increasingly recognised that contemporary global organisations are characterised by unprecedented levels of complexity and variability. As the world has become more 'bumpy' in relation to the geographical points of origin of multinational companies (MNCs) – with the BRIC (Brazil, Russia, India and China) nations beginning to rival the dominant patterns of Western and Japanese ownership of MNCs – so stereotypical notions of international staffing are called into question. Further, as Wadhwa (2009) implies, the traditional definition of MNC organisation as a linear parent/subsidiary relationship is losing credibility: major corporations around the world in sectors such as software design, pharmaceuticals and financial services are recognising the competitive advantages of disaggregating operational activities and sourcing differentiated reservoirs of available talent across geographical spaces, including from developing and emerging countries.

In these circumstances, it may be argued that unidirectional conceptions of international staffing are increasingly redundant, as international networks of knowledge exchange become more pronounced across previously remote territories. These paradigm shifts in modes of international operation have led to a multifaceted picture of the international mobility of people, blurring the traditional dividing line between 'expatriation' and 'migration'. It is also the case that the traditional expatriate has most often been portrayed as relatively youthful, Caucasian and male. While many expatriates undoubtedly do comply with this characterisation, given the emergence of highly cosmopolitan, multilayered and 'flattened' international business models, this ethnically and gender laden human profile of the international staffing community may be regarded as unsustainably **ethnocentric** and insensitively imperialistic in the modern era.

ethnocentrism A strategic assumption in the MNC that tried-and-tested approaches to management can be extended from the country of origin to operating sites in other countries. Underlying this is a wish to retain power in the country of origin.

In this chapter, we first provide an overview of the nature and rationality of 'traditional' expatriation and consider alternative and emergent forms of international assignment in a rapidly changing global business context. Second, we ask the question 'Who are the international assignees?' and observe that stereotypical notions about the identity of expatriate managers and similar staffing categories should be opened up for review. Third, we question the validity of the pervasive, yet rather simplistic, parent/subsidiary typology of MNC organisational form. We suggest that we can gain more nuanced and sophisticated insights into the realities of international staffing and mobility when we recognise the emergence of web-like international business linkages that allow MNCs to source talent from a range of widely dispersed global locations. Finally, we present an original case study of an MNC in the process of relocating a primary research and development (R & D) site to China. In this on-the-ground study, we bring to the fore the complexities associated with the intimate combination of diverse ethnic groupings within a single enterprise, an international staffing experiment that prompted its participants to contestation, as well as to collaborate in highly effective ways.

▪ Key actors in international organisation

It has been recognised (Hollinshead, 2009) that the nature of the deployment of principal managerial agents within the MNC is fundamentally conditioned by its strategic purpose and orientation as it straddles international boundaries. Accordingly, highly centralised or ethnocentric (Perlmutter, 1969) organisational forms are prone to rely heavily on managerial emissaries from headquarters in implementing corporate **mandates** in the subsidiary context. Meanwhile, devolved or **polycentric** configurations are associated with local managers and workers at the level of the subsidiary being entrusted with the conduct of corporate affairs. Undoubtedly, much of the IHRM literature to date has placed considerable emphasis on expatriates as critical human actors in instigating processes of control, coordination and socialisation across the MNC (Harzing, 2001). Expatriates may typically be defined as parent-country nationals (PCNs) engaged in international assignments for a predefined, specified period. In the wake of the global financial crisis, the Global Relocation Trends Survey (Brookfield Global Relocation Services, 2010: 1) reflected buoyancy in the international 'traffic' of expatriation, reporting an almost 50 per cent increase in international assignments over the previous year in its participating group of MNCs and stating that:

> assignment activity outside the headquarters country location continued to rise hitting 46%, an all-time high, and another sign that companies are diversifying their sources for talent and looking farther afield for new market opportunities.

In seeking to unravel the corporate rationality that underlies the deployment of expatriates, Colakoglu and Caligiuri (2008) posit that a major role of international managerial assignees is to engage in the transfer of knowledge from headquarters to subsidiary, and to exert strategic leadership through **boundary spanning** activities (Edström & Galbraith, 1977; Bonache & Brewster, 2001). The role expatriates play as **cultural carriers** is significant, particularly in the startup phase of overseas operations, because it catalyses the dissemination of corporate values and the building of trust across organisational components, which are embedded in institutionally and culturally

mandate An authoritative course of action, or strategy formulation, that the senior managers of an MNC typically define.

polycentrism A strategic assumption in MNCs that local managers and employees are best placed to formulate policies that reflect local needs, with a preference for decentralisation and autonomy at operating sites.

geocentrism The idealised status of a truly global concern, combining local and international strengths. Managers are able to take a global view of the organisation, both responding flexibly to local needs and transcending them, in the pursuit of corporate goals and values at international level.

boundary spanning The fostering of networks and linkages across diverse international organisational units.

cultural carriers Internationally mobile individuals who diffuse the primary norms and values of the MNC across its organisational subunits.

diverse territories, thus serving to minimise strategic risk (Harzing, 2001; Balgia & Jaeger, 1984; Boyacigiller, 1990; Kogut & Zander, 2003). As Riusala and Suutari (2000) point out, expatriates may also serve as conduits for the 'inward' transfer of knowledge and locally contextualised information from subsidiary to parent.

In their seminal work, Edström and Galbraith (1977) reinforce the notion that international management assignees are closely involved in the diffusion of corporate norms and values throughout the international organisation. In this way, such assignees assist with the process of organisational development and potentially contribute towards the growth of the subsidiary within the corporate value chain. Edström and Galbraith (1977) recognise the strategic significance of expatriation and suggest that its objective may also be highly functional. Colakoglu and Caligiuri (2008) concur, recognising that international assignments may be primarily operational in their orientation; for example, in the case of carrying out an assigned financial, marketing or HR project, or providing advice relating to new technical systems. Edström and Galbraith (1977) also suggest that international assignments may be instigated in order to foster management development, as international experience augments the skill set of an international executive who seeks career progression.

In summary, following Edström and Galbraith (1977), expatriation may be regarded as serving three major purposes. First, it contributes to international organisational development by facilitating the coordination and control of corporate philosophies and practices throughout geographically dispersed subsidiary units of MNCs (Harzing, 2004). Second, international mobility provides expatriates themselves with opportunities to acquire international experience and develop a global vision. Third, expatriation can ensure the transfer of specific areas of know how across the MNC to compensate for gaps in expertise and skill in various operational locations.

■ Alternatives to expatriation, devolving to the subsidiary and the 'new Argonauts'

Although 'traditional' expatriation has occupied a pivotal position in the IHRM literature, it is a relatively high-risk international staffing strategy, particularly in the light of growing cultural and institutional distances between headquarters and subsidiaries in developing countries, which create a risk of 'adjustment' problems. The resourcing of international assignments is also a relatively expensive business, as considerable time and money (at least in theory) is needed for investment in the selection, training and motivation of expatriates, and possibly into support for their spouses or partners and families. In such circumstances, and given advances in virtual forms of communication, MNCs are now able to review critically the need for traditional expatriation and to opt for more flexible alternatives (see table 3.1), including the use of international commuters, employees on short- and medium-term foreign postings, international transferees (who move from one subsidiary to another), migrants, contract expatriates or virtual international employees in cross-cultural project teams

Table 3.1 Types of international assignee	
Assignee category	**Description**
International commuter	A person who moves on a daily or weekly basis between subsidiary units, within the same continent.
Short- or medium-term foreign posting	A person who transfers within an MNC for a fixed period of time (typically between one month and three years).
International transferee	A person who undertakes temporary assignments abroad, which may occur on a serial basis throughout their career. Such assignments may occur to facilitate the startup of an overseas operation.
Migrant	A person who is engaged in remunerated employment in a region to which they have moved. The term typically refers to workers rather than managers, and the assignment may be for an unlimited time.
Contract expatriate	A person who is posted overseas to fulfil the requirements of a particular contract, and who is remunerated for completion of the contract. The posting is for a fixed term and is often seen in fields such as construction and information technology.
Virtual international employee	A person who remains in their home base but interacts frequently with international counterparts through various means, such as video conferencing and Skype.

(Zimmerman & Sparrow, 2007). In Europe, the deregulated airline industry has made it realistic for people – at least at executive level – to commute regularly across the continent to work. So, a person may pursue an international assignment with minimal disruption to their home, personal life and career.

Such international staffing categories may provide cost-effective and functional alternatives to traditional expatriation, and yet an increasing number of academics and practitioners recognise that the fundamentally unidirectional and 'exportative' (Reiche, Kraimer & Harzing, 2009) model of international staffing is outliving its usefulness, given the plethora of organisational structures and configurations that are emerging in the global economy, and the international reservoirs of talent and skill that are available.

Scholars have now begun to recognise high levels of complexity in international organisations, implying a pressing need to reframe the existing orthodoxy which places expatriates centre stage in the discourse and practice of IHRM. Reiche, Kraimer and Harzing (2009) argue that, in the current era of globalisation, MNCs are seeking to capitalise on new opportunities in developing and emerging economies. Where sites of operation are institutionally and culturally remote from headquarters, the use of traditional expatriation may be seen not only as a risky and expensive staffing instrument, but also as an insensitive and inappropriate option from the perspective of the indigenous population. As Harvey, Novicevic and Speier (2000) argue, host-country nationals (HCNs) may represent an invaluable source of context-specific, and frequently tacit, knowledge at the local site, and are thereby uniquely equipped to engage in cross-unit brokerage (Harvey & Novicevic, 2004;

Kostova & Roth, 2003). Complying with Perlmutter's (1969) notion of polycentricity, Harzing (2004) concurs that HCNs may contribute invaluable resources to international companies, particularly relating to socioeconomic, political and legal circumstances and to business practices in the host environment.

As an alternative to HCNs or in combination with them, there are now more third-country nationals (TCNs) in many MNC structures. Coming neither from home nor host country, TCNs can nevertheless fill knowledge and skill gaps as well as offering cultural neutrality where corporate ethical partisanship is an issue. The pools of managerial and technical talent emerging in India, China, Brazil and Russia may be fruitfully sourced by MNCs seeking third-country participation in their corporate structures. In a study of a new joint venture between Turkish and Serbian partners in the brewing industry in Serbia, Hollinshead and Maclean (2007) found that TCNs from Scandinavia and the Netherlands were able to inject state-of-the-art marketing, R & D and technical knowledge in the early stages of the merger. The intervention of the Northern European industrial experts over a protracted period offered an impartial and modern perspective on the introduction of new technologies and managerial systems.

bicultural A person who identifies with two or more cultures, having internalised more than one set of cultural schemas.

inpatriate An international assignee, usually from the less developed regions of the world, who is an HCN. Inpatriates share their more diverse cultural and educational backgrounds with employees in the HQ.

returnee A highly skilled knowledge or managerial worker who has typically migrated to a highly developed Western economy from an emerging economy such as India or China but later returns home.

reverse brain drain The trend towards a shift of human capital from industrialised/developed to emerging/developing economies.

Various forms of bicultural engagement, associated with the 'network' form of international organisation (Dicken, 2011), are becoming more common. According to Brannen and Thomas (2010), biculturals may be defined as individuals who 'identify with two (or more) distinct cultures because [they have] internalised more than one set of cultural schemas'. The following groups may be regarded as bicultural assignees or migrants. **Inpatriates** are managers or workers who are seconded from the MNC host environment to headquarters (that is, a form of 'reverse' expatriation) in order to gain exposure to, and familiarity with, norms and values in the 'parent' locality; they are then able to disseminate to their home locale the embedded knowledge they have gained from the MNC country of origin (Harzing, 2004). **Returnees** are highly skilled knowledge or managerial workers who have typically migrated to highly developed Western economies from emerging nations such as India or China, and have been tempted to return home, in a form of **reverse brain drain** (Wadhwa, 2009). As the case study in this chapter demonstrates, this staff resource is vital for emerging economies because it potentially combines exposure to state-of-the-art Western business and scientific models with cultural, linguistic and institutional familiarity with the subsidiary milieu.

In a compelling work, which is perhaps emblematic of the 'new world order' in international organisation, Saxenian (2006) describes the critical role Chinese and Indian immigrants are playing at the helm of companies engaged in high-tech operations in Silicon Valley, California. Such 'new Argonauts' have compensated for deficits in the United States talent pool by galvanising innovative activity in the 'Golden State' and beyond. Similarly, Indian managers and consultants now occupy many senior positions in the US financial services industry. Undoubtedly, such highly placed immigrants in the West retain an ethnically based affinity with their home countries and, in the most recent phase of global development, have been tempted to contribute to the ascent of India and China through innovative and creative thinking, either directly (through reverse migration) or indirectly (through virtual methods or networking). The transcendent nature of these ethnically based networks of talent, which straddle advanced and emerging economies, acts to intersect conventional and bounded organisational configurations, and arguably makes superfluous the ethno-centric assumptions that underpin traditional patterns of international staffing.

In summary, simple models of expatriation predicated on the notion of exporting experts from Western nerve centres to dispersed subsidiaries are becoming obsolete given the growing complexity of the international business world. Instead, a multi-directional and multifaceted pattern of international mobility is becoming apparent and making an impact on 'traditional' ethnic divides.

Diversity and international mobility

Although the bulk of the literature on expatriation focuses on organisationally assigned expatriates, other 'subsets' in the international organisational community may contribute readymade capital and skills generated through life experiences, outside of the parameters of the 'normal' expatriation process. For the purpose of this chapter we will focus first on women and secondly on migrants, ethnic minorities and self-initiated expatriates (SIEs).

Women

While there has been a discernible increase in the number of female expatriates in recent years, with women representing some 20 per cent of international assignees in 2009, this figure has recently declined to a mere 17 per cent (Brookfield Global Relocation Services, 2010). This decline corresponds to a general reduction in the number of expatriates worldwide due to recession (Brookfield Global Relocation Services, 2010). Nonetheless, the low level of female representation within the expatriate community is disappointing given the increasing numbers of women in management roles within organisations, a situation that is even more surprising because female expatriates have proven to be remarkably successful in their assign-ments (Linehan, 2000). In this section, we draw on the published literature to explore real and perceived barriers to women's engagement with the expatriation process.

The reasons posited for lack of female participation in expatriation are many and varied and tend to be in keeping with Adler's (1984a; 1984b; 1987; 2007; 2011) widely discussed 'myths' that: 'Women don't want to go abroad'; 'companies do not want to send women abroad'; 'foreigners are so prejudiced that women would not succeed even if sent'; 'dual-career marriages make expatriation impossible for most women' (Adler 2011: 511). These barriers to participation in international assignments are still more debilitating for women in a career-development environment that extols the virtues of global organisations and the 'international manager' and in which expatriation is regarded as a 'valuable career opportunity' (Shortland, 2011). Adler (2011) succinctly sums up the situation for women. Situating expatriation in a context where global assignments are increasingly associated with successful careers, she argues that for women (Adler, 2011: 510) this means that:

> what had been a nice-to-have international experience that was often denied to them, and then became a must-have international experience that was often denied to them, became a must-have international experience that was becoming more open to them, but which was still more frequently offered to men.

A significant barrier to female expatriation is the 'glass ceiling' that confronts women wishing to access senior management positions, diminishing the pool of human resources from which international assignees are typically selected. Statistics from Germany demonstrate that, despite the fact that the number of women in management is increasing, such positions are at the lower levels of management (Vogel, 2012). Clearly, if women are inadequately represented in the formal and informal networks from which expatriates are selected, then the stereotype and reality of the male expatriate will be further perpetuated. Of course, the claim that women's non-availability is a reason for the scarcity of female expatriates would need to be challenged were the number of senior female managers in general to grow. We argue that excuses such as this are a covert form of discrimination, since gender stereotypes frequently underpin lack of female representation.

The first of these stereotypes is the view that women do not want to go abroad to work. The growth in the number of female expatriates demonstrates that women do apparently wish to work abroad if given the opportunity. Linehan (2006) and Adler (2011) have identified that, rather than women not wanting to work abroad, they are generally not asked to do so, meaning that women tend to initiate an international assignment themselves. Shortland's (2011) work identifies networking as a useful tool for expatriates in general and women in particular. She asserts that women utilise both formal and informal networks to raise the profile of their social capital; however, some of the participants in her study were concerned that women-only networks might 'reinforce gender divisions' (Shortland 2011: 271).

It is likely that informal selection and networking processes may prove an even greater disadvantage for women from some cultural backgrounds, who may not be seen as being suitable 'Western' expatriates. For these women, their cultural and gender identities may intersect negatively, since those selecting expatriates are prone to perceive a woman from a male-dominated background as one who 'would not wish' or 'would not be allowed' to move abroad. More pejoratively, even if selectors accept that the woman in question might be willing to relocate, they may still assume that her 'dominant male' spouse or partner would not wish to be a **trailing spouse**.

A further constraint that women in general face is the perception that they will feel 'uncomfortable' working in cultures that are different and distant from their own, particularly in Middle Eastern countries. Harrison and Michailova (2012) challenge this preconception, finding that in fact Western expatriate women are indeed successfully living and working in the United Arab Emirates. Confounding the expatriation 'myths', it would actually appear that if women are offered the opportunity to move they may well do so, even to some ostensibly less hospitable global territories. The failure to involve women fully in international staffing programs is perplexing, particularly in the light of growing multiculturalism in Western society, which offers a wealth of potentially highly adept and flexible international resources.

> **trailing spouse** The 'inactive' partner who accompanies a (typically male) expatriate for the duration of the assignment.

■ *Self-initiated expatriation, migration and ethnicity*

The extant literature reveals various theoretical and methodological approaches towards the investigation of self-initiated expatriation. Studies to date tend to focus on the areas of career development (Inkinson & Arthur, 2001; Hall, 2002, 2004); the boundaryless nature of the global career paradigm (Ikson, Pringle & Barry, 1997); and options, motivations and opportunities as conceptualised through the dimensions of psychological orientation and physical mobility (Briscoe, Hall & DeMuth, 2006; Sullivan & Arthur, 2006). In considering self-initiated expatriation, it is important to establish definitions and clarify the distinctions between SIEs and migrants. Al Ariss (2012) has explained this conceptual distinction by suggesting that the term 'migrant' is often associated with an emphasis on work or employment (rather than a career), often under harsh conditions of employment or even unemployment. In contrast, the career choices and outcomes available to SIEs are frequently seen as 'boundaryless' (Al Ariss, 2012). While an SIE is defined as a motivated individual who has not been forced to move abroad, the concept of migration is profoundly conditioned by institutional and organisational barriers, which constrain physical mobility across socially constructed and geographical territories.

The SIE and migration literature has also tended to place a primary focus on (Caucasian) men, a discourse that subsumes women and people of different ethnicities. Although research into women expatriates has been ongoing for over 20 years (Izraeli, Banai & Zeira, 1980; Adler, 1984a, 1984b), much of this analysis has centred on the barriers women confronted as spouses or partners of male expatriates (Bikos et al., 2007). Phizacklea (2003) argues that mainstream literature has thus adopted a 'gender-neutral' or 'gender-blind' tenor, assuming women to be dependants 'who are following men' in moves abroad (p. 26).

The study of SIEs who are ethnic minorities from developing countries is a neglected area of the literature (but see Al Ariss, 2010; Harvey, 2011). However, this apparent omission does not mean that the phenomenon does not exist. It is therefore vital that IHRM theorists establish clearer distinctions and connections between international migration and SIEs, and understand the movement of SIEs from developing and emerging economies. SIEs from the developing world may be oppressed and subject to processes of discrimination (Berry & Bell, 2011; Nkomo, 1992), or they may be from privileged, white ethnic groups, for whom colonialist perceptions have also had a mobilising effect (Grimes, 2001). We must account for the specific histories and sociopolitical contexts that affect all demographic groupings of SIEs from developing countries, in order to understand broader patterns and trends in national and international mobility and migration (Al Ariss, 2010; Al Ariss & Özbilgin, 2010; Bell, Kwesiga & Berry, 2010; Carr, 2010).

A further factor that provides insight into the related phenomena of mobility and displacement is the skill level of affected individuals. In general, knowledge workers are at an advantage because global trends towards outsourcing and automation affect them only lightly. The international dispersal of advanced technology tends to substitute low-skilled jobs, while highly skilled jobs such as those in medicine, engineering, finance and education require extensive human contact. Such modernisation of work processes, in conjunction with rapid demographic change in emerging economies, is increasing the role of highly skilled, flexible and adaptable human resources such as SIEs. 2013 research by McKinsey & Company has highlighted the global significance of the emergence of pools of local talent in developing economies in determining the international investment decisions of MNCs, and in facilitating competitive advantage (Lund, Manyika & Ramansway, 2012).

■ Conceptual departures and notions of social spaces in MNCs

In a welcome conceptual departure, which seeks to cast the critical relationship between parent and subsidiary in a more nuanced theoretical light, Edwards and Kuruvilla (2005) invoke the idea of **international division of labour** as a sense-making device in unravelling contemporary international organisation. This notion relates to the capability of the MNC, both in manufacturing and service provision, to stratify productive activities into discrete functional areas and to relocate each into appropriate geographical regions. As Macionis and Plummer (2012) describe, as people in single societies perform specialised work, so labour functions and contributions vary across regions, with high-income countries typically dominating 'high-value' or scientific activity and utilising the most complex technologies. The concept of **global commodity chains** (GCCs) (Gereffi, 1999) – also known as global value chains (GVCs) (Gereffi & Kaplinsky, 2001) – provide valuable insights into why certain firms 'touch-down' in

international division of labour The capability of the MNC, both in manufacturing and service provision, to stratify productive activities into discrete functional areas and to relocate each into appropriate geographical regions.

global commodity chain Worldwide networks of labour and production processes, which form a tightly interlocked 'chain' of all pivotal production activities to yield a finished product. These networks connect a product, from its creation out of raw materials to the final customer purchase.

certain localities, and, more generally, how the internal functions of international organisations may be both disaggregated and coordinated.

Giddens (2006: 55) has pointed out that such GCCs or GVCs are associated with what he calls a 'Global Production Network' (see also Gereffi, 1995; Hopkins & Wallerstein, 1996; Appelbaum & Christerson, 1997), which he describes as:

> the worldwide networks of labour and production processes which yield a finished product. These networks consist of all pivotal production activities that form a tightly interlocked 'chain' that extends from the raw materials needed to create the product to its final customer.

Illustrating the concept of the GCC or GVC, Giddens refers to the manufacture of 'Barbie Dolls'; toys whose various features are systematically sourced, assembled or moulded in Saudi Arabia, Taiwan, China, India, Japan, Malaysia, China, Hong Kong and the United States. So, for example, Barbie starts life in Saudi Arabia, where oil is used to create her plastic body; she is assembled in various Asian regions and the United States (the latter contributing the 'highest value' features to her anatomical 'shaping'); her hair is sourced from Japan and her clothing from China.

GVC analysts draw attention to systems of governance in MNCs, which coordinate and control networks of production across socially embedded and regionally dispersed organisational units. An underlying asymmetry in power relationships is also a facet of the geographical distribution of productive activities within the MNC, with creative functions (often with a higher perceived value) tending to be retained in the advanced country of origin, and more routine operations being devolved increasingly to subsidiaries in the developing and emerging world. The recognition that the organisational fabric of the MNC is constructed through social relationships inevitably brings to the fore the significance of human and institutional agents in moulding the social contexts that MNCs occupy. In particular, the state can play a significant role in determining the nature of an MNC's engagement in the countries it operates within, through making investments and interventions in education and training. The state may also be instrumental in providing the regulatory climate for the conduct and tenor of industrial relations (Edwards & Elgar, 1999).

Building on notions of asymmetry in the construction of multinational organisational linkages, Dörrenbächer and Geppert (2011) stress the significance of **human agency** and power relationships in defining **social spaces** in MNCs, emphasising that they are dynamic and negotiated, rather than purely structural. These authors assert that we should see formal authority and power structures in MNCs as fragmented, combining domains of knowledge and expertise emanating from various host contexts. In effect, as Morgan and Kristensen (2006) assert, there is a 'federation of national companies'. Following from this, local resource-building activities are critically significant to our understanding of how managers (and workers) in the subsidiary environment seek to mobilise and negotiate mandates that come

human agency The capability of human actors to engage, in an autonomous and self-determined fashion, with broader social, institutional and regulative structures.
social spaces The MNC seen as a variety of cellular units, each with its own identity, vested interests and objectives.

coercive comparisons A direct yet insidious practice, in some multinational headquarters, of comparing performance aspects in one subsidiary with equivalents in another.

micro-politics The use of formal or informal power by individuals or groups in organisations in order to maintain or further their status.

from headquarters and elsewhere. **Micro-political** 'game playing' represents a crucial dynamic within the socio-political fabric of the MNC. Such political contestation typically involves key actors from headquarters and subsidiary and may relate to how HQ allocates budgets, mandates change, decides relocations, benchmarks systems and makes **coercive comparisons** between subsidiaries (Becker-Ritterspach & Dörrenbächer, 2009; Dörrenbächer & Geppert, 2009; Kristensen & Zeitlin, 2001, 2005; Morgan & Kristensen, 2006). In this chapter's case study, based on empirical research by one of the chapter authors, we investigate issues of expatriation, biculturalism, the implementation of GVCs, and the contestation of social spaces at organisational and workplace levels, in a recently established R & D subsidiary based in China.

■ Conclusion

In focusing on key players in IHRM, our chapter has suggested that the theatre in which the major protagonists are interacting is subject to an ongoing program of reconstruction. While much literature in the field has tended to assume that lead actors have emanated from Western nerve centres and followed quite linear trajectories across international platforms, we have suggested that the voices of actors from far-flung and diverse territories are now being heard in the corridors of the international enterprise. As we have suggested, host countries and TCNs are playing a significant role in ensuring that eclectic and diverse forms of international knowledge are contributing to the fine tuning of decision-making in networked forms of international organisation. Moreover, given the emergence of exemplary pools of talent in emerging economies such as China and India, it is evident that reverse and alternative patterns of migration are occurring with, for example, Indian engineers catalysing innovative and entrepreneurial activity in Silicon Valley and often returning home to assist in regenerating economic growth. Indeed, an overall message of our chapter is that the 'stage' for IHRM is created by human agents, either those who are directly involved in formulating policies, practices and philosophies in the MNC itself, or those extraneous to the enterprise, for example in government, who create the context for MNC investment and local embeddedness. As the backcloth for IHRM is painted in more detail, so we realise that the identities of the major actors assumes paramount significance, extending to issues of ethnicity and gender. Further, in common with interactions between people in all walks of life, it cannot be assumed that human relations will be ordered or predictable. Instead, the script of IHRM is punctuated with contestation, power plays and potential misunderstandings. We would therefore assert that MNC strategies cannot be formulated in a 'clean' and disembodied fashion but rather need to acknowledge the unpredictable realities of human behaviour across international boundaries.

▪ Take-home messages

- A variety of actors play a significant role in the conduct of the MNC, including home-, host- and third-country nationals. Configurations and combinations of international staffing are subject to change as international organisation itself evolves.
- The significance of gender and ethnicity in IHRM tends to have been neglected, and stereotypical views of international staffing may be regarded as insensitive and inappropriate in the modern, diverse world of international business.
- The organisation of MNCs across regional borders is becoming increasingly complex, more frequently taking the form of 'global value chains' (GVCs), thus contributing to the level of diversity in the international organisation and raising the significance of a range of actors at the local level.
- A micro-level picture of the realities of international staffing reveals that combining home, host and other varieties of international staff is highly complex and carries with it the possibility of organisational conflict and intergroup tensions.

▪ Closing the learning loop

1. Why may 'traditional' expatriation be inappropriate in the modern era?
2. Why has the stereotype of the Caucasian male expatriate persisted in international business circles, and how is it inappropriate?
3. What is the impact of global value chains (GVCs) on international staffing?
4. What problems may confront individuals who are part of the 'reverse brain drain' to emerging economies?
5. Discuss this statement: 'Women make better expatriates than men.'

CASE STUDY 3.1   R & D DISCOVERY CHINA

Mission and growth

The origins of R & D Discovery China* may be traced back to late 2005, when the board of UniCo* decided to establish an R & D presence in an emerging economy. Following consideration of alternative global locations, including India, Russia and South America, the corporation opted to locate in China and made an initial investment of £300 million in a 'green field' facility in Shanghai. Undoubtedly, the establishment of R & D Discovery China was a bold and ambitious move by the corporation, entailing the construction of an 'end-to-end', fully integrated, custom-built and state-of-the-art facility. Over the first year of the site's operation in 2007, major developments occurred at a

* We have used pseudonyms to protect the anonymity of survey participants. The authors are grateful to the anonymous colleagues who helped facilitate access to the case company and in the acquisition of data.

'dragon speed', including its formal inauguration in Shanghai, the appointment of the company head and senior scientific positions, the transfer of major product lines and legal entity submission and the commencement of more generic recruitment.

The scientific acumen and creativity of its staff ultimately determine the credibility of R & D Discovery China. A further distinctive operational aspect of R & D Discovery China is its strategy of pursuing up to 10 projects simultaneously, each at a different stage of advancement, thus placing a demand for dynamic and flexible work orientation on the part of staff.

As R & D Discovery China has grown, and as it has increasingly demonstrated innovative capability, so there has been progressive localisation of key managerial and scientific responsibilities to the site. This trend is perhaps most obviously manifested in the field of HR, which was initially the responsibility of two expatriate managers from the United Kingdom and United States, but which has now been devolved to a team of six locally hired specialists. The strategy of localisation is also potentially fruitful as it permits the tapping into *guanxi*, or local networks. Interviewees referred to the nurturing of privileged relationships with universities and scientific institutes for recruitment purposes, representation of corporate interests at local, regional and national governmental levels through political networking, through strong and reciprocal links with scientific counterparts in Chinese-based scientific institutes.

Capabilities and knowledge resources

R & D Discovery China's distinctive, hybridised approach towards scientific discovery has necessitated the combination of staffing and knowledge resources from East and West. The chairperson of R & D Discovery China is a renowned scientist from Shanghai, who has strong relationships with the Academy of Sciences in China and local and national government and who repatriated from a senior R & D position in the United States approximately eight years ago. Reporting relationships at the site are organised around the chairperson, a charismatic and influential leader who represents the interests of the site at global corporate level.

The organisational structure of the site has been designed from the Centre of UniCo and essentially uses Western nationals and Chinese returnees at higher management level, returnees and locals at lower management level, and only locals as scientists. Those participants in our study who were present at the firm's startup suggested that an emphasis was placed on sourcing returnees (known locally as 'sea turtles') to fill senior positions, as they possessed vital managerial and strategic skills and were able to act as scientific mentors. Such individuals were typically Chinese nationals who had graduated from prestigious Chinese scientific institutes, who had been working in equivalent operations in the West and who were recruited to R & D Discovery China through company web advertisements.

Turning to the recruitment and composition of 'bench' scientists, HR specialists reported that there was little difficulty in attracting local and high quality reserves of scientific talent, through tapping into the reservoir of doctoral graduates in the labour market. Virtually all recruits were young (less than 30 years old) and comprised both men and women. Such laboratory scientists were required to serve a three-month probation period and were then employed on the basis of three-year renewable contracts.

The majority of managers and scientists participating in our onsite study were conscious of manifesting extraordinarily high levels of commitment to their work and to the 'mission' of R & D Discovery China. A number, including repatriates, referred to the excitement of potentially 'making history' through winning new patents in a particularly challenging field of R & D, and where breakthroughs would benefit consumers not just in China but around the world. Returnees were able to draw comparisons between organisational culture and work ethics in the United States and China, stating that the working context in the US was more functionalised and bureaucratic, with less drive to achieve results. A number of interviewees alluded to the significance of corporate culture, or the fundamental principles of the company, as a motivational factor. It became clear from our encounters with managers and scientists that their work environment encouraged them in an ongoing sense of urgency, a huge appetite for change and high energy levels. It was also mentioned that employees' readiness to mix personal and professional life was regarded as a considerable virtue at R & D Discovery China. One of our study participants asserted that the environment at the site was 'contagious', and that it frequently shocked new starters.

One senior informant highlighted the significance of 'synergy', stating that organisational actors steeped in Eastern and Western scientific and organisational traditions could learn from each other. This participant referred to a new and optimal balance between socialism and capitalism being manifested at enterprise level, with 'socialism having strong government and capitalism being good for businesses'. The significance of R & D Discovery China as a 'learning institution' was stressed, this being manifested through strong links with universities and other scientific bodies, with academic speakers offering lectures and seminars on company premises.

Challenges and perceived risk

While a number of interviewees spoke of the productive benefits of implementing the 'socialist market paradigm' at corporate level, involving the dynamic combination of Eastern/Western staffing and knowledge resources in both clinical and organisational domains, others suggested that some practical dysfunctions arose from the hybridised, culturally complex model. It was observed, in particular, that in China, 'people tended to jump' without taking 'due' time for systems changes and innovation, and this caused some consternation among Western organisational counterparts. Some also felt that 'the quickest solution was not always the best one' and that sometimes actions were taken without allowing for sufficient dialogue. Accordingly, while the Centre of UniCo welcomed the hunger for innovation that R & D Discovery China staff exhibited, it was evident that some radical, locally inspired initiatives were taking place outside its purview.

It was also revealed that the site had experienced serious employee relations difficulties as international returnees had been remunerated at significantly higher levels than locally hired staff. A two-tier status in pay and other conditions was clearly in evidence at the site, with more privileged positions resting on possession of internationally based knowledge and experience. A requirement to speak English in formal corporate settings and meetings reinforced this 'glass ceiling' for local hires, as not all bench scientists could do so.

Despite their relatively privileged status, a number of the bicultural 'sea turtles' we interviewed expressed reservations concerning their return home. Some referred to existing in a state of 'psychological limbo' as they had not fully re-integrated into Chinese life and culture, operating only in the somewhat rarefied atmosphere of a Western-owned MNC. Others believed that they had been financially penalised through repatriation, and that family issues had been difficult to manage. One participant candidly admitted that the internationalisation strategy adopted in the sectors would not be sustainable in the long term, that the pendulum had shifted too rapidly to the East and that a new equilibrium needed to be found between Western and Eastern operational platforms.

Discussion

We argue that firms can only access the extraordinary Chinese work orientation with certain inevitable preconditions and costs. First, such capabilities cannot be realised without a corresponding localisation agenda, which effectively draws on the social capital generated through *guanxi*. In the case of R & D Discovery China, the most obvious examples of the critical significance of networking included the incorporation of the Chinese national chairperson into prestigious corridors of government and science, and the appointment of a Chinese local HR department, which was finely attuned to the nuances of the local labour market. Second, the case demonstrates that the raw and unbridled work orientation of the company's local Chinese scientists needed to be tapped, institutionalised and 'branded' through the ethnocentric agency of Western expatriates on the site, to enable it to contribute to the corporate mission as envisaged by senior management at UniCo HQ. In pursuit of this objective, the Western interests on the site orchestrated an array of Western inspired and 'rationalistic' HR and performance management techniques, which ultimately foundered on a rock of passive resistance among the local employees. Bicultural 'sea turtles', the company's repatriating Chinese senior scientists and managers, could be regarded as pivotal human actors in the fledgling enterprise. Such individuals acted not only as scientific mentors but as 'cultural carriers' and agents of socialisation for the corporate entity.

However, there were two critical indications, in the area of international resourcing, that parties from 'emerging' and 'advanced' institutional settings may not always be combined sympathetically at microlevel, providing continued evidence of the site's 'shallow integration' into its international corporate value chain. First, the status gap between internationally experienced and locally based staff rendered the notion of a unified enterprise fictitious, and may have jeopardised the level of future employee commitment. Second, the position of repatriating scientists and managers, who performed the vital role of bridging Western and Eastern interests in the enterprise, was precarious. A number of 'sea turtles' appeared to occupy a transnational and transitional space that was neither 'here' nor 'there', personifying the paradoxes associated with transposing Western capitalistic values and techniques to release embedded reserves of Chinese know how and inventiveness.

Case study questions

1. Why did UniCo decide to set up an R & D operation in China, and what were its major strategic objectives in doing so?
2. Draw an organisational pyramid of staffing categories at R & D Discovery China, indicating the ethnicities of categories you depict.
3. What were the causes of tension between the operation's staff groupings?
4. How far do you think the company will eventually achieve its strategic objectives? Explain your response.
5. What can other organisations learn from the experiences of UniCo and R & D Discovery China?

>> **ACTIVITIES**
....

Group PEST analysis

Break into groups. Imagine that you are members of an MNC's senior management team, which is planning to outsource key business functions to China from
headquarters in the United Kingdom. As a group, conduct a political, economic,
social and technological (PEST) analysis of the major factors likely to facilitate or
constrain this international corporate initiative. Where possible, draw on the local
knowledge of your group's members.

Mapping social spaces in an organisation

Present a diagram that maps 'social spaces' in an organisation familiar to you
(preferably an international organisation). Explain where points of tension exist
within the organisation you have mapped, and show why they exist.

Online resources

- For instructors: answers to activities; long media article with questions; additional
  questions and answers.
- For students: further reading; answers to case study.

Acknowledgement

The authors wish to thank Dr Francesca Gagliardi at the University of Hertfordshire
for assisting with the collection of case study materials.

References

Adler, N. J. (1984a). Expecting international success: Female managers overseas *Columbia Journal of World Business*, 19(3): 79–85.

Adler, N. J. (1984b). Women do not want international careers: And other myths about international management, *Organizational Dynamics*, Autumn: 66–78.

Adler, N. J. (1987). Pacific Basin managers: A *gaijin*, not a woman, *Human Resource Management*, 26(2): 169–91.

Adler, J. (2007). Competitive frontiers: Women managing across borders. In Mendenhall, M. E.,
Oddou, G. R. and Stahl, G. K. (eds), *Readings and cases in international human resource management*, 4th edition. London: Routledge.

Adler, N. (2011). Women leading and managing worldwide. In Harzing, A-W. and
Pinnington, A. H. (eds), *International human resource management*, 3rd edition. London: Sage.

Al Ariss, A. (2010). Modes of engagement: Migration, self-initiated expatriation, and career development, *Career Development International*, 15(4): 338–58.

Al Ariss, A. (2012). Ethnic minority migrants or self-initiated expatriates? Questioning assumptions in international management studies. In Andresen, M., Al Ariss, A. and Walther, M. (eds), *Self-initiated expatriation, individual organisational and national perspectives.* London: Routledge.

Al Ariss, A. and Özbilgin, M. F. (2010). Understanding self-initiated expatriates: Career experiences of Lebanese self-initiated expatriates, *Thunderbird International Business Review*, 52(4): 275–85.

Appelbaum, R. P. and Christerson, B. (1997).Cheap labor strategies and export-orientated industrialization: Some lessons from the East Asia/Los Angeles apparel connection, *International Journal of Urban and Regional Research*, 21(2): 202–17.

Balgia, B. R. and Jaeger, A. M. (1984). Multinational corporations: Control systems and delegation issues, *Journal of International Business Studies*, 15: 25–40.

Becker-Ritterspach, F. and C. Dörrenbächer (2009), Intra-firm competition in multinational corporations: Towards a political framework, *Competition and Change*, 13: 199–213.

Bell, M. P., Kwesiga, E. N. and Berry, D. P. (2010). Immigrants: The new 'invisible men and women' in diversity research, *Journal of Managerial Psychology*, 25(2): 177–88.

Berry, D. and Bell, M. (2011). 'Expatriates': Gender, race and class distinctions in international management, *Gender, Work and Organisation*, 19(1): 10–28.

Bikos, L., Ciftci, A., Guneri, O, Demir, C., Summer, Z, Danielson, S., DeVries, S., Bilgen, W. (2007). A repeated measures investigation of the first-year adaptation experiences of female expatriate spouses living in Turkey, *Journal of Career Development*, 34(1): 5–26.

Bonache, J. and Brewster, C. (2001). Knowledge transfer and the management of expatriation, *Thunderbird International Business Review*, 43: 143–68.

Boyacigiller, N. (1990). The role of expatriates in the management of interdependence, complexity and risk in multinational corporations, *Journal of International Business Studies*, 21(3): 357–81.

Brannen, M. Y. and Thomas, D. C. (2010). Bicultural individuals in organizations: Implications and opportunity, *International Journal of Cross-cultural Management*, 10(1): 6.

Briscoe, J. P., Hall, D. T. and DeMuth, R. L. F. (2006). Protean and boundaryless careers: An empirical exploration, *Journal of Vocational Behavior*, 69: 30–47.

Brookfield Global Relocation Services (2010). *Global relocation trends survey 2010*, www. articles.totallyexpat.com/global-relocation-trends-survey-2010/. Retrieved 7 March 2012.

Carr, S. (2010). Global mobility and local economy: It's work psychology, stupid! In S. Carr (ed.), *The psychology of global mobility* (125–50). New York: Springer.

Colakoglu, S. and Caligiuri, P. M. (2008). Cultural distance, expatriate staffing and subsidiary performance: The case of US subsidiaries of multinational corporations, *International Journal of Human Resource Management*, 19(2): 223–39.

Dicken P. (2011). *Global shift: Reshaping the global economic map in the 21st century*, 6th edition. London: Sage.

Dörrenbächer, C. and Geppert, M. (2009), Micro-political games in the multinational enterprise: The case of mandate change, *Management Revue*, 20: 373–91.

Dörrenbächer, C. and Geppert, M. (2011), Introduction. In Dörrenbächer, C. and Geppert, M. (eds), *Politics and power in the multinational corporation*. Cambridge: Cambridge University Press.

Edström, A. and Galbraith, J. R. (1977). Transfer of managers as a coordination and control strategy in multinational organizations, *Administrative Science Quarterly*, 24: 248–63.

Edwards, P. and Elgar, T. (eds) (1999). *The global economy, national states and the regulation of labour*. London: Mansell.

Edwards, T. and Kuruvilla, S. (2005). International HRM, national business systems, organizational politics and the international division of labour in MNCs, *International Journal of Human Resource Management*, 16(1):1–21.

Gereffi, G. (1995). Contending paradigms for cross-regional comparison: Development strategies and commodity chains in East Asia and Latin America. In Smith, P. H. (ed.), *Latin America in comparative perspective: New approaches in methods and analysis*. Boulder, CO: Westview Press.

Gereffi, G. (1999). International trade and industrial upgrading in the apparel commodity chain, *Journal of International Economics*, 48: 37–70.

Gereffi, G. and Kaplinsky, R. (2001). The value of value chains: Spreading the gains from globalisation, *IDS Bulletin*, 32(3): n.p.

Giddens, A. (2006). *Sociology*. Cambridge: Polity Press.

Grimes, D. (2001). Putting their own house in order: Whiteness, change and organization studies. *Journal of Organizational Change Management*, 14(2): 132–49.

Hall, D. T. (2002). *Careers in and out of organisations*. Thousand Oaks, CA: Sage

Hall, D. T. (2004). The Protean career: A quarter-century journey, *Journal of Vocational Behaviour*, 65: 1–13.

Harrison, E. C. and Michailova, S. (2012). Working in the Middle East: Western female expatriates experiences in the United Arab Emirates, *International Journal of Human Resource Management*, 23(4): 625–44.

Harvey, M. and Novicevic, M. M. (2004). The development of political skill and political capital by global leaders through global assignments, *International Journal of Human Resource Management*, 15(7): 1173– 88.

Harvey, M., Novicevic, M. M. and Speier, C. (2000). Strategic human resource management: The role of inpatriate managers, *Human Resource Management Review*, 10(2): 153–75.

Harvey, W. S. (2011). British and Indian scientists moving to the United States, *Work and Occupations*, 38(1), 68–100.

Harzing, A. W. (2001). Of bears, bumble- bees and spiders: The role of expatriates in controlling foreign subsidiaries, *Journal of World Business*, 36(4): 366–79.

Harzing, A. W. (2004). Composing and international staff. In Harzing, A. W. and Van Ruysseveldt, J. (eds), *International human resource management*, 2nd edition. London: Sage.

Hollinshead, G. (2009). *International and comparative human resource management*. Maidenhead, Berkshire: McGraw-Hill.

Hollinshead, G. and Maclean, M. (2007). Transition and organizational dissonance in Serbia, *Human Relations*, 60(10): 1551–74.

Hopkins, T. H. and Wallerstein, I. (1996). *The age of transition: Trajectory and the world system, 1945–2025*. London: Zed Books.

Ikson, K., Pringle, J. and Barry (1997). Expatriate assignment versus overseas experience: Contrasting models of human resource development, *Journal of World Business*, 32: 351–68.

Inkinson K. and Arthur M. (2001). How to be a successful career capitalist, *Organisational Dynamics*, 30(1): 48–61.

Izraeli, D., Banai M and Zeira, Y (1980). Women executives in MNC subsidiaries, *California Management Review*, 23(1): 53–63.

Kogut, B. and Zander, U. (2003). Knowledge of the firm and the evolutionary theory of the multinational corporation, *Journal of International Business Studies*, 24(2): 625–45.

Kostova, T. and Roth, K. (2003). Social capital in multinational corporations and a micro–macro model of its formation, *Academy of Management Review*, 28(2): 297–317.

Kristensen, P. H. and Zeitlin, J. (2001). The making of a global firm: Local pathways to multinational enterprise. In Morgan, G., Hull Kristensen, P. and Whitley, R. (eds), *The multinational firm*. Oxford: Oxford University Press.

Kristensen, P. H. and Zeitlin, J. (2005). *Local players in global games: The strategic constitution of a multinational corporation*. Oxford: Oxford University Press.

Linehan, M. (2000). *Senior female international managers: Why so few?* Aldershot: Ashgate.

Linehan, M. (2006). Women in international management. In Scullion, H. and Collings D. G. (eds), *Global staffing*. London: Routledge.

Lund, S., Manyika, J. and Ramansway, S. (2012). Preparing for a new era of work, *McKinsey Quarterly*, McKinsey Global Institute, www.mckinseyquarterly.com/Economic_Studies/ Productivity_Performance/Preparing_for_a_new_era_of_knowledge_work_3034. Retrieved 25 February 2013.

Macionis, J. J. and Plummer, K. (2012). *Sociology: A global introduction*. Harlow, Essex: Prentice Hall.

Morgan, G. and P. H. Kristensen (2006), The contested space of multinationals: Varieties of institutionalism, varieties of capitalism, *Human Relations*, 59(11): 1467–90.

Nkomo, S. M. (1992). The emperor has no clothes: Rewriting race in the study of organizations, *Academy of Management Review*, 17(3): 487–513.

Perlmutter, H. (1969). The tortuous evolution of the multinational corporation, *Columbia Journal of World Business*, 4(1): 9–18.

Phizacklea A (2003). Gender, ethnicity and migration. In Andall, J. (ed.), *Gender and ethnicity in Europe*. Oxford: Berg.

Reiche, B. S. Kraimer, M., and Harzing, A. W. K. (2009). Inpatriates as agents of cross-unit knowledge flows in multinational corporations. In Sparrow, P. (ed.), *Handbook of international human resource management: Integrating people, process and context*, 151–70. Oxford: Blackwell.

Riusala, K. and Suutari, V. (2000). Expatriation and careers: Perspectives of expatriates and spouses, *Career Development International*, 5(2): 81–90.

Saxenian, A. (2006). *The new Argonauts: Regional advantage in a global economy*. Massachusetts: Harvard University Press.

Shortland, S. (2011). Networking: A valuable career intervention for women expatriates?, *Career Development International* 16(3): 271–92.

Sullivan, S. E. and Arthur, M. B. (2006). The evolution of the boundaryless career concept: Examining physical and psychological mobility, *Journal of Vocational Behavior*, 69: 19–29.

Vogel, S. (2012). More women attain management roles in companies, *EIRO Online*, www.eurofound.europa.eu/eiro/2012/09/articles/de1209019i.htm. Retrieved 7 March 2012.

Wadhwa, V. (2009). A reverse brain drain, *Issues in Science and Technology*, Spring: 45– 52.

Zimmerman, A. and Sparrow, P. (2007). Mutual adjustment processes in international teams: lessons for the study of expatriation, *International Studies of Management and Organisation*, 37(3): 65–88.

4

Recruitment and selection in the international context

Kristina Potočnik, Maria Felisa Latorre Navarro, Beliz Dereli and Blanka Tacer

■ Learning objectives

- To outline the specifics of recruitment and selection in the international context.
- To describe categories of international employees.
- To identify and explain the international recruitment and selection process.
- To illustrate potential challenges of international selection and recruitment from the employee and company perspectives.

■ Learning outcomes

After reading this chapter, students will be able to:
- develop an international recruitment and selection plan for different types of multinational company
- create a set of interview questions for an international post
- determine a set of selection criteria for different types of international employees
- evaluate indicators of selection and recruitment effectiveness.

▦ Introduction

Careful planning is needed to ensure that international **recruitment**, and **selection** can deploy the right candidates to international posts. Failure to do so may result in inefficient use of time, financial losses or even risk to a company's reputation. HR managers in multinational companies (MNCs) should consider various issues when preparing for international recruitment and selection, mainly because of cultural or national differences between the country in which an MNC is headquartered (the parent country) and the countries in which they have subsidiaries (host countries). These differences affect international recruitment and selection because:

- employment legislation varies across countries
- the pool of job applicants for international posts is wider – MNCs can choose from parent-country nationals (PCNs), host-country nationals (HCNs) and third-country nationals (TCNs) as well as, increasingly, **self-initiated expatriates** (SIEs) and **skilled migrants** (SMs)
- a thorough and specific job analysis for international posts is required, even if the same type of post is advertised (for instance, the competencies a manager needs in Australia might be different from those a manager needs in another cultural context)
- needs specific to advertising international posts drive MNC selection practices, from filling a position to developing the managerial skills of existing staff (Brookfield Global Relocation Services, 2012).

International recruitment and selection challenges are visible at the macro-, meso- and micro-levels. A macro-level challenge relates to institutional arrangements or legal factors (e.g. employment and health and safety laws), national culture and social factors (e.g. education system and career attitudes). The meso-level comprises an organisation's recruitment and selection policies, procedures and practices, the developing employer brand and the evaluation of international recruitment and selection effectiveness. The micro-level refers to the HR competencies for international recruitment and selection, job analysis and person–organisation fit; and competencies for working in and adjusting to an international work environment. Micro-level challenges in the international recruitment and selection also include job candidates' reactions to a company's HR practices and initiatives, such as their reactions to different selection methods.

In this chapter, we address these challenges and discuss recruitment and selection practices in the international context. We first review the different categories of international employees MNCs can target in their international posts, before analysing in detail a four-stage process model of international selection and recruitment.

....

recruitment Practices designed to attract a suitable number of qualified job applicants.

selection Choosing the best candidate for the available post from the pool of job candidates.

self-initiated expatriate A person who moves abroad for work on their own initiative.

skilled migrant A well-educated individual who moves from a developing to a developed country for work.

....

◼ Categories of international employee

A number of approaches are available in international recruitment, which Perlmutter (1969) describes as ethnocentric, polycentric, geocentric and regiocentric (see chapter 1). Before an MNC designs its recruitment and selection practices, it must decide on a general approach to international recruitment and selection. Under any of these approaches, the MNC will need to target a category of international employees in their selection and recruitment. We summarise the characteristics of the main categories of international employee in table 4.1.

Table 4.1 Advantages and disadvantages of using categories of international employees (based on Al Ariss & Seyed, 2011; Reiche & Harzing, 2011; Dowling et al., 2008; Froese, 2012)

Approach	International employees	Advantages	Disadvantages
Ethnocentric	PCNs	Deep understanding of the MNC's goals, practices and procedures Facilitation of communication between headquarters and subsidiaries Specialised skills and knowledge needed to achieve an MNC's objectives	Difficulties in adapting to the host-country environment High costs involved with maintaining PCNs and their families in host countries Limited job and career opportunities for the HCNs (local communities may not accept the subsidiaries if they only employ PCNs)
Polycentric	HCNs	Deep understanding of local practices, policies and broader culture Facilitation of job opportunities for the local workforce Lower costs compared to hiring PCNs or TCNs	Difficulties in communication with headquarters Reduced control of the headquarters over the subsidiaries' operations Limited opportunities for PCNs to gain international experience
Geocentric and regiocentric	TCNs	Deep understanding of the local culture compared to PCNs Hiring highly qualified employees (TCNs are frequently career managers) Lower costs compared to hiring PCNs Less expensive to maintain TCNs and their families abroad	Host-country governments may resent hiring TCNs Limited job and career opportunities for HCNs Superficial understanding of the company's goals, practices and procedures
	SIEs	Highly motivated individuals eager to get international exposure Limited family and financial concerns Better cultural adjustment (SIEs frequently relocate for personal reasons, such as travelling and adventure)	Lack of work experience (SIEs are frequently young individuals or recent graduates) Lower satisfaction if the motivation to expatriate is a poor labour market in the home country Poorer work adjustment and less support at work, especially when SIEs work in traditional versus international companies
	SMs	Highly educated and skilled individuals	Strict immigration legislation may prevent migration of skilled individuals

Different factors determine which approach, and consequently which category of international employee, the MNCs will eventually target: for example, cultural distance between the headquarters and its subsidiaries; living costs in the host country; immigration issues; and role expectations of the international employees (Dowling, Festing, & Engle, 2008; Harzing, 2004; Sparrow, 2007). For instance, MNCs may focus on PCNs because they expect them to assume certain roles (Dowling et al., 2008), such as:

1. network builders, who strengthen and develop interpersonal linkages and contacts abroad
2. boundary spanners, who represent their companies in the host countries and gather host-country information for the headquarters
3. agents of direct control, who engage in direct supervision to ensure compliance of the HCNs
4. agents of socialisation, who transfer the corporate culture (i.e. shared values and beliefs) to the host-country organisation
5. language nodes, who speak a host country's language and so are able to deal effectively with queries from the HCNs.

In general, using PCNs can help MNCs achieve their targets and objectives in the host country, and all these roles involve transfer knowledge and competencies from the headquarters to the subsidiaries located in host countries (Dowling et al., 2008). However, Shaffer and colleagues (2012) have recently suggested that, due to new demands in the globalised labour market, MNCs must consider alternative categories of international employees to fill positions (see table 4.2). Organisations use these groups to make international posts simpler and more flexible, both for employees and organisations.

Table 4.2 Alternative contemporary types of international employee (based on Shaffer et al., 2012; Mayerhofer et al., 2004; Maznewski et al., 2006)

International employee type	Tasks	Advantages	Disadvantages
Short-term assignee	Developing a specific task or project Skill/technology transfer Problem-solving Management control/ development	Cost-effectiveness Global boundary spanner	Separation stress Lack of integration with HCNs
Flexpatriates	Visiting foreign markets and/or clients Team supervising Skill/technical transfer Problem-solving	Cost-effectiveness Global boundary spanner Global perspective	Separation/travel stress (health issues, work–family conflict) Time-zone differences (jetlag) Lack of social integration at home and host locations

Table 4.2 (cont.)			
International employee type	Tasks	Advantages	Disadvantages
International business travellers	Visiting foreign markets and/or clients Supervising units and/ or projects Negotiation Meeting conferences	Global boundary spanner Relationship maintenance with home-country colleagues	Separation/travel stress Time-zone differences Host-country relationships limited to work colleagues
Global virtual team members	Flexibility of schedule	Cost-effectiveness Global boundary spanner	Extended work schedule Work–family conflict

In summary, MNCs can target different types of international employee. Importantly, as we explore next, the choice of the targeted applicants will have a significant impact on the MNC's recruitment and selection practices.

Process model of international recruitment and selection

In this section, we propose a holistic four-stage process model of the international recruitment and selection process, starting with determining the competencies of the HR professionals who recruit and select international employees and concluding with an evaluation of its effectiveness (see figure 4.1). The feedback from the last stage can be used to improve the practices and procedures of the first three stages in future. Each stage of this process model comprises macro-, meso- and micro-levels, and every level raises specific challenges. Here, we discuss these challenges in detail.

short-term assignee An employee appointed to an international post for a short period, usually less than one year.

flexpatriate An employee who travels for brief assignments, away from their home base and across cultural or national borders.

international business traveller An employee who makes frequent international business trips for short periods of time.

global virtual team member A team member based in a different geographical location to other team members, and who works on interdependent tasks, communicating mainly through information and communication technologies (ICTs).

■ *Stage 1: Determining competencies of HR professionals for international recruitment and selection*

In the first stage, MNCs should determine the competencies of the HR managers who will be responsible for the international recruitment and selection. A macro-level challenge here is the anticipation of the recruitment and selection practices in the host country (e.g. whether or not psychometric assessment is a common practice in the host country). Defining an international HR competency profile based on its strategic goals is a meso-level challenge for the organisation. The HR managers who perform different international HR-related tasks need specific competencies (e.g. linguistic abilities, cultural sensitivity). The international HR

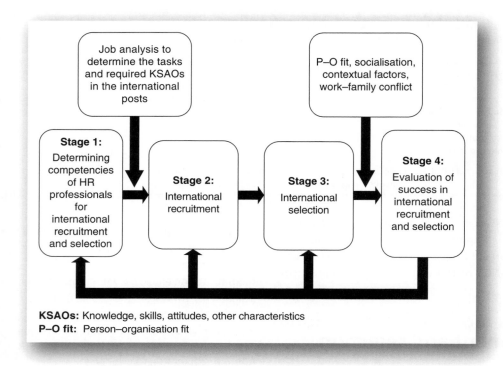

Figure 4.1 A four-stage process model of international recruitment and selection

competency profile differs depending on the stage of international development an organisation has reached. For example, an MNC with only two subsidiaries, in culturally similar countries, needs an HR manager with additional linguistic skills, while an MNC with global staffing needs a more complex international HR competency profile. At the micro-level, the development of international recruitment and selection competencies is a task for each manager and member of the HR department; these competencies include knowledge, skills, attitudes, abilities, personality traits and other characteristics for effective work in international recruitment and selection.

The scope of international recruitment and selection is related to the company's stage of internationalisation (see chapter 1 for discussion of these stages). In the early stages of internationalisation, HR managers are involved in the recruitment and selection of HCNs and TCNs, raising challenges such as how to comprehend the local legislation and culture. In contrast, in MNCs with already-developed local HR departments, the recruitment and selection challenges often relate to cross-cultural collaboration between subsidiaries and headquarters. Importantly, HR managers at the headquarters need an intimate understanding of the organisational strategy to effectively design job posts (i.e. to identify the required competencies and skills) and make decisions regarding international recruitment and selection. For instance, in the case of a pharmaceutical company deciding to open a new subsidiary focused on sales, international posts will mostly be connected with marketing and the HR manager will need to design job competencies based on this strategic aim.

International recruitment and selection calls for competencies that address the special challenges that characterise the international environment. The international recruitment and selection manager needs to possess specific competencies for several reasons:

- Cross-cultural situations require adaptation of recruitment and selection methods and flexible interpretations of communications, values and behaviours (Tarique & Schuler, 2010).
- The international HR manager needs to consider the local institutional environment, especially legal matters (Festing & Eidems, 2011).
- International recruitment and selection connect with coordinating different staffing interests. Local managers' interests do not always align with the global interests of MNCs. For instance, a manager in Mexico may not support the international transfer of a team member because they need that person's competencies for the local company.
- Building an international network is crucial to respond to the continued shortage of required competencies in MNCs (Farndale, Scullion & Sparrow, 2010).
- Diverse forms of international mobility dictate the approach to international recruitment and selection (Meyskens et al., 2009).

Building on Roe's (2002) model of competency architecture, we derive a competency profile for the HR manager responsible for international recruitment and selection. In addition to knowledge, skills, attitudes and other characteristics (KSAOs), the model allows consideration of abilities, personality traits, competencies and subcompetencies as psychological determinants of job performance, as shown in table 4.3.

Table 4.3 A competence profile for international recruitment and selection managers (based on Roe, 2002)

Profile area	Specific attributes and skills
Knowledge	IHRM theory Recruitment and selection theory Core business of MNC Comparative management
Skills	Cross-cultural and cross-functional cooperation Verbal communication Non-verbal communication Fluency in MNC's official language Systems thinking Observation
Attitudes	Positive toward diversity Positive toward MNC Comfortable with changes Able to reconcile viewpoints

Table 4.3 (cont.)	
Profile area	**Specific attributes and skills**
Other characteristics	Interested in people from different cultures Motivated to work in an international environment Committed to teamwork Able to be mobile Free from prejudices
Abilities	Emotional intelligence Verbal reasoning Analytical reasoning
Personality traits	Open Responsible Adaptable Self-confident Proactive Emotionally stable
Competencies	International internal and external employer branding Cross-cultural integration of workforce planning Cross-cultural internal and external selection system design Local adaptation of recruitment and selection methods International networking Cross-cultural collaboration with local HR departments and local managers Coordination and monitoring of international recruitment and selection
Subcompetencies	International and local job market mapping Cooperating across departments to develop and maintain employer brand Planning international assignments Interviewing international candidates Assessing international candidates Evaluating international work experiences, education and competencies Managing the mobility of international assignees Balancing the global standardisation and local adaptation of recruitment and selection practices

Once a company has an HR manager in place to lead international recruitment and selection, it needs a recruitment strategy to attract the best talent to the applicant pool.

■ *Stage 2: International recruitment*

Recruitment practices are essential to attract the right talent in the highly competitive international market (Ma & Allen, 2009). At this stage, researching the legal, social and cultural environments in the host country is the main macro-level challenge, while designing a recruitment strategy and developing the employer brand are important meso-level issues. At the micro-level, the main challenges are job analysis and remuneration planning.

Recruitment starts with job specification and analysis to define a set of character-istics and competencies a person needs to perform effectively in the available interna-tional post. Thorough job analysis of the international post should also inform the approach to international staffing that the MNC adopts, for instance by providing information about the availability of the HCNs for a specific post, the need for close surveillance of the headquarters, or potential risks to local cultural adjustment. The job analysis identifies such issues by drawing on multiple sources, including in-depth interviews with the HCNs and PCNs who will collaborate with newly appointed employees. In this context, we emphasise that future-oriented job analysis focuses on dynamic and changeable requirements of international posts (Landis, Fogli & Goldberg, 1998). These aspects must thus be considered when designing the recruit-ment strategy for the company's international posts, together with questions such as the size of the targeted applicant pool, the length of the commitment sought in the post (short-term or long-term) and the budget available for salary and other benefits. The success of the recruitment strategy (i.e. whether the company attracts a sufficient number of highly skilled and qualified candidates) will depend on the quality of the employer brand reference. That is, the company has to develop a unique image with which potential job candidates value and identify, linked to the company's values and policies (think of Google or Coca-Cola, for example).

Employer branding is mainly used to attract external candidates, but it can also be used internally to stimulate already employed talent to apply for the company's international posts. Next, we review international recruitment strategies for PCNs, HCNs and TCNs (including SIEs and SMs), respectively.

International recruitment of PCNs

Recruitment of PCNs may focus on candidates already employed by the company (**internal recruitment**) or target anyone in the parent country's labour market (**external recruitment**). Internal recruitment relies on certain prac-tices and sources, such as internal job vacancy ads pub-lished on staff boards or intranets, career planning and internal networking. It has many advantages, including

internal recruitment Recruitment focused on candidates already employed by the company.
external recruitment Recruitment focused on any candidate in the labour market.

low costs, higher employee motivation to excel at work (i.e. to increase the probability of getting the international offer) and increased company attractiveness and reputa-tion (Briscoe, Schuler & Tarique, 2012). Nevertheless, this strategy can be very restrictive because it can limit the number and quality of the candidates in the applicant pool.

An HR manager can overcome these limitations by expanding the recruitment strategy outside the company. Some common practices of external recruitment are attendance at job fairs, job vacancy ads published on the company website, news-papers and social media (e.g. LinkedIn, Facebook), recommendations from employ-ees and focus on competitors' PCNs (Briscoe et al., 2012). Although external recruitment can reach more highly skilled applicants, their lack of knowledge about the company is a potential drawback. A combination of internal and external recruitment may be the best strategy when focusing on PCNs.

International recruitment of HCNs and TCNs

The literature indicates a need to recruit HCNs for international managerial posts to develop international talent (Ma & Allen, 2009), while paying attention to a number of issues.

1. Analysis of the host country's labour market to determine the quantity of suitable candidates for the available posts. MNCs should invest effort and resources in their external employer branding. This is important because having a unique image which the HCNs and TCNs value and are fond of will attract a greater number of better qualified candidates to the applicant pool.

2. Analysis of common recruitment and selection practices in other local or international companies. For instance, Chinese firms usually recruit through informal channels or networks (Han & Han, 2009). Indian private-sector organisations usually recruit using social networking (Budhwar & Khatri, 2001). In the United States, job applicants are more likely to search for job ads in newspapers or on websites (Ma & Allen, 2009).

3. Adapting recruitment practices to local cultural values (Ma & Allen, 2009). In countries with strong collectivist values (e.g. China, Latin American countries), ads should include group-focused activities, such as teamwork and team-based rewards. In contrast, ads targeting applicants from individualistic countries (e.g. United States, United Kingdom) should emphasise individual-based activities, remuneration and benefits.

Some MNCs are concerned primarily with getting the best possible employees for their international posts regardless of nationality, and these companies can also target TCNs. However, cultural differences can be harder to control in these cases (Moore, 2001).

Once the company is satisfied with the quality and size of the applicant pool, it begins the process of selection, the third stage in our four-stage model.

■ Stage 3: International selection

In this section, we review relevant selection criteria and selection methods in the international context. Here, macro-level challenges are related to the adaptation of selection methods to the host country environment; meso-level challenges include the choice of selection methods MNCs will use for their international posts, and micro-level challenges reflect different selection criteria for international posts.

Selection criteria

Capacity for cultural adjustment

Cultural adjustment helps lessen the intensity of the stress an employee experiences during acculturation and changes the candidate's expectations so that they may adjust more easily to the new situation. Black, Mendenhall and Oddou (1991) have suggested three kinds of adjustment for PCNs:

1. Work adjustment to job requirements, working conditions, management styles and performance expectations.
2. Interaction adjustment that emphasises establishing good relationships with HCNs and therefore underlines the need to use the HCN's language adequately.
3. General living adjustment – for example, adjustment to accommodation facilities, shopping and local foods (Huang, Chi & Lawler, 2005).

Family situation

Family situation is an important criterion that affects whether a PCN decides to accept an international post and later how he or she performs in the job (Harvey & Novicevic, 2001). Effective family communication (i.e. the ability to share and discuss opinions clearly and develop constructive solutions for conflicts that arise) and strong emotional support among family members reduce stress intensity and facilitate adaptation to the new environment (Caligiuri, Hyland, Joshi & Bross, 1998).

The need for couples to consider their **dual careers** is becoming an increasingly important factor in applicants' decision-making about an international job offer (Riusala & Suutari, 2000). Some MNCs resolve this problem by resourcing career counselling, job search and work permit arrangements, or even covering education expenses for a spouse (Dowling et al., 2008). Spouses most often desire relocation support in the form of networking information (e.g. a list of employment agencies and Western companies that use English-speaking staff) and career counselling. Yet, according to a recent study of PCN spouses from Australia, Asia, Canada, Europe, the United Kingdom and the United States, employment assistance programs for spouses are very rare indeed (Cole, 2011). If the spouse of a relocating PCN does not move, it is important that the MNC covers the family's travel and communication costs (Ntshona, 2007). MNCs should also consider other family constraints on a candidate's acceptance of the international job offer, such as disruption to children's education, lack of care services for aged family members and the adverse effect of relocation on family members (Osiecka, 2001).

> **dual-career perspective** The aim of maintaining both spouses' careers when one partner relocates.

Linguistic ability

A UK–German study by Marx has reported linguistic ability as the fifth most important selection criterion, ranked after sociability, openness, **cultural adaptation** and professional perfection (cited in Osiecka, 2001). Although language differences are recognised as having a negative impact on cross-cultural communication and job performance and may even cause PCNs to return earlier than planned from an international post (Jordan & Cartwright, 1998), some MNCs consider linguistic abilities to be non-essential attributes.

> **cultural adaptation** Changes in the individual that facilitate his or her adaptation to the new environment.

Experience in the international context

Applicants who have experience in the international context are better able to develop realistic expectations about the international post, which reduces the risk of uncertainty and stress due to acculturation issues (Black et al., 1991). Extensive experience of travelling and relocation also helps in adjusting to a new environment, responding to new tasks and establishing relationships (Groesch, 2004).

Personality traits

The role of the 'Big Five' personality characteristics in PCNs' job performance and their adaptation to international posts is well recognised (Caligiuri, 2000a; Harvey & Novicevic, 2001; Huang et al., 2005; Jordan & Cartwright, 1998). These characteristics describe the extent to which an individual is:

1. extroverted – asserts him or herself in the environment by being outgoing, sociable and talkative
2. agreeable – a team player, warm and trustworthy
3. conscientious – organised and hard working
4. emotionally stable – calm and able to cope with areas of stress in his or her life
5. open and intellectually able – imaginative, able to adapt to a changing environment.

The weighting the selection process for international assignments attaches to each of these characteristics may vary from one culture to another. For example, introverts may be preferred over extroverts in cultures where modesty and conservatism are accepted as fundamental values (Huang et al., 2005).

Mendenhall and Oddou's (1985) model posits four dimensions that link specific behavioural tendencies to potential performance in international posts (Dowling et al., 2008):

1. Self-oriented dimension – the extent to which an expatriate expresses concern for self-preservation, self-enjoyment and mental hygiene.
2. Perceptual dimension – a PCN's expertise in correctly understanding HCN behaviours, successfully combining all their previous perceptual and appraisal experiences.
3. Others-oriented dimension – the extent to which a PCN is concerned about their HCN peers and intends to cooperate with them.
4. Cultural-toughness dimension – a PCN's adaptive ability, or their sensitivity to the new environment, determined by the degree of similarity between the host and parent countries' cultures. Subcultures within each country also affect the degree of similarity between host and parent countries.

Knowledge, skills and competencies

Some studies have found that soft skills – including global awareness, an ethical understanding of conducting business in foreign countries, cultural empathy, cross-cultural team building, international negotiation skills and self-confidence – are essential for successful performance in international posts (see, for example,

Harvey & Novicevic, 2001). Technical competence is another essential criterion in international selection. Technically competent international employees can more easily manage job uncertainty, have fewer work-related problems and build trustworthy and cooperative relations with HCNs (Groesch, 2004).

Person–organisation fit

Job applicants are attracted to organisations that fit with their personal values (Kristof, 1996). Due to the differences between host and parent countries' organisational cultures, accurate assessment of person–organisation fit makes success more likely in international posts (Rian & Ulf, 2012). The alignment of applicants' personal values with a host country's organisational values fosters employee job satisfaction (Kristof-Brown, Zimmerman, & Johnson, 2005) and organisational commitment (Tsai, Chen, & Chen, 2012).

Selection methods

When the HR department has established the selection criteria, it chooses appropriate selection methods, which may involve tests, interviews, the use of **assessment centres** (ACs) and cooperation with HR consultancies.

assessment centres In-house or external location for evaluating behaviour using multiple tests and exercises for different purposes, including employee selection.

Tests

Psychometric tests are used for personality and competence assessment, linguistic ability assessment and cultural adjustment and flexibility assessment, among others (Briscoe et al., 2012; Moore, 2001). When using tests in international selection, we should consider using both assessments of specific competencies and skills for international posts and culture-free tests or tests adapted to HCN and TCN applicants' culture of origin. Certain tests have been translated, validated and standardised in a diverse range of cultures, and these are preferred in international selection; they include the Big Five Personality Questionnaire (Schmitt, Allik, McCrae, & Benet-Martínez, 2007) and the Wechsler Adult Intelligence Scale (Bowden, Saklofske & Weiss, 2011).

Interviews

All selection procedures include some sort of interview. Structured interviews are more effective with applicants from high-power distance cultures (e.g. Latin and Asian countries), while less structured interviews are more effective with applicants from low-power distance cultures, such as Anglo and Germanic countries (Ma & Allen, 2009). It is recommended that the interview panel includes representatives from different departments of the company, to enable a balanced assessment of the applicants (Briscoe et al., 2012; Moore, 2001). The interview provides an opportunity to assess and probe applicants' ability to adapt to different cultural contexts. It can also be conducted using video conferencing, which may help ensure diversity among panel members. However, applicants do not favour virtual selection methods (Chapman, Uggerslev & Webster, 2003), and it is debatable how reliably such an environment can aid examination of their abilities.

Assessment centres

ACs comprise standardised evaluation of cognitive abilities and personality tests, structured interviews and exercises such as leaderless group discussion, in-basket exercises, case studies and role-playing (in an in-basket exercise, job candidates receive a set of items related to their future post and are asked to indicate how they would prioritise and deal with each; the exercise simulates tasks that an employee might do on returning from a holiday). Applicants engage in exercises both individually and in groups (Searle, 2003). The assessors may be HR personnel or line managers from the recruiting organisation, external HR consultants, psychologists or job experts (Edenborough, 2005; Guion & Highhouse, 2006). In the international context, assessors should be included from both parent and host countries, to address cultural and national aspects of applicant selection (Briscoe, 1997). Many MNCs around the world use this method, including Shell, Siemens, HSBC and BASF (Jansen & Jongh, 1997). Some companies prefer to outsource to ACs because of a lack of experienced staff or adequate facilities in-house. Outsourcing may also prevent biases: if the selection is carried out among the internal candidates and the company uses in-house assessment, then assessors' individual relationships with candidates may affect the objectivity of their evaluations. The AC's exercises should also test critical skills for managerial success in a multicultural environment (e.g. the candidate's flexibility or adaptability).

Cooperation with HR consultancies

Some MNCs are inclined to outsource their recruitment and selection to HR consultancies, especially for managerial posts. A consultancy's success and past experience with recruitment and selection, and their knowledge of the MNC, are essential factors in determining whether using a consultancy is appropriate (Ballantyne & Povah, 2004). The decision to use a specific HR consultancy also depends on how well it fares in terms of credentials and positive references; track record; size and number of employees; client base; national or international presence; and cost-efficiency and time management (Schoye & Rasmussen, 1999). A consultancy may also need to be located centrally for ease of access. Some MNCs prefer to work with only one consultancy to reduce costs and ensure the integrity of the selection process, while others prefer consultancies that have specific experience with particular positions or occupations or that have a strong portfolio in a particular region. In that case, an MNC may choose a different consultancy depending on the type of post or the region they are recruiting for at that moment.

Specific issues in selection methods

It is possible to ease the international employee selection process in two ways (Caligiuri & Tarique, 2006, cited in Caligiuri, Tarique & Jacobs, 2009). First, a company can provide a candidate with a realistic preview of the post; for example, by arranging interviews with repatriates who formerly occupied the same post. This may reduce the risk of the employee completing their post prematurely. Second, applicants can use self-selection tools to help them critically evaluate themselves, especially regarding personality and individual characteristics and career and family issues. Such tools may help create an applicant pool for potential future international posts by considering applicants' availability, technical knowledge, skills and abilities, job and life experiences and preferences for international positions. However, Caligiuri, Tarique and Jacobs (2009) caution that self-assessment may be ineffective when there are few job opportunities in the labour market, since applicants may overestimate their competencies and preferences for working in other countries due to the difficulty of finding jobs in their own countries.

Final selection decision and job offer

The selection process concludes with a final selection decision and job offer to the successful applicant. HR managers may or may not make the final decision personally, depending on the level and purpose of the international post, and in any case they will be required to recommend the best candidate for the job. The top management team or the CEO may then make the final selection decision.

A candidate's acceptance of the job offer depends on various factors but mainly on the content of the offer, which is comprised of objective aspects (e.g. pay, holidays, job title) and subjective aspects (e.g. person–organisation and person–job fit). It has been argued that applicants from **masculine cultures** (e.g. the United States, the United Kingdom) pay more attention than others to objective factors such as salary and holiday allowance when considering a job offer (Ma & Allen, 2009).

> **masculine culture** A society in which 'emotional gender roles are clearly distinct: men are supposed to be assertive, tough, and focused on material success; women are supposed to be more modest, tender, and concerned with the quality of life' (Hofstede & Hofstede, 2005: 402). A high score in the masculine dimension implies that the society is driven by competition, achievement and success. According to Hofstede (2001), Japan, Mexico, UK, Germany, the United States and Australia are the most masculine societies.

Once the selected applicant accepts the employment offer, the company must socialise the newcomer. This will to a large extent determine the success of the international recruitment and selection in the last stage of our four-stage model.

■ Stage 4: Evaluation of success in international recruitment and selection

The fourth and final stage of international recruitment and selection is evaluation of the success of the process. Here, we look at the main indicators of successful selection and the actual costs for the headquarters, subsidiary and international employee. Macro-level challenges at this stage comprise a continuous exploration of contextual factors in the host country, which affect international recruitment and selection. Meso-level challenges relate to establishing a system of success evaluation and improving organisational HR practices related with international selection (e.g. a review of medical packages, socialisation programs or mentoring). Micro-level challenges include the analysis of recruitment and selection effectiveness for the individual employee (e.g. job satisfaction). These challenges are related to an employee's successful completion of the international post. At the micro-level, selection was successful if the employee completed their international post and adjusted to the new culture (Bhaskar-Shrinivas et al., 2005; Bonache, Brewster & Suutari, 2007). The evaluation of success should also consider the employee's performance level, not merely whether they completed their post, including how far they fulfilled or even overachieved against organisational goals. A number of factors improve the performance of international employees and diminish their intention to quit: adjustment to the host country's culture; certain personality traits; and the level of support PCNs and their families receive from the MNCs and their subsidiaries (Bhaskar-Shrinivas et al., 2005; Takeuchi, 2010). Next, we discuss some of these indicators.

Indicators of selection and recruitment success

Family and couple adjustment

The ability of individuals, couples and children to adjust to a foreign environment and new customs is one of the most critical aspects of expatriate success (Hays, 1974). Among the work- and family-related factors that may influence employee performance levels are children's wellbeing, family satisfaction and the quality of family and marital life in the new setting (Takeuchi, 2010).

Headquarters' HR practices and policies

As Takeuchi (2010) points out, headquarters may have a comprehensive HR strategy that facilitates the process of adjustment in terms of international logistic assignation (e.g. providing housing support or spouse relocation resources) and organisational support (e.g. mentoring, career development support, training, availability of global mobility managers in-house or externally, or other benefits).

The role of HCNs

HCNs can support PCNs in achieving their objectives to a greater extent by developing better relationships with them (Bhaskar-Shrinivas et al., 2005). In this sense, HCNs and PCNs may perceive higher supervisory support and develop an effective leader–member relationship, regardless of who is the supervisor and who is the subordinate; this may lead to improved attitudes and behaviours from the perspectives of HCN satisfaction with a supervisor (Shay & Baack, 2004) and good PCN adjustment and job performance (Kraimer & Wayne, 2004). Some subsidiaries also implement practices such as onsite mentoring of PCNs by HCNs. Mezias and Scandura (2005) suggest that onsite mentoring ensures the fulfilment of PCNs' basic needs in the new country (e.g. getting advice about supermarkets, restaurants, banks, government taxes) and helps them adjust to their new work role (e.g. participation in company events, becoming aware of informal procedures in the subsidiary).

Individual factors

A smooth cross-cultural adjustment process corresponds to individual satisfaction with work and non-work aspects of the relocation; a commitment to the organisation; reduced intention to return early; and more effective performance (Takeuchi, 2010). Other factors also influence a person's level of adjustment, including their ability with languages; educational attainment level; multicultural experience; interpersonal skills; sociability and extraversion; flexibility; self-efficacy; cultural intelligence; openness to experience and new learning; and resilience to stress and tolerance of uncertainty (Caligiuri, Tarique & Jacobs, 2009; Bonache et al., 2007).

Costs of failure in recruitment and selection

There is an economic cost to headquarters when an appointed international employee's relocation fails. PCNs are the key to knowledge transfer in areas such as product design, distribution, know how, skills and innovative customer service (Subramaniam & Venkatraman, 2001). Failure in the selection process diminishes the benefits and networks of the headquarters and weakens the subsidiary–headquarters relationship.

For the host-country organisation, the failure of an international employee may decrease productivity, profitability and sales growth, and may even influence customer satisfaction and market penetration; the extent of its impact on these outputs depends on the person's competencies in the position and on his or her job status. Last, it may have negative effects on the employee who has failed, in terms of reduced self-efficacy and self-esteem and increased work–family conflict (Takeuchi, 2010).

▓ Conclusion

A range of factors drive recruitment and selection practices in the international context, including cultural differences between parent and host countries and varying linguistic and legislative contexts. MNCs can target different types of international employee in their recruitment and selection efforts, ranging from PCNs, HCNs and TCNs to more recently developed categories such as flexpatriates and short-term assignees. In this chapter, we proposed and explained our four-stage model, which encapsulates the process of international recruitment and selection as follows:

- Stage 1 – MNCs should recruit and select HR managers in the headquarters to design international recruitment and selection for subsidiaries, including conducting a thorough job analysis.
- Stage 2 – A recruitment strategy to attract the best talent to the applicant pool is designed and conducted.
- Stage 3 – The selection of the best candidate to fill the available international post is conducted, considering the criteria that will determine the success of the applicant in the post.

- Stage 4 – The evaluation of the success of implemented recruitment and selection practices is conducted, including indicators such as cultural adjustment and the quality of PCN–HCN relationships.

The costs of getting recruitment and selection wrong can be very high for both the MNC and the appointed employee. As international posts and the need for global employees will only grow in future, MNCs should prioritise ensuring the success of the international recruitment and selection process.

■ Take-home messages

- HR managers should conduct an in-depth job analysis when planning recruitment and selection in the international context, to determine what category of international employee to target (e.g. PCN, TCN, HCN, short-term assignee) and what competencies he or she will need to perform well in the post.
- HR professionals who have extensive knowledge of both headquarters (e.g. organisational culture) and host-country culture and regulations (e.g. employment legislation) should manage the recruitment and selection of international employees.
- HR managers selecting for international posts should consider the different competencies and social and personal skills that facilitate an individual's adjustment to the host country.
- MNCs should develop programs and practices that help international employees and their families adapt to new cultural environments (e.g. socialisation programs, mentoring by an HCN, relocation allowances).
- Poor selection and recruitment for international posts may lead to significant financial losses and the failure of an MNC's strategic goals (e.g. through reduced productivity or lost business deals).

■ Closing the learning loop

1. What are the key features of international recruitment and selection?
2. What are the main advantages and disadvantages of different categories of international employees?
3. Explain the four-stage process model of international recruitment and selection.
4. Discuss selection criteria that may determine employee success in an international post.
5. How can we best evaluate the success of international recruitment and selection?
6. Critically assess the consequences of getting international recruitment and selection wrong.

CASE STUDY 4.1   MERCATOR GROUP

Mercator Group (www.mercator.si) is a Slovenian corporate group and one of the largest retail chains in Southeastern Europe. It focuses on fast-moving consumer goods, home products and technical devices. Its retail network includes shopping malls, hypermarkets, supermarkets and convenience stores operating in Slovenia and eight other European markets: Albania, Bosnia and Herzegovina, Bulgaria, Croatia, Kosovo, Macedonia, Montenegro and Serbia. It also owns several distinguished private labels. Mercator Group's international scope is embedded in the following fundamental strategic goals (Mercator Group, 2011):

1. Strategic goals in the domestic market (Slovenia):
   - To retain the position of the leading fast-moving consumer goods retailer.
   - To consolidate the position of the second-largest retailer of home products.
   - To develop supplementary trade services related to their customer loyalty system.
2. Strategic goals in existing foreign markets (Serbia, Croatia, Bosnia and Herzegovina, Montenegro):
   - To consolidate or attain the position of the second-largest fast-moving consumer goods retailer.
   - To rank among the top three retailers of home products.
   - To develop supplementary trade services related to their customer loyalty system.
3. Strategic goals in new foreign markets (Bulgaria, Albania, Macedonia, Kosovo):
   - To rank among the top five retailers of fast-moving consumer goods.

Today, Mercator Group employs more than 24 000 people. Its IHRM strategy has developed in accordance with the company's international development. In the early phases of internationalisation, there were only few international posts. The first subsidiaries were established in Croatia, Serbia and Bosnia and Herzegovina between 1998 and 2003. In the beginning, the subsidiaries were small, each one starting with a single shopping mall and usually staffed with two international posts: one role to supervise marketing, category management and operations and the other to manage finances, investments and HRM. The headquarters in Slovenia recruited and selected international assignees from an internal talent pool, rarely from the external labour market. The HRM department at headquarters also played a significant role in the recruitment and selection of local employees in subsidiaries, including a management team and shop attendants.

As Mercator Group's international operations grew, its approach to international recruitment and selection gradually changed. Subsidiaries established their own HR departments and now handle recruitment and selection locally. The HR department in the headquarters only becomes involved in selection for key management positions. The number of international posts expanded and is no longer limited to internal talent from headquarters. International assignees are selected from the company's entire talent pool. The HR department at headquarters still selects them, but local HR departments perform the recruitment and pre-selection. Thus, local HR departments play a key role in the recruitment and selection of local employees, as well as in international recruitment and selection.

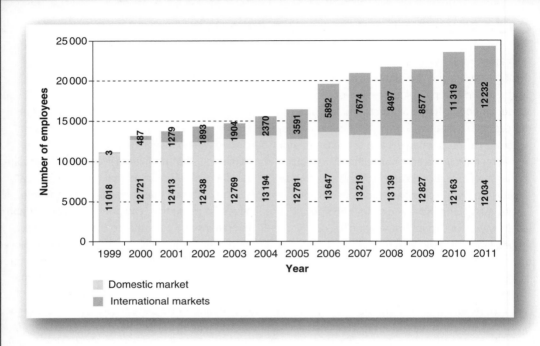

Figure 4.2 Number of employees in Mercator Group (adapted from www.mercator.si)

Case study questions

1. In what ways does Mercator Group's current international HRM strategy emphasise local integration in its subsidiaries?
2. What was the company's philosophy on international recruitment and selection in the early phases of its internationalisation, and how has it changed?
3. A geocentric approach to international recruitment and selection may have advantages and disadvantages for Mercator Group. Which approach would you recommend, and why?

» *ACTIVITIES*

Conducting an international interview

Break into small groups. Imagine that Mercator Group is seeking to fill the position of board member for a subsidiary in Bulgaria. Review the description of the role below. Next, consider the profile of Ivan Vasiljev, a potential candidate for this position. How would you conduct an interview with this candidate? Develop a set of suitable questions.

Board member responsibilities

- Supervises marketing, category management and operations departments. Works closely with department heads, provides strategic guidelines and leadership.
- Implements and adapts local policies for marketing, category management and operations from headquarters.
- Leads business development and growth in Bulgaria.
- Actively participates in annual evaluation and planning activities.
- Establishes both short and long-term business goals.
- Works closely with departments in the headquarters in order to ensure suitable management for different projects.
- Works closely with other Mercator Group's markets.
- Visits headquarters in Slovenia and other markets in which Mercator operates.
- Regularly attends board meetings.

Candidate profile

Ivan Vasiljev, 37, has an MBA from the Faculty of Economics at the University of Ljubljana, Slovenia, and 12 years of professional experience. He started out with a Slovenian retail company, where he worked as a merchandiser before progressing to category manager and non-food category director. He then spent two years as a country manager in Slovenia for an MNC that supplied non-food products to all significant retail companies in Slovenia. For the past six years, he has been a sales director for another MNC, and has completed two international assignments: four years in Hong Kong and a further four years in Singapore. In his current role, he has responsibility for business development in the fast-moving consumer goods sector. Today, Ivan is married and has two daughters. His hobbies are golf, skiing and tennis. He is fluent in English and Croatian and knows basic Chinese.

Developing a recruitment plan

Break into small groups. Imagine that Mercator Group wishes to enter the Romanian market and plans to open a shopping mall in its capital city, Bucharest. The company has a strong employer brand in all its existing markets, but not yet in Romania. You are working in Mercator Group's HR department and must prepare the recruitment plan for the new shopping mall, including profile descriptions for several roles that you will recruit in two stages, as follows.

Stage 1

- Local director of Romanian subsidiary
- Category manager (three positions)
- Accountant (two positions)
- Marketing manager
- Information technology associate
- Secretary

Stage 2

- Shopping mall head
- Line manager (six positions)
- Sales team members (75 positions)

How would you approach recruitment in this scenario? Discuss and develop an action plan in your group. Remember to support your plans with strong arguments.

▪ Online resources

- For instructors: answers to activities; long media article with questions; additional questions and answers.
- For students: further reading; answers to case study; IHRM in practice.

▪ References

Al Ariss, A. and Seyed, J. (2011). Capital mobilization of skilled migrants: A relational perspective, *British Journal of Management*, 22: 286–304.

Ballantyne, I. and Povah, N. (2004). *Assessment and development centres*, 2nd edition. London: Gower.

Bhaskar-Shrinivas, P., Harrison, D. A., Shaffer, M. A. and Luk, D. M. (2005). Input-based and time-based models of international adjustment: Meta-analytic evidence and theoretical extensions, *Academy of Management Journal*, 48: 257–81.

Black, J. S., Mendenhall, M. and Oddou, G. (1991). Toward a comprehensive model of international adjustment: An integration of multiple theoretical perspectives, *Academy of Management Review*, 16: 291–317.

Bonache, J., Brewster, C. and Suutari, V. (2007). Knowledge, international mobility, and careers, *International Studies of Management and Organization*, 37: 3–16.

Bowden, S. C., Saklofske, D. H. and Weiss, L. G. (2011). Invariance of the measurement model underlying the Wechsler Adult Intelligence Scale-IV in the United States and Canada, *Educational and Psychological Measurement*, 71: 186–99.

Briscoe, D. R. (1997). Assessment centers: Cross cultural and cross national issues, *Journal of Social Behavior and Personality*, 12: 261–70.

Briscoe, D., Schuler, R. and Tarique, I. (2012). *International human resource management*. London: Routledge.

Brookfield Global Relocation Services (2012). *Global relocation trends: 2012 survey report*. USA: Brookfield Global Relocation Services, http://espritgloballearning.com/wp-content/uploads/2011/03/2012-Brookfield-Global-Relocations-Trends-Survey. pdf. Retrieved 22 March 2013.

Budhwar, P. S. and Khatri, N. (2001). A comparative study of HR practices in Britain and India, *International Journal of Human Resource Management*, 12: 800–26.

Caligiuri, P. M. (2000). The Big Five personality characteristics as predictors of expatriate's desire to terminate the assignment and supervisor-rated performance, *Personnel Psychology*, 53(1): 67–88.

Caligiuri, P. M., Hyland, M. A., Joshi, A. and Bross, A. S. (1998). Testing a theoretical model for examining the relationship between family adjustment and expatriates' work adjustment, *Journal of Applied Psychology*, 83: 598–614.

Caligiuri, P., Tarique, I. and Jacobs, R. R. (2009). Selection for international assignments, *Human Resource Management Review*, 19: 251–62.

Chapman, D. S., Uggerslev, K. L. and Webster, J. (2003). Applicant reactions to face-to-face and technology-mediated interviews: A field investigation, *Journal of Applied Psychology*, 88: 944–53.

Cole, N. D. (2011). Managing global talent: Solving the spousal adjustment problem, *International Journal of Human Resource Management*, 22: 1504–30.

Dowling, P. J., Festing, M. Engle, A. D. (2008). *International human resource management*, 5th edition. Hong Kong: Cengage Learning EMEA.

Edenborough, R. (2005). *Assessment methods in recruitment, selection and performance*. London: Kogan Page.

Farndale, E., Scullion, H. and Sparrow, P. (2010). The role of the corporate HR function in global talent management, *Journal of World Business*, 45: 161–68.

Festing, M. and Eidems, J. (2011). A process perspective on transnational HRM systems: A dynamic capability-based analysis, *Human Resource Management Review*, 21: 162–73.

Froese, F. J. (2012). Motivation and adjustment of self-initiated expatriates: The case of expatriate academics in South Korea, *International Journal of Human Resource Management*, 23: 1095–112.

Groesch, N. (2004). *Validation of a biodata inventory for expatriate selection: Assessing cross-cultural adaptability*, doctoral dissertation, Auburn University.

Guion, R. M. and Highhouse, S. (2006). *Essentials of personnel assessment and selection*. New York: Lawrence Erlbaum Associates.

Han, J. and Han, J. (2009). Network-based recruiting and applicant attraction in China: Insights from both organizational and individual perspectives, *International Journal of Human Resource Management*, 20: 2228–49.

Harvey, M. and Novicevic, M. (2001). Selecting expatriates for increasingly complex global assignments, *Career Development International*, 6: 69–87.

Harzing, A. W. (2004). Composing and international staff. In Harzing, A. W. and van Ruysseveldt, J. (eds), *International human resource management*, 2nd edition, 251–282. London: Sage.

Hays, R. D. (1974). Expatriate selection: Insuring success and avoiding failure, *Journal of International Business Studies*, 5: 25–37.

Hofstede, G. (2001). *Culture's consequences: Comparing values, behaviors, institutions and organizations across nations*. Thousand Oaks, CA: Sage.

Hofstede, G. and Hofstede, G. J. (2005). *Cultures and organizations: Software of the mind*. New York: McGraw-Hill.

Huang, T. J., Chi, S. C. and Lawler, J. J. (2005). The relationship between expatriates' personality traits and their adjustment to international assignments, *International Journal of Human Resource Management*, 16: 1656–70.

Jansen, P. and Jongh, F. (1997). *Assessment centres: A practical handbook*. New York: John Wiley.

Jordan, J. and Cartwright, S. (1998). Selecting expatriate managers: Key traits and competencies, *Leadership and Organization Development Journal*, 19: 89–96.

Kraimer, M. L. and Wayne, S. J. (2004). An examination of POS as a multidimensional construct in the context of an expatriate assignment, *Journal of Management*, 30: 209–37.

Kristof, A. L. (1996). Person-organization fit: An integrative review of its conceptualizations, measurement, and implications, *Personnel Psychology*, 49: 1–49.

Kristof-Brown, A. L., Zimmerman, R. D. and Johnson, E. C. (2005). Consequences of individuals' fit at work: A meta-analysis of person–job, person–organization, person–group, and person–supervisor fit, *Personnel Psychology*, 58: 281–342.

Landis, R. S., Fogli, L. and Goldberg, E. (1998). Future-oriented job analysis: A description of the process and its organizational implications, *International Journal of Selection and Assessment*, 6: 192–7.

Ma, R. and Allen, D. G. (2009). Recruiting across cultures: A value-based model of recruitment, *Human Resource Management Review*, 19: 334–46.

Mayerhofer, H., Hartmann, L. C., Michelitsch-Riedl, G. and Kollinger, I. (2004). Flexpatriate assignments: A neglected issue in global staffing, *International Journal of Human Resource Management*, 15: 1371–89.

Maznewski, M., Davison, S. C. and Jonsen, K. (2006). Global virtual team dynamics and effectiveness. In Stahl, G. K. and Björkman, I. (eds), *Handbook of research in international human resource management*, 364–84. Northampton, MA: Edward Elgar.

Mendenhall, M. and Oddou, G. (1985). The dimensions of expatriate acculturation: A review, *Academy of Management Review*, 10: 39–47.

Mercator Group (2011). *Annual Report 2011*, www.mercatorgroup.si/en/za-vlagatelje-en-us/porocila-in-objave-en-us. Retrieved 15 October 2013.

Meyskens, M., Von Glinow, M. A., Werther, J. W. B. and Clarke, L. (2009). The paradox of international talent: Alternative forms of international assignments, *International Journal of Human Resource Management*, 20: 1439–50.

Mezias, J. M. and Scandura, T. A. (2005). A needs-driven approach to expatriate adjustment and career development: A multiple mentoring perspective, *Journal of International Business Studies*, 36: 519–38.

Moore, F. (2001). Recruitment and selection of international managers. In Edwards, T. and Rees, C. (eds), *International human resource management: Globalization, national systems and multinational companies*, 2nd edition, 184–205. Harlow, Essex: Prentice Hall.

Ntshona, S. (2007). *Expatriate management within a context of best practice in the Africa division of a multinational bank*, unpublished master's thesis, University of Pretoria, http://upetd. up.ac.za/thesis/available/etd-04232010115134/ unrestricted/dissertation.pdf. Retrieved 5 October 2012.

Osiecka, A. (2001). *International transfer of knowledge in multinational enterprises: The role of international human resource management in transferring tacit knowledge across borders*. Munich: Grin Verlag.

Perlmutter, H. V. (1969). The tortuous evolution of the multinational corporation, *Colombia Journal of World Business*, 4: 9–18.

Reiche, B. S. and Harzing, A. W. (2011). International assignments. In Harzing, A. W. and Pinnington, A. H. (eds), *International human resource management*, 3rd edition, 185–226. London: Sage.

Rian, D. and Ulf, H. (2012). Cultural distance or cultural positions? Analysing the effect of culture on the HQ–subsidiary relationship, *International Business Review*, 21: 383–96.

Riusala, K. and Suutari, V. (2000). Expatriation and careers: Perspectives of expatriates and spouses, *Career Development International*, 15: 81–90.

Roe, R. A. (2002). Competences: A key towards the integration of theory and practice in work psychology, *Gedrag en Organisatie*, 15: 203–24.

Schmitt, D. P., Allik, J., McCrae, R. R. and Benet-Martínez, V. (2007). The geographic distribution of big five personality traits: patterns and profiles of human self-description across 56 nations, *Journal of Cross-Cultural Psychology*, 3: 173–212.

Schoyen, C. and Rasmussen, N. (1999). *Secrets of the executive search experts*. New York: Amacom.

Searle, R. H. (2003). *Selection and recruitment: A critical text*. Basingstoke: Palgrave Macmillan.

Selmer, J. and Lauring, J. (2012). Reasons to expatriate and work outcomes of self-initiated expatriates, *Personnel Review*, 41: 665–84.

Shaffer, M. A. Kraimer M. L., Chen, Y. P. and Bolino, M. C. (2012). Choices, challenges, and career consequences of global work experiences: A review and future agenda, *Journal of Management*, 38: 1282–327.

Shay, J. P. and Baack, S. (2004). Expatriate assignment, adjustment and effectiveness: An empirical examination of the big picture, *Journal of International Business Studies*, 35: 216–32.

Sparrow, P. R. (2007). Globalization of HR at function level: Four UK-based case studies of the international recruitment and selection process, *International Journal of Human Resource Management*, 18: 845–67.

Subramaniam, M. and Venkatraman, N. (2001). Determinants of transnational new product development capability: Testing the influence of transferring and deploying tacit overseas knowledge, *Strategic Management Journal*, 22: 359–78.

Takeuchi, R. (2010). A Critical review of expatriate adjustment research through a multiple stakeholder view: Progress, emerging trends, and prospects, *Journal of Management*, 36: 1040–64.

Tarique, I. and Schuler, R. S. (2010). Global talent management: Literature review, integrative framework, and suggestions for further research, *Journal of World Business*, 45: 122–33.

Tsai, W. C., Chen, H. Y. and Chen, C. C. (2012). Incremental validity of person–organization fit over the big five personality measures, *Journal of Psychology: Interdisciplinary and Applied*, 146: 485–509.

5 Cross-cultural training and development for overseas assignments

*Aykut Berber, Yasin Rofcanin
and Yitzhak Fried*

■ Learning objectives

- To emphasise the prevalence of international assignments in today's integrated business settings.
- To explain and evaluate cross-cultural training programs for international assignees, emphasising differences between expatriates and inpatriates.
- To acknowledge that successful overseas assignment and relocation require the joint efforts of both international human resource managers and the focal employee assigned to the new destination.

■ Learning outcomes

After reading this chapter, students will be able to:
- understand and evaluate cross-cultural training programs designed for international assignees
- understand and appreciate training tools, learning mechanisms and socialisation programs to manage and minimise culture shock
- comprehend that the success of long-term international assignees is heavily influenced by the joint efforts of international human resource managers and the relocated employee
- appreciate the need to develop individualised and cross-culturally appropriate training programs for overseas assignees before, during and after their arrival in a host country.

▪ Introduction

Effective management of international assignees (Reiche, 2011) in the global business setting is one of the most challenging tasks for international HR managers. Integrated, fierce and innovation-driven markets characterise today's business environment (Moeller, Harvey & Williams, 2010); international assignees are key actors who share knowledge in multinational companies (MNCs) and who act as boundary spanners in a range of MNC units (Reiche, Harzing & Kraimer, 2009). Combining the perplexity of managing international assignees with the rising predominance of MNCs across the globe (Van der Heijden, van Engen & Paauwe, 2009), IHR managers need to plan training and development of international assignees for a global context – hence **cross-cultural training** and development programs (Mezias & Scandura, 2005). However, employees who are assigned international responsibilities should also adopt a global mindset, as it is the joint responsibility of IHR managers and focal employees to share mutual benefits in the global training and development context (Lazarova & Caligiuri, 2001). In this chapter, our main aim is to evaluate, understand and present key concepts, tools and processes used in cross-cultural training and development programs across international work settings.

cross-cultural training Training designed for international assignees to help them adapt to, and integrate with, the host country's business setting and social context. Such programs are sequential and take place before, during and after the arrival of the assigned employee in the host country.

Appropriate selection and cross-cultural training of international assignees are critical because of the direct and indirect costs to companies in cases of failure (Hocking, Brown & Harzing, 2007). Direct costs include the expense of relocating and returning the assignee, compensation packages and return-related administrative costs. Indirect costs include potential relational damages with employees, customers, suppliers and the organisational community. Hence, IHR managers should identify and select employees who are likely to perform effectively in new cultural contexts; who have a learning orientation; who have flexible and global mindsets; and who are very culturally intelligent (Harvey et al., 2005). In other words, the selection criteria of IHR managers should go beyond the assignee's technical knowledge to focus on aspects related to his or her adaptability and potential for learning in different cultural settings, as evidenced in research (Harvey, Ralston & Napier, 2000) and current practice. A survey conducted with 60 managers from 13 countries confirmed that adaptability was seen as the most central criteria for the success of international assignees (Moeller, Harvey & Williams, 2010). Another study revealed that assessment centres (ACs) may be used to identify potential employees who could be assigned international duties (Moeller, Harvey & Williams, 2010).

Overseas assignments: expatriates and inpatriates

Employees are assigned to overseas positions in many ways (Moeller, Harvey & Williams, 2010). Expatriation and inpatriation (Peterson, 2003; Reiche, Harzing & Kraimer, 2009) are the two typical forms of international assignment (see chapter 3), and both refer to managerial-level employees working overseas on permanent or semi-permanent bases. In a similar vein, both **expatriates** (known as 'expats') and **inpatriates** (known as 'inpats') experience and encounter issues when they undergo **culture shock**, **cultural adaptation** and integration processes in their new cultural context (Reiche, 2011). However, expatriates and inpatriates are different: the former is a parent-country national (PCN) assigned overseas for duties in a foreign subsidiary (Feldman & Thomas, 1992), and the latter is a host-country national (HCN), usually a subsidiary manager in the host country, relocated to headquarters for a specified period of time (Harvey, 1997). Third-country nationals (TCNs) are also sometimes relocated in managerial roles, being a citizen neither of the country where the headquarters are located nor of the destination to which they are assigned. Overall, the most distinctive and significant difference between expatriation and inpatriation is that inpatriation defines the overseas relocation process in which HCNs from the foreign subsidiaries are assigned to headquarters, whereas expatriated PCNs are assigned from the headquarters to a subsidiary. Table 5.1 summarises the essential differences between inpatriates and expatriates.

expatriates International assignees who are usually from more developed parts of the world and who are PCNs. They share similar cultural and educational backgrounds with employees at headquarters.

inpatriates International assignees who are usually from the less developed regions of the world and who are HCNs. They share more diverse cultural and educational backgrounds with employees at headquarters.

culture shock The sense of shock employees encounter in an unfamiliar context, such as a new country or company, mainly due to lack of sufficient experience with, or knowledge and information about, the host country.

cultural adaptation The final stage of the adaptation process for an assigned employee, in which they adapt to, and reflect, culturally consistent behaviours in their new business and country setting.

The differences between inpatriates and expatriates are critical for international assignees considering their socialisation, international training and development needs (Hocking, Brown & Harzing, 2007). IHR managers should develop training and development programs that will meet the unique needs of inpatriates and expatriates. Additionally, IHR managers should emphasise aspects such as the free choice of accepting the new responsibility, security of repatriation and the provision of individualised and attractive compensation packages in the new cultural context (Mezias & Scandura, 2005). However, the assigned employee should also make every effort to adapt to their new context. The support and efforts of the home-country managers (IHR managers and the immediate supervisors and colleagues of the assigned employee) and the individualised efforts, mindsets, behaviours and

Table 5.1 Differences between expatriates and inpatriates	
Expatriates	**Inpatriates**
Assigned from headquarters to foreign subsidiaries, and so, generally considered PCNs.	Relocated to headquarters from local subsidiaries, and so, generally considered HCNs.
Receive attractive compensation package and a better status compared to their previous positions.	Do not necessarily receive attractive compensation package and status; this depends on the importance of the subsidiary from which they have come.
Do not generally face corporate culture shock due to their familiarity with the headquarters' corporate culture.	Face cultural adjustment challenges both concerning the corporate and country cultures.
Constantly coordinate with the headquarters team.	Integrated into the HQ management team only temporarily.
Usually come from developed economies.	Usually come from developing economies, mainly due to cheap labour and production costs in such countries.
May be dual-career couples.	Generally not dual-career couples, since working spouses are still not common in inpatriates' home countries.
More diverse range of business education and professional experiences.	Less diverse range of business education and professional experiences.
Reflect a dominant ethnocentric orientation in the MNC.	Reflect a dominant polycentric orientation in the MNC.

attitudes of the employee concerning the new cultural context jointly shape the international assignee's successful performance.

Accordingly, it is a key strategic imperative for international HR managers to assign the right people to appropriate jobs in a global context. At one time, research (e.g. Bhawuk & Brislin, 1992; Adelman, 1988) and practice focused solely on the technical abilities of employees who were relocated for international positions. However, as Earley and Ang (2003) argued more recently, when employees are relocated they should acknowledge cultural differences and adapt their behaviours according to the norms, values and general culture of their new position and the host country. Bhawuk and Brislin (1992) also emphasised that the newly relocated employee should show sensitivity to, and understanding of, the different context they are encountering (Harvey, Novicevic & Speier, 1999). In this respect, IHR managers should encourage and select employees who have a global mindset, who show appreciation of new and distinct cultures and who make some effort to adapt their behaviour to the new norms and societal expectations of both the national and corporate culture.

cross-cultural socialisation The adaptation process through which international assignees familiarise themselves with company cultural contexts and the norms, behaviours and expectations of the host country.

IHR managers share responsibility for the assigned employee's full integration before, during and after arrival in the host country. Therefore, IHR managers should encourage the assignee and offer **cross-cultural socialisation**, training and development opportunities that address more than the assignee's technical abilities. Moreover, cross-cultural training and development programs should also integrate the parents, spouses and partners of the relocated employee, as appropriate.

The socialisation process for overseas assignments

The full integration process of overseas assignees starts with their socialisation. Socialisation helps to ensure the assignee's correct knowledge and experience about the host country or company cultures. Recent research (e.g. Moeller, Harvey & Williams, 2010; Reiche, 2011) and practice emphasise that socialisation should be modified to meet the different needs of expatriates and inpatriates. First, inpatriates often come from developing economies around the world and HCNs may not give them the same level of respect and credibility as their expatriate peers (Reiche, 2011). The socialisation process for inpatriates should underline the linking and bridging roles of the inpatriate between the home and host-country contexts. Second, inpatriates face greater country and company-specific challenges than expatriates do (Harvey et al., 2005). For this reason, the inpatriate socialisation process should include elaborative processes to ensure the assignee's successful integration with country and company contexts. Third, as Reiche (2006) has argued, inpatriates come from different cultural backgrounds than that of the host organisation, while expatriates usually share common cultural habits and backgrounds with their new organisational and country context. Therefore, socialisation steps should initiate a greater integration and appreciation of the more diverse cultural and educational backgrounds of inpatriates.

Cross-cultural training and development

With the rapid pace of internationalisation, more companies have explored opportunities to expand businesses in emerging economies (e.g. China, India, Mexico, Brazil, Turkey and many of the South/Southeast Asian and Eastern European regions). For instance, a study by Colakoglu and Caligiuri (2008) revealed that around 850 000 subsidiaries of MNCs operate around the globe, and these operations are mostly clustered around the late-developing markets. Therefore, international assignee positions have become prevalent ways for MNCs to utilise managers with global mindsets. Previous research showed that around 150 000 employees from the United States were sent to overseas assignments. In same way, a recent relocation survey (Moeller, Harvey & Williams, 2010) revealed that the number of international assignee positions is expected to rise, as the success of companies in global competition is highly dependent on a competent and experienced workforce.

The central goal of cross-cultural training programs is to equip employees with appropriate forms of behaviours in their new cultural settings and work environments (Mezias & Scandura, 2005). However, we argue that the international assignment is a process that encompasses different stages of adaptability and performance. Scholars and practitioners generally agree (Moeller, Harvey & Williams, 2010; Reiche, 2011) that international assignees go through two main stages that as they settle to their new responsibilities. These include pre-departure preparations and post-arrival (early-arrival and late-arrival) experiences.

Relatedly, Selmer (1998) identified four distinct and sequential phases of international assignees' adjustment process. First, they show ethnocentric attitudes; second, they experience culture shock; third, they develop conformist behaviours; and fourth, they become culturally adjusted. Selmer (1998) argued that international assignees need to be trained at various stages of the assignment, to fit different social contexts more closely and to perform effectively. Similarly, as the learning capability, needs and receptivity of employees differ in each of the four adjustment stages, the timing and content of the cross-cultural training should fit with the assignee's phase at a given time. The successful management of this continuum determines the success or failure of international assignees. Below, we discuss cross-cultural training with respect to the four phases of cross-cultural adaptation (Selmer, 1998) and with emphasis on the pre-arrival and post-arrival experiences of international assignees.

In the pre-departure period, international assignees are reluctant to develop in-depth understanding of the particular cultural context, mainly because the new context is not salient to them at that moment. Assignees experience only trivial cultural differences that do not necessarily require cognitive and behavioural readjustment (Mendenhall, Dunbar & Oddou, 1987). Employees in this stage lack a sufficient frame of reference about the host culture and do not have enough experience or knowledge to determine what constitutes a culturally significant issue in that country (Reiche, Harzing & Kraimer, 2009). More specifically, in-patriates lack information and experience about the country and company cultural contexts where they will be relocated. As expatriates are already familiar with the corporate culture of headquarters, they tend to encounter challenges mostly during adaptation to the country context. For this reason, pre-departure training programs for inpatriates should include specific information about country and corporate culture.

Regardless of the form of international assignment, pre-departure training and development programs should predominantly focus on two key areas: enhancing cultural awareness and decreasing the level of ethnocentrism (Mezias & Scandura, 2005). While the number of pre-departure training programs has increased especially over the past 20 years, there are still not enough comprehensive cross-cultural training programs designed for employees and their families (Moeller, Harvey & Williams, 2010). Cross-cultural training programs should go beyond simply offering basic culture orientation, language training and some environmental briefings. IHR managers should emphasise cross-cultural training that raises awareness of the local norms, values, ways of behaving and other appropriate cultural codes.

As international assignees are exposed to comprehensive cross-cultural training activities, they usually adapt to their new business settings easily and will eventually modify their behaviours in accordance with the ways of living and doing business in their new environment (Peterson, 2003). The international assignee is likely to achieve full adaptation when he or she starts viewing the world from the lens of the host-country context.

Successful pre-departure training and development programs include cross-cultural adaptation and social processes not only for the international assignee but also for his or her spouse and parents (Van der Heijden, van Engen & Paauwe, 2009). Examples of activities undertaken during this process encompass training in dealing with the new environment; managing stress; understanding and adapting to new behavioural norms; developing relationships, non-verbal and verbal communication skills for use in the new culture; and practising non-judgement about others in the new environment (Adelman, 1988). In this regard, pre-departure training and development activities are usually aimed at developing the individual and others, and modifying perceptions the international assignee and the parents or spouse may have of the new cultural context (Bhagat et al., 2002). Previous research (Reiche, 2006; Reiche, Harzing & Kraimer, 2009) revealed that culture-contrast learning (a learning approach that emphasises the cross-cultural similarities and differences), and fact-oriented training are among the most effective cross-cultural training tools for expediting the daily transition of assignees at work and at home. Therefore, the international assignee is exposed to initial knowledge about the host country, and develops understanding and acknowledges cultural awareness about ways of working and living in their new environment.

Once the employee is assigned to the new position (usually defined as the early-arrival stage), he or she will start viewing the new environment with idiosyncratic perspectives and implicit assumptions (Harvey, 1997). During the early periods of arrival in a host country, the newly assigned employee retains his or her home country–driven confidence and ethnocentrism (Carraher, Sullivan & Crocitto, 2008); therefore, he or she applies new behaviours only gradually. This stage is marked by culture shock, in which the assignee is still unfamiliar with the new norms, rules, behaviours, and overall cultural expectations of their new environment (Bonache, Brewster & Suutari, 2001). International assignees are exposed to many different experiences and impressions that require cognitive reframing. In other words, as the assignee receives different cognitive elements from the host environment, he or she experiences cognitive inconsistency and therefore tries to reframe the new cultural context in his or her mindset (Bhaskar-Shrinivas et al., 2005). In more specific terms, inpatriates experience culture shock as they adapt to company and country cultural contexts. They face challenges and make extra effort to reframe their cognitive mindsets given the unfamiliarity of the country and company cultures. On the contrary, a new expatriate's culture shock is most likely limited to the new country context.

Therefore, training during the period of culture shock needs to respond to the different degrees of familiarity and integration inpatriates and expatriates may have with their new surroundings. Training conducted during the culture shock phase should reduce the uncertainty related to cross-cultural expectations and facilitate cognitive reframing of international assignees. At the end of this stage, the assignee will generally have developed a flexible mindset, in which he or she can appreciate behaviours specific to the host country and develop norms consistent with its prevalent cultural context. Training modules for this stage should include practical information about ways of living and working in, and determining the expectations of, the host culture. The experiential learning approach, including simulations, role-plays and situational exercises, is a highly appropriate tool in the host-culture context. Overall, international assignees experience simultaneous uncertainty and cognitive ambiguity, which is why cross-cultural training tends to be most effective during this phase. The overarching goal is to make sure that the assignee manages his or her culture shock.

The latter stages of an assignee's arrival phase are usually composed of conformist and cross-cultural adjustment stages. During these stages, the international assignee accommodates the norms and expectations of the host culture (Moeller, Harvey & Williams, 2010) but is not fully confident about behaving in ways that are different to behaviours in the home country. Therefore, training in this phase should help assignees to learn by doing as people do in the host country. In this way, assignees engage in an interactional mode of learning and develop culturally sensitive skills necessary to adapt to their work and home lives. Research suggests that during the conformist stage, international assignees interact with trainees, HCNs and/or experienced expatriates. These structured and unstructured interactions enable assignees to incorporate and develop cross-cultural competencies.

During the cross-cultural adjustment phase, the international assignee is expected to develop an integrative and flexible understanding of the host-country context. Local values, norms, expectations and behaviours are accepted in an open-minded manner and the learning experience triggers new ways of thinking in an unfamiliar cultural context. In cross-cultural training, the international assignee can expand his or her portfolio of attitudes and behaviours to fit new contexts, which will also be relevant during repatriation.

In addition to cross-cultural training programs, IHR managers should develop and implement individualised cross-cultural development programs, which will help them to keep and utilise the skills of international assignees (Briscoe, Schuler & Ibraiz, T., 2012). IHR managers and the assigned employees should keep in mind that development is a long-term process, aimed at creating a cadre of global executives who possess global mindsets (Schuler & Briscoe, 2004). In a successful international assignment, the employee adapts to the host-country context through appropriate training programs, and repatriates when he or she has completed the assignment. In this respect, cross-cultural training and development programs should be directed towards keeping and utilising the talented international assignees in the long run, after repatriation. In this way, the IHR manager can avoid the indirect and direct costs of failure in international assignments (Schuler & Briscoe, 2004).

■ Conclusion

In this chapter, our central aim was to define, discuss, exemplify and offer practical guidelines on key concepts in cross-cultural training, including socialisation, adjustment processes and culture shock. To fulfil this goal, we first discussed and differentiated between inpatriates and expatriates, the two most commonly observed groups in overseas assignments. We then discussed cross-cultural socialisation and training designed for international assignees and examined issues involved in cross-cultural training pre-arrival and post-arrival employees.

Throughout, we emphasised that the frequency and success of cross-cultural training programs are heavily influenced by the support of the headquarters; the provision of appropriate learning materials and training tools by international HR managers; the resources available in the headquarters; the learning abilities and learning styles of the focal employees; and the joint input of international HR managers and overseas assigned employees in maintaining a successful assignment and relocation process. Therefore, assigned employees and international HR managers can be said to share responsibility for managing global careers in new cultural contexts.

■ Take-home messages

- International assignments are increasingly seen in today's integrated markets, particularly given the fast pace of globalisation and more dynamic work settings.
- Expatriation is not the only method for sending employees overseas; organisations also commonly use inpatriation and self-initiated expatriation, as recent scholarship has noted. MNCs use international assignees extensively to fill overseas positions.
- Despite their similarities, expatriate and inpatriate employees are different in terms of their cultural and educational backgrounds; their positions and compensation packages in the host country; their reasons for overseas assignment; and their need for cross-cultural training and development.
- Training, development and adaptation needs differ among expatriates, inpatriates and self-initiated expatriates, most importantly support with issues around culture shock and the integration process. It is imperative for international HR managers to develop and implement cross-cultural socialisation, training and development programs to meet these different needs, and to offer repatriation programs for returning employees.
- International HR managers should design individualised training and development programs to ensure that overseas assignees are able to adapt to their new context; reduce their ethnocentric orientations; and fully integrate with their new country and company settings.

- The assigned employee should adopt a flexible and global mindset; reduce his or her ethnocentric viewpoints regarding the company and cultural context; and adapt his or her behaviours to respect local norms, expectations and behaviours.
- It is the shared responsibility of international HR managers and assigned employees to maintain successful overseas assignment and repatriation; their joint efforts lead to successful overseas assignments and relocations, in which cultural adaptation is achieved and relocation is secured.

■ Closing the learning loop

1. Critically discuss the following statement: 'Expatriates adapt to their host country's culture better and faster than inpatriates do.'
2. What challenges may be involved in the socialisation process for expatriates and inpatriates? How should international HR managers manage these challenges?
3. Identify two differences between inpatriates and expatriates, and discuss how cross-cultural training can be adapted to meet each group's needs.
4. What is the employee's role in the cross-cultural socialisation and training process, compared to the manager and HR department's role?

CASE STUDY 5.1   A CAREER IN TEXTILE DESIGN

Nour was born in Cairo, Egypt, where her Jordanian father was working as an engineer in a British construction company when he met Nour's mother, Julia. Nour was raised in Liverpool and rarely left the United Kingdom, except for a few occasional visits to her grandparents in Jordan's capital city, Amman. She always had a passion for textile goods and studied the subject at the University of Birmingham. She was then accepted on a master's degree program to study the use of furnishing textiles in Switzerland and Japan. Her years spent in these two different cultures were fruitful: she attended various aesthetics courses and improved her skills in design workshops; she learnt to speak French and Japanese; and she developed relationships with several local designers in both countries. Nour decided to get an MBA degree and lived in California and Hawaii for a year, where she had the chance to work with two different fabric and furnishing manufacturers that shared Nour's passion for Pacific and Japanese cultures.

Returning to the UK, Nour successfully applied for a position with City & M, an international fabric design company. Established in 1956 and originally English-owned, City & M went international in 1985, maintaining its London headquarters but extending to more than 30 countries. The company now has branch offices in Buenos Aires, Doha, Delhi, Frankfurt, Istanbul, Kyoto, Los Angeles, Milan and Shanghai. Nour felt lucky to work in a company with such an extensive international network. She started working on design projects, focusing on reviving traditional designs for Swiss-style kitchen furniture by using concepts from Japanese design.

The City & M managers repeatedly assigned Nour to duties that involved Middle Eastern countries, despite her specific interest in Swiss and Japanese styles of art and design elements. She travelled to many countries in the Middle East and was responsible for designing fabric products manufactured for customers in these markets. Yet her real passion was in designing for European and Japanese markets. One day, when Nour's manager asked her to visit a customer in Doha, she said no and suddenly quit her job, saying that she would like to pursue her own career goals.

Case study questions

1. In this chapter, you read about issues and challenges faced in career development. Discuss the career challenges Nour faced in light of recent trends and her background as described in the case study.
2. What could Nour's employer have done to attempt to retain her in the company? In your response, consider cross-cultural development and training.
3. Evaluate Nour's career development path from the company and Nour's perspectives.
4. Do you think that Nour was right to quit her job? Why or why not?

» *ACTIVITY*

Role-play

Overview

Break into groups of five. In each group, two students assume the roles of international HR managers of a MNC, one of whom is responsible for recruitment and the other for training and development. Three students assume the roles of employees who are applying for an international assignment.

Objective

The objective of this role-play scenario is to emphasise the importance of selecting the right employee for an overseas position and engaging in providing continuous cross-cultural training and development program for the focal employee.

Directions

Building on the background information provided below, the role-play will show three interviews, after which one manager will select the best employee for the overseas position and the other will design a training and development program for the chosen employee.

- First, read the background information about the company, the position and the three candidates.

- Second, role-play separate interviews between the recruitment manager and each of the candidates.

- Third, role-play a meeting between the two HR managers, at which the recruitment manager explains whom he or she has selected, and the training and development manager suggests an appropriate support program for the selected candidate.

Background

Company information: The role-play characters work for a company called Speedy, a leading MNC in the fast-moving consumer goods (FMCG) sector. The company has been in operation for 17 years, and manages operations across 14 different countries. The company is headquartered in North America and all five employees are employed at headquarters. The organisational structure of Speedy is based around product categories, each of which has client relations, sales and operations divisions. The company outsources its finance and accounting functions. Due to stiff competition and dynamic nature of the FMCG sector, employees work long hours and frequently travel abroad. Despite these work-related challenges, roles in FMCG in general and client relations in particular receive a high number of competent applications from MBA-qualified and other graduate candidates.

Position description: The vacant position is a client account manager position based in Romania. The account manager will constantly interact with clients and is required to manage long-term relationships. Therefore, the job demands cultural adaptability and communication skills in the host-country context.

Employee 1 (Eli): Eli has been with Speedy for two years. Before joining the company, he worked for McKinsey & Company in the business development department for emerging economies. Currently, he oversees the client relations on the west coast of the United States and in China. His main goal is to increase the number of clients in each region and try to generate as much revenue as possible, to enhance the profitability of Speedy in these areas. He is also responsible for client interactions – that is, the quality of communication with the clients. He holds a bachelor degree from the University of Michigan and immediately entered the MBA program at Boston University. During his studies, he stayed in Singapore for four months, where he studied at the Singapore Management University.

Employee 2 (Rohanna): Rohanna has worked at Speedy for seven years. She worked in the finance department for two years before transferring to the sales division, in which has been the sales manager of the Europe, Middle East and Africa (EMEA) region for five years. Previously, she worked in a wide variety of sectors: she held finance-related responsibilities at a position with the World Bank and sales responsibilities in her other jobs, including the energy and cosmetics industries. She has a bachelor degree from Catholic Leuven University and an MBA from Rutgers University, where she received a full scholarship. She has travelled extensively in Europe as part of her current job.

Employee 3 (Tarique): Tarique has recently been hired in, and promoted, from Speedy's management trainee program. He has been in the company for two years and is working in his first role after graduating with a degree in industrial engineering from the Middle East Technical University, where he came top of his class. In Speedy's management trainee program, he has worked in a range of departments, including finance, marketing and sales. He is the youngest of the three candidates and has relatively limited work experience.

Discussion questions

1. From the perspective of the recruitment HR manager, which of the candidates would you select for the vacant position and why? Discuss the strengths and weaknesses of each candidate in turn.

2. From the perspective of the training and development HR manager, describe the cross-cultural training and development program you would prepare for each of the candidates. Outline the challenges you would address during these programs.

3. From the perspective of the training and development manager, if the selected employee showed unsatisfactory performance on the job, what steps would you take?

Online resources

- For instructors: answers to activities: long media article with questions.
- For students: further reading; answers to case study; IHRM in practice.

References

Adelman, M. B. (1988). Cross-cultural adjustment: A theoretical perspective on social support, *International Journal of Intercultural Relations*, 12: 183–204.

Bhagat, R.S. et al. (2002). Cultural variation in the cross-border transfer of organizational knowledge: An integrative framework, *Academy of Management Review*, 27(2): 204–21.

Bhaskar-Shrinivas, P. et al. (2005). Input-based and time-based models of international adjustment: Meta-analytic evidence and theoretical extensions, *Academy of Management Journal*, 48: 257–81.

Bhawuk, D.P.S., and Brislin, R. (1992). The measurement of intercultural sensitivity using the concepts of individualism and collectivism, *International Journal of Intercultural Relations*, 16(44): 413–36.

Bonache, J., Brewster, C., and Suutari, V. (2001). Expatriation: A developing research agenda, *Thunderbird International Business Review*, 43(1): 3–20.

Briscoe, D., Schuler, R. and Ibraiz, T. (2012). *International human resource management: policies and practices for multinational enterprises*. New York: Routledge.

Carraher, S.M., Sullivan, S.E. and Crocitto, M.M. (2008). Mentoring across global boundaries: An empirical examination of home- and host-country mentors on expatriate career outcomes, *Journal of International Business Studies*, 39(8): 1310–26.

Colakoglu, S. and Caligiuri, P. (2008). Cultural distance, expatriate staffing and subsidiary performance: The case of US subsidiaries of multinational corporations, *International Journal of Human Resource Management*, 19: 223–39.

Earley P.C. and Ang, S. (2003). *Cultural intelligence: Individual interactions across cultures*. Stanford, CA: Stanford University Press.

Feldman, D.C. and Thomas, D.C. (1992). Career management issues facing expatriates, *Journal of International Business Studies*, 32: 271–94.

Harvey, M. (1997). Inpatriation training: The next challenge for international human resource management, *International Journal of Intercultural Relations*, 21: 393–428.

Harvey, M., Novicevic, M.M., Buckley, M.R. and Fung, H. (2005). Reducing inpatriate managers' 'liability of foreignness' by addressing stigmatization and stereotype threats, *Journal of World Business*, 40(3): 267–80.

Harvey, M., Novicevic, M.M. and Speier, C. (1999). Inpatriate managers: How to increase the probability of success, *Human Resource Management Review*, 9(1): 51–81.

Harvey, M., Ralston, D., and Napier, N. (2000). International relocation of inpatriate managers: Assessing and facilitating acceptance in the headquarters' organization, *International Journal of Intercultural Relations*, 24: 825–46.

Hocking, J.B., Brown, M.E. and Harzing, A.W. (2007). Balancing global and local strategic contexts: Expatriate knowledge transfer, applications and learning within a transnational organization, *Human Resource Management*, 46(4): 513–33.

Lazarova, M. and Caligiuri, P. (2001). Retaining repatriates: The role of organizational support practices, *Journal of World Business*, 36(4): 389–401.

Mendenhall, M., Dunbar, E. and Oddou, G.R. (1987). Expatriate selection, training and career pathing: A review and critique, *Human Resources Management*, 26(3): 331–45.

Mezias, J.M. and Scandura, T.A. (2005). A needs-driven approach to expatriate adjustment and career development: A multiple mentoring perspective, *Journal of International Business Studies*, 36(5): 519–38.

Moeller, M., Harvey, M. and Williams, W. (2010). Socialization of inpatriate managers to the headquarters of global organizations: A social learning perspective, *Human Resource Development Review*, 9(2): 169–93.

Peterson, R.B. (2003). The use of expatriates and inpatriates in Central and Eastern Europe since the wall came down, *Journal of World Business*, 38(1): 55–69.

Reiche, B. S. (2006). The inpatriate experience in multinational corporations: An exploratory case study in Germany, *International Journal of Human Resource Management*, 17(9): 1572–90.

Reiche, B. S. (2011). Knowledge transfer in multinationals: The role of inpatriates' boundary spanning, *Human Resource Management*, 50(3): 365–89.

Reiche, B. S., Harzing, A. W. and Kraimer, M. L. (2009). The role of international assignees' social capital in creating inter-unit intellectual capital: A cross-level model, *Journal of International Business Studies*, 40(3): 509–26.

Schuler, R. and Briscoe, D. (2004). Global ethics and international human resources management, *Competitiveness and Ethics*, 12: 269–85.

Selmer, J. (1998). Expatriation: Corporate policy, personal intentions and international adjustment, *International Journal of Human Resource Management*, 9: 996–1007.

Van der Heijden, J. A. V., van Engen, M. L. and Paauwe, J. (2009). Expatriate career support: Predicting expatriate turnover and performance, *International Journal of Human Resource Management*, 20(4): 831–45.

6 International reward

Glenville Jenkins

■ Learning objectives

- To provide a concise introduction to international reward management.
- To appraise the key concepts that inform international reward management.
- To illustrate the design architecture of reward systems at macro-, meso- and micro-levels.
- To identify the key strategic international reward issues in multinational companies.
- To explain how reward policies and practices are employed to motivate employees on international assignments.

■ Learning outcomes

After reading this chapter, students will be able to:
- understand the nature of international rewards
- critically evaluate the architecture of international reward systems at macro-, meso- and micro-levels
- compare and contrast the main approaches to reward management in multinational companies
- comprehend the complexity and diversity of rewarding international assignees.

Introduction

Sparrow (2006) argues that multinational companies (MNCs) require a specific HRM architecture to operate successfully in an international context. In terms of reward management, the foundations of this architecture are built around designing the reward system to reward employees for their knowledge, skills and aptitudes.

Economic and social factors strongly influence the design of reward systems as does the frame of reference of international managers. In recent years, the 'new pay' agenda (Heery, 2000; Lewis, 2000), in line with a neo-liberal, free enterprise ideology, has strongly influenced managerial perceptions about rewarding people, with its emphasis on 'individual market value, flexibility and performance' (Corby, Palmer & Lindop, 2009: 7). Central to this approach is the idea that reward systems should be designed strategically to reward results and behaviour that are con-sistent with the goals of the organisation (Schuster & Zingheim, 1992). The suggested means for doing this is **variable pay**, where pay is tied closely to individual or team behaviour or to the achievement of organisational goals. Lawler (1995), one of the central architects of the 'new pay' approach, stressed that 'new pay' was not a pre-scription to success, but a way of thinking about reward design to make the organisation more effective. He argued: 'It is entirely possible to design a reward system that moti-vates people to work and satisfies them while at the same time contributing to organizational effectiveness' (see also Lawler, 1995:178; Armstrong & Murlis, 2007: 5).

> **variable pay** Pay contingent on performance, contribution, competence or skill of individual, team or organisation.

Still, the traditional goals of reward systems to motivate, recruit and retain employees have not gone away, although the means by which these goals are achieved are highly contested. Traditionally, rewards have been classified into pay and non-pay benefits, the former including wages and salaries and the latter comprising health insurance, pensions and holidays. The scope of rewards was later widened and classified into extrinsic and intrinsic rewards. **Extrinsic rewards** are pay and benefits (see below) that meet employ-ees' basic need for security and recognition. Extrinsic motivation, satisfaction and com-mitment may stem from these instrumental rewards, but these tend to be short-lived rewards; financial gain, not satisfaction derived from work, is what motivates employees. **Intrinsic rewards** are the psychological benefits derived from well-designed jobs that meet the employee's needs and aspirations. They may derive from the employee's level of discretion in the job; how meaningful the job is; the quality of the employee's working life; and the extent to which he or she achieves work–life balance. Intrinsic motivation, satisfaction and commitment also arise from an employee's greater direct participation in the work, security status and job satisfaction (Armstrong & Murlis, 2007). Rewards can

> **extrinsic rewards** Rewards derived from, for example, pay and fringe benefits, promotion or advancement opportunities in the organisation, the social climate and physical working conditions.
>
> **intrinsic rewards** Rewards derived from the job itself, such as variety, challenge and autonomy.
>
> **transactional rewards** Financial rewards in the contract of employment.
>
> **relational rewards** Rewards such as recognition, autonomy, learning and development, quality of working life and work–life balance.

also be described as **transactional** and **relational rewards**. Transactional rewards arise from the *economic* contractual relations of work and include the tangible rewards of pay and benefits. Relational rewards arise from the *psychological* contractual relations of work and include intangible rewards such as individual work experience or learning and development (Armstrong & Murlis, 2007).

total reward approach Considering the contribution of every reward as a way of generating employee motivation, satisfaction or commitment.

We can also consider the totality of extrinsic/intrinsic or transactional/relational rewards in reward design, which is known as the **total reward approach** (Thompson, 2002). This approach allows us to consider the contribution of each reward as a way of generating employee motivation, satisfaction or commitment.

▪ The foundations of reward systems

The foundations of reward systems generally comprise three constituent elements: basic pay, variable pay and benefits. In this section, we look at each in turn.

▪ *Basic pay*

Basic pay or base pay is a wage or salary negotiated as part of the contract of employment. Most basic pay is time-based pay and in essence is a standardised monetary rate for the job. A number of factors influence the scope of basic pay, including:

basic pay A fixed rate of pay for the job.

- the time a person needs to do the job
- external regulation (e.g. minimum wage, health and safety regulations)
- internal regulation (e.g. trade union negotiations)
- labour market comparability – the relationship between the pay of one employee and another in the same occupation
- differentials between salary and wage levels in the organisation hierarchy (e.g. differences between train drivers and track workers)
- competence and capability levels – skill, knowledge and aptitudes needed to do the job.

The base salary for expatriate managers normally reflects the parity of pay for a comparable position in the parent country. Base salary also provides a reference point for establishing employee benefits and provides the employee with a comparison to peers in the parent country. If the base salary is in line with reward practices in the parent country over the term of an international assignment, it will smooth the assignee's transition when they are later repatriated.

One of the key issues in international reward is the influence of labour market comparability on base pay. Varying employee expectations of reward in different national contexts make comparability and differentials difficult issues for the international reward manager (Parker & Janush, 2001). Similarly, different external and internal regulation may also make comparison difficult. As with other contexts, base pay is a key part of all reward systems and can also be linked to variable pay and/or other employee benefits in a 'reward package'.

■ *Variable pay*

Variable pay is pay linked to the performance, contribution, competence or skill of the individual, team or organisation. Many reward systems link pay directly to employee performance outputs or productivity. The main argument in favour of pay for performance is that pay motivates the employee to achieve performance objectives and gives recognition for his or her effort in achieving them. However, despite support for variable pay in the 'new pay' paradigm, variable pay puts an employee's total reward at risk. Employee risk increases as a greater proportion of pay is made contingent on individual, team or organisational performance. The employee cannot predict his or her pay as easily as when pay is linked with time, and his or her basic need for security and recognition may be threatened. A focus on variable pay may also weaken intrinsic rewards because of the absence of employee participation in the design of reward systems (Heery, 2000). Indeed, researchers have for some time voiced concerns that variable pay undermines intrinsic motivation, satisfaction and commitment (Pfeffer, 1998).

The variation in country use of pay for performance and increasing variation in international assignments have led to increasing pressure to reward expatriates for their role and performance through variable pay systems. However, measuring expatriate performance is fraught with difficulties (Harzing & Christensen, 2004). First, it can be difficult to define clearly the aims and objectives of the assignment; second, it is challenging to make a fair assessment of the extent to which the assignee has achieved them (Kessler, 1994; McKenna & Richardson, 2007). The limitations of variable pay have also been noted in international reward; for example, Tahvanainen and Suutari (2005: 101) argue that the level of expatriate dissatisfaction with incentives, particularly in the form of performance-related pay, compounds these issues. Tahvanainen and Suutari (2005) have shown that not every expatriate values the offer of extra money, instead complaining that 'the way of measuring achievement of the incentive objectives was invalid' or not set for the right job functions; the relationship between goals and incentive objectives was not always clear; and, for project expatriates, the incentive was paid months after the assignment had ended. For some expatriates, such incentives have a diminishing marginal utility and lose their motivational effect over time (Gunkel, Lust & Wolff, 2009). Indeed, researchers have concluded from case study analysis that 'different institutional frameworks generate different individual levels of satisfaction for employee incentives', arguing that 'in some cases, an incentive in one country is, in fact, a non-motivator in the other' (Gunkel, Lust & Wolff, 2009: 308).

■ *Benefits*

Benefits are sometimes called fringe benefits or indirect rewards, and include:
- car leasing and usage
- company discounts

benefits Rewards that an employee receives on top of their basic cash pay.

- employee insurance
- healthcare provision
- paid leave or holiday time
- performance or merit elements
- share options
- superannuation or pension arrangements
- training grants.

For expatriates on international assignments, benefits may also include:

- cost-of-living allowances
- housing provision or allowances
- return flights to the home country
- school and education costs
- tax relief to offset an assignee's liability in the host country (if higher than in the parent country).

Konopaske and Werner (2005) found that benefits are an important component in encouraging prospective expatriates to accept international (and particularly long-term) assignments. However, Lovewell (2010) highlighted a sharp increase in the number of MNCs operating a global benefits strategy that enables expatriates to receive a consistent reward package wherever their job may take them.

◾ Designing an international reward system

In designing an international reward system, an HR manager must consider macro-, meso- and micro-level implications and concerns.

◼ *Macro-level implications and concerns*

Legal compliance

In national and international contexts, reward systems exist in a legal environment in which all employment organisations must operate. In liberal economies, reward systems must comply with an increasing amount of employment legislation and with indirect legislation that affects the employment relationship. National cultures influence legal frameworks and the accepted social norms and values of that culture determine what inclusions are acceptable and unacceptable in a reward system.

In developed economies, employment is highly regulated and there is a range of employee rights, such as the right to be a member of a trade union and the right not to be discriminated against in employment due to one's sex, ethnicity or other social characteristics. However, the degree of employment legislation and extent of the **floor of rights** accorded to employees varies considerably between nations. In the less developed economies, there may be only the minimum level of employment legislation and few employee rights that constrain the employer in allocating rewards to employees. Here, the employment relationship tends to be regulated voluntarily between employer and employee.

floor of rights Basic statutory employment rights and minimum standards that benefit all employees.

At an international level, the principles and rights contained in the conventions of the International Labour Organization (ILO) have attempted to provide a set of international employment standards to promote minimum rights for ILO Treaty signatories (Servais, 2009). The ILO conventions have a broad focus and relate to reward policy on such issues as freedom of association and social dialogue, equality of opportunity, wages and working time. Not all countries have signed the treaty, and signatory states must act to enforce it at national level. The conventions also have no direct regulatory effect on MNCs in a global context. MNCs therefore are legally responsible to the legislatures of the countries in which they operate, in complying with ILO conventions.

■ *Meso-level implications and concerns*

Internal equity

Management decisions about rewards, whether made unilaterally or collectively with trade unions, must take into account the requirements of internal equity. Internal equity is concerned that people in organisations are rewarded appropriately for their contribution when compared with others (Milkovich & Newman, 2008) and that comparisons and differentials between jobs are seen as fair. In designing reward systems, this implies that rewards in the organisation have been distributed in accordance with the contribution of employees (distributive justice) and that employee rewards should not be based on arbitrary or biased management decisions but that such decisions should be made consistently and transparently (procedural justice) (Heery, 2000).

Some organisations adopt formal and systematic approaches to achieve **internal equity**, determining the relative values of different jobs and roles in the organisation. The primary method of determining the relative value of jobs is that of job evaluation. Armstrong and Murlis (2007: 147) stated: 'It could be claimed that, every time a decision is made on what a job should be paid, a form of job evaluation is required. Job evaluation is therefore unavoidable...' Job evaluation introduces a hierarchical, rational organisational structure of reward linked to jobs, and provides a potential defence against claims of wage discrimination in developed economies.

internal equity Employee reward comparisons with similar or different jobs within an organisation.

External equity

External equity is primarily concerned with aligning internal job values with similar job values in the labour market at local, national and international levels. External equity is based on the principle of labour market equilibrium and the equilibrium wage. The value of any job may be decided by supply and demand for that job when the market is in equilibrium (i.e. market-driven). This is sometimes referred to as the 'rate for the job'. External equity is concerned with market competitiveness and

external equity Employee reward comparisons with similar jobs in the labour market at local, national and international levels.

comparisons between what different employers will pay for the same job. An employer who pays more than the market value of the job may be perceived as uncompetitive.

Some employers may reject formal procedures such as job evaluation, and may base their decisions on fairness, consistency and transparency or purely on external equity. Such reward decisions, however, have led to gender inequalities when the market value of female employment is lower than that of male employment in the same job. Where market values are high, this may put pressure on job evaluation schemes and market supplements may be required to more closely reflect the market or equilibrium rate. Also, an employer may need to pay wage differentials to attract workers to unattractive jobs in the labour market, compensating for the unattractive elements of a job, such as when an expatriate is asked to work in a country experiencing civil unrest. We must recognise such tensions between internal and external equity, and make transparent reward decisions whenever they arise (Milkovich & Newman, 2008).

Alignment with corporate strategy

Bloom, Milkovich and Mitra (2003: 1350) identify two major pressures that MNCs face in their international operations, the first of which is the pressure of **alignment**. They argue that there is pressure on international managers to develop a 'more integrated global organization that aligns management structures with the MNC's organisational context, especially its global strategy'. Second, there is the pressure of **conformance** – that is, the conditions that compel MNCs to conform to the local host contexts in which they operate. Each of these pressures influences reward decisions to some degree. These propositions assume that there is a deterministic pressure on strategic reward decision-makers, emanating in each case from the internal environment (alignment) or from the external environment (conformance).

alignment Aligning reward decisions with the strategic goals of the MNC.
conformance Conforming to the various host-country contexts in which MNCs operate.

The alignment proposition views international managers as rational actors in their environment, who make strategic choices about business goals and the means by which they will achieve them (Trevor, 2009). This rational choice model informs the 'new pay' assumptions (Lawler 1984, 1990, 1995). Lawler (1984) has argued that three critical elements need to be aligned with business goals for a reward system to be effective. First, rewards must be strategically aligned to the organisation's core values (e.g. honesty, fairness, equity, trust). Management's espoused values take on symbolic and instrumental significance but are aligned primarily to the product or service market; they take various forms, including quality of product or service and cost reduction (Legge, 2005). Second, rewards must be aligned to the organisational structure (e.g. the degree of centralisation; the locus of decision-making; the relationship between internal and external equity; hierarchical levels). Third, reward must be aligned to process design (e.g. management style, communication systems, participation and involvement in decision-making).

Imperial, federal and hybrid approaches

Following Perlmutter (1969), Loveridge (1983) and Ferner (1997), we can identify three substantive approaches to international reward management that reflect alignment and conformance: the imperial, federal and hybrid approaches.

The imperial approach

Some organisations have an imperial approach to international reward – that is, they tend to emphasise the conquest of corporate culture over national culture (Boxall, 1995). From an HR perspective, an MNC's organisational structure may reflect managers' values about geographical sourcing of the management team (Perlmutter, 1969: 11). An **ethnocentric organisation** (see chapter 1) focuses its HR efforts on selecting key positions overseas from the parent country's internal labour market. In such organisations, management knowledge and understanding are informed by the parent-country nationals (PCNs). These managers are viewed as superior to the host country nationals (HCNs).

> **ethnocentric organisation** An organisation that emphasises the subordination of host-country cultural values to corporate cultural values or those of the parent country.

This approach presents an *exportive* strategic orientation (Taylor, Beechler & Mapier, 1996; Scullion & Starkey, 2000) and ensures that alignment and control are maintained through PCNs, who share the espoused values and cultural orientations of managers in the parent country as well as their leadership ideology and management knowledge. In the imperial view, such control is essential in reducing the level of uncertainty (e.g. communication, HCN expertise or experience) and risk (economic and political) involved in conducting business abroad (Hocking, Brown & Harzing, 2007; Harzing, 2001). The imperial approach emphasises the subordination of host-country cultural values to corporate cultural values or those of the parent country.

Morgan and Kristensen (2006) found that MNC managers transfer practices, people and resources to subsidiaries in order to maintain control and achieve their strategic objectives. The host-country subsidiaries have differential capacities to resist these transferred practices or to develop them in their own interests. However, they argue, such resistance is rare and MNCs generally produce subsidiary 'clones'. In studying Turkish–United States relations, Sayim (2010: 2648) saw a 'straightforward transfer of US multinational corporate policies in reward management to the Turkish subsidiaries, without significant resistance from managers or need for translation'. He further argued that a critical majority of studies identify the US as 'the "dominant" exporter of management knowledge and practice'; what Legge (2005: 3) has called an applied 'US academic imperialism'. In reward management terms, the US MNCs are generally found to have set highly centralised and formalised policies for their subsidiaries, pursuing a 'one world, one strategy' approach (Sayim, 2010: 2632; see also Björkman & Furu, 2000; Bloom, Milkovich & Mitra, 2003; Almond et al., 2006). For example, the automobile manufacturer General Motors adopted this approach in the past but has become more hybrid in recent years.

Almond and colleagues (2006) have modified this unidirectional model, stating that US MNCs must conform to host-country expectations and also need to adapt their reward management policies and practices in some host countries due to specific sectoral or occupational labour markets, unionisation, or the limiting power of collective bargaining in such countries. Nonetheless, Almond and colleagues (2006) conclude that US MNCs are determined to overcome host-country effects, particularly in the area of pay for performance.

The federal approach

In contrast to the imperial approach, the polycentric organisation of HR practices tends to conform to host-country cultures and will give foreign subsidiaries a degree of autonomy, staffing them with HCNs. The parent organisation's HR department accepts the limitations of the organisation's internal labour market and recruits instead from labour markets in the host country. The organisation presents an *adaptive* strategic orientation, where HR buys into an existing network of management knowledge and skills. Uncertainty and risk are 'externalised' from the parent organisation by legal and financial means; by spreading risk across separate units and incorporating the HCNs' knowledge management and understanding of local values and cultural orientations (Harzing, 2001). Such organisations have a *federal* approach to international reward, one that builds on the already existing economic and social foundations of the host country and rests on 'shared understandings and joint decision-making through "mutuality"' (Loveridge, 1983: 105–6). For HR managers, the delegation of local HR to HCNs has the advantages of avoiding the cultural adjustments of PCNs and their expense, while also offering cost savings by removing the need to develop a parent managerial hierarchy with standardised control systems.

To be sure, Scullion and Starkey (2000) argue, MNCs that have decentralised HR structures tend to have smaller HR departments and are less strategic. Westerman and colleagues (2009: 770) argue that matching HR practices to a country's culture is important because this process:

- conveys cultural awareness and sensitivity
- conveys expectations of and rewards for employee behaviour consistent with ingrained patterns of acceptable behaviour
- results in higher levels of company financial performance.

Westerman and colleagues (2009) conclude that MNCs should consider tailoring their rewards to fit the culture of their workforce and temper the 'one-size-fits-all' approach to reward design. A good example of this approach is Gillette, which, through its International Graduate Training Program, recruits top business students from host-country universities.

Lowe and colleagues (2002), in examining reward practices in 10 countries, challenged the use of ethnocentric exportation of reward practices and argued that MNCs should focus on what employees in a given culture want from a reward system. Similarly, Gunkel, Lust and Wolff's (2009) study of reward practices in China,

Germany, Japan and the United States found that different institutional frameworks generate different individual levels of satisfaction for employee incentives, and argued that it is unwise for MNCs to transplant reward practices from the parent country to others.

Hybrid approaches

In geocentric organisations (see chapter 1), HR espouses meritocratic values and places more importance on an employee's levels of competence and capability than on his or her nationality. Such organisations reduce uncertainty and risk by employing 'talent', and consistently maintain alignment and control through sophisticated communication channels. Regiocentric organisations (see chapter 1) also adopt a federal approach, but base it on regional labour markets; recruitment is then meritocratic but restricted to the specific regional labour market and, as in the polycentric organisation (see chapter 1), regions enjoy a degree of independence. Again, HR accepts the limitations or constraints that the regional labour market imposes (Perlmutter, 1969; Heenan & Perlmutter, 1979; Adler & Ghadar, 1990; Kelly, 2001).

Alignment further implies that the espoused value, for example the value of customer service quality, is reinforced through the organisational process design of *re-education* through communication and training; *replacement* through selection, promotion and redundancy; and *reorganisation* through redesign of the reward and performance management systems. For example, this may involve re-educating employees to embrace variable pay linked to customer satisfaction, even though this effectively transfers some element of the market risk to the employees; or linking an employee's movement up salary bands to a performance appraisal system that includes customer service measures; or reassessing job values in relation to customer service (Legge, 2005).

Some have criticised this view of strategic alignment. Cross-cultural research has pointed to the limitations of ethnocentric alignment strategies, claiming that it creates problems of internal equity when PCNs and HCNs are offered different rewards. This can generate intergroup conflict and hamper the adjustment of PCNs in the host country (Mahajan, 2011).

Nonetheless, the rational model suggests that there is some, if constrained, strategic choice for reward decision-makers in defining the reward architecture and a key indication of alignment is the development of a **global reward strategy** (Bloom et al., 2003). Reflecting on Scullion and Starkey's (2000) viewpoint, the 2008 WorldatWork Global Compensation Practices survey (WorldatWork, 2008)

> **global reward strategy** Policies and strategies that are applied uniformly in all operations around the world unless individual country compliance dictates otherwise.

painted a picture of the increasing centralisation of reward decisions but also reported that organisations are split between developing centralised structures (53 per cent) and non-centralised structures (47 per cent). Also, 59 per cent of organisations in the survey said they had a 'global compensation strategy' – that is, 'policies and strategies that are applied uniformly in all operations around the world unless individual country compliance dictates otherwise' (WorldatWork, 2008). In this, the WorldatWork survey closely matched the 2006–2007 Mercer Global Compensation Strategy and Administration Survey, which put the figure at 61 per cent (Mercer HR Consulting, 2007). This evidence, though limited, suggests that MNCs are employing both imperial and federal approaches.

Both surveys highlighted companies' use of a dual reward strategy, in which they offered a global reward strategy for executives and some senior managers and a local reward strategy for other employees, such as professionals, contractors and sales. For many, the pattern was mixed, suggesting a hybrid strategic approach, and some companies indicated they saw potential for opportunistic change in the future (see Ferner, 1997). Also, Europeans led in developing global reward strategies but lagged behind the United States in applying such strategies to managers and other employee groups (Mercer HR Consulting, 2007). The majority of MNCs saw the Asia–Pacific region as the most challenging in which to implement a global reward strategy (WorldatWork, 2008).

From this evidence, we can say that the strategic alignment of reward practice at a global level seems rather constrained. Only limited homogenisation and convergence have been possible in reward strategies, structures and processes, and MNCs' are perceived as managing executive reward and the reward of others in divergent ways (Mahajan, 2011).

■ Micro-level implications and concerns

■ *The expatriate role and international assignments*

The expatriate employee is generally a PCN who works in another country to support an MNC's strategic objectives. Most expatriation arrangements are long term (usually between one and five years): according to KPMG's 2012 Global Assignment Policies and Practices Survey, 96 per cent of MNCs employ expatriates on assignments of this type (KPMG, 2012). Other expatriate assignments tend to be short term, and 86 per cent of organisations use this type of assignment. However, nearly half of organisations (47 per cent) also make permanent transfers of an indefinite length. In 2012, KPMG reported that 'Over the last two years organisations are increasingly using commuter assignments and rotational assignments' (KPMG, 2012: 14). These alternatives to long-term assignments are viewed as ways to reduce the cost of the long-term assignment and to encourage greater return on investment (Johnson, 2005; McNulty & Tharenou, 2004).

It is common for MNCs to offer informal assessment by line management or the HR department, or no assessment at all (KPMG, 2012: 17). Bonache and Fernandez (2005) believe this underlines the 'trustworthiness' of the expatriate and the level of 'company specific knowledge', while others emphasise 'loyalty' and the exchange of benefits and rewards in the psychological contract. Indeed, Yan, Zhu and Hall

(2002) argue that relational rewards are just as important as transactional rewards in ensuring expatriate success. Warneke and Schneider (2011) also suggest that the increasing heterogeneity of expatriates, in terms of their age, gender, occupational background and country of origin (Altman & Shortland, 2008; Mayrhofer, Kuhlmann & Stahl, 2005; Shaffer and Ferzandi, 2006), means that companies have to induce potential candidates to relocate by designing individual reward packages to meet each employee's demands. Perkins and Shortland (2006: 185) and Perkins and White (2011: 383) argue that the individualisation of expatriate reward moves away from the traditional approach of reward for effort and more towards compensatory reward for an employee's acceptance of lifestyle changes, hardship and so on. This points more to a need for 'persuading' or 'incentivising' employees to engage in an international assignment rather than employees actively seeking such roles.

It is not surprising, therefore, that research on the long-term expatriate has emphasised the importance of comparability; that is, ensuring that a PCN enjoys a standard of living no worse than in his or her home country (Brewster & Suutari, 2005; Dowling, Welch & Schuler, 2004). It has also emphasised the use of the balance-sheet approach, which we examine in the next section.

The balance-sheet approach

MNCs commonly use the **balance-sheet approach** to determine the pay and benefits of PCNs (Watson & Singh, 2005). The basic objective of the approach is the maintenance of the PCN's prior living standard, to which is added a financial inducement to take on the international assignment. The levels of a PCN's parent-country pay and benefits are the foundations of this approach. Adjustments are also made to offset any additional expenses the PCN will incur in the host country. Financial incentives can also be added to make the package more attractive. This approach is considered to be cost-effective (Bonache & Fernandez, 2005). However, it must be frequently reviewed to ensure the parity of cost-of-living rates (Dowling, Welch & Schuler, 2004).

balance-sheet approach Expatriate reward based on the market value of the parent country.

As such, the approach provides 'the benefits of equity for the expatriate between the assignments and better facilitates repatriation' (Watson & Singh, 2005: 33). It is also easy for prospective expatriates to understand what transactional reward they will need to live abroad and to match their base pay to parent-country standards. Financial benefits may also include performance-related pay, travel expenses for trips home and use of a company car. Arguably, this approach is as much about repatriation as expatriation because it eases the assignee's homeward transition when their international assignment ends (Yan, Zhu and Hall, 2002). Despite these benefits, there is no consensus on the use of the balance-sheet approach. Researchers have put forward a number of views about its strengths and weaknesses, including that it is:

- an administrative tool that ensures assignments can be filled (McKenna & Richardson, 2007)
- too complex and expensive (Watson & Singh, 2005)
- not an effective means of attracting and retaining the best expatriates (Phillips & Fox, 2003; Stanek, 2000)
- a path to expatriate dissatisfaction (Bonache, 2005)
- unrelated to the expatriate role and the aims of the assignment (Phillips & Fox, 2003).

transpatriate An employee who is not employed in the parent country, including employees formerly labelled as expatriates or host-country nationals.

Phillips and Fox (2003: 470) and Watson and Singh (2005) agree that the approach needs to be reformed, but they offer different solutions. Phillips and Fox (2003: 475) state that the approach 'must be replaced by a globalised **transpatriate** compensation system, based largely on host-country levels and traditions but influenced by a global market for transnational employees'. In contrast, Watson and Singh (2005) argue for a focus on corporate culture and business strategy rather than on national culture and local conditions.

going-rate approach Expatriate rewards are based on the market value of the host country

Going-rate approach

An alternative method is the **going-rate approach**. This is primarily based on host-country market pay rates (Dowling, Welch & Schuler, 2004; Watson & Singh, 2005). Here, the base salary is linked to the salary structure in the host country. The approach relies on local survey comparisons of:

- local HCNs
- expatriates of the same nationality (e.g. all Canadians working in Japan)
- expatriates of all nationalities.

Additional payments may supplement base pay and benefits in low-pay countries.

The advantages of the going-rate approach are its simplicity, its provision of external equity, and its use in identifying the expatriate more closely with the host country. It also supports equity among different nationalities (Watson & Singh, 2005). However, it also has a number of drawbacks, including variations in pay and benefits between assignments for the same employees and between expatriates of the same nationality in different countries. The first occurs when, for example, the expatriate is transferred from a developed economy such as the United States to a developing economy. In this situation, the expatriate may reject the international assignment because of the lack of parity between parent-country and host-country rewards. Expatriates are also likely to compete for work in countries where the standard of living is higher; assignments in countries with a lower standard of living are likely to be rejected. Unlike the balance-sheet approach, the going-rate approach does not help to ease the repatriation process (Dowling, Welch & Schuler, 2004).

Conclusion

In this chapter, we have built on the foundations of rewards to construct a broader understanding of the complexity and diversity of international reward practices in MNCs. In examining the need for strategic alignment, we have noted that a number of approaches can be applied. The design architecture of international reward systems is complex and reflects variability in reward practices worldwide. In considering expatriate rewards, we are reminded of the need to encourage employees to undertake international assignments and the problems that can occur if the reward package does not meet their expectations.

We have also seen that an examination of cross-national comparisons of reward practices forces practitioners and students to re-evaluate what is considered normal practice within their own context. They may then question the nature and meaning of the reward management practices they employ, as well as the institutions that regulate rewards. Comparisons inevitably lead to a better understanding of the similarities and differences in rewards and to better theoretical understanding of international reward management.

Take-home messages

- An understanding of the foundations of reward systems helps to explain how employees are rewarded on international assignments.
- Internal and external equity are important in understanding how expatriates value their rewards.
- There is considerable variation in how international organisations align their reward policies and practices to the corporate strategy.
- Rewards assist in recruiting, retaining and motivating international employees.

Closing the learning loop

1. What is the difference between extrinsic and intrinsic rewards?
2. Why are intrinsic rewards important in motivating international employees?
3. What are the advantages and disadvantages of variable pay?
4. What are the key elements of the imperial, federal and hybrid approaches?
5. Why are the expectations of international employees so important in reward determinations?
6. Why do MNCs prefer to use the balance-sheet approach to rewarding expatriates?

CASE STUDY 6.1   RELUCTANCE TO RELOCATE

Alice Lee, 25, a talented executive working for an international insurance company, had progressed fairly quickly in the organisation's hierarchy and was now a mid-level executive with very good career prospects. She had aspirations to become one of the senior managers in the firm and was keen to impress her peers and her mentor, Paul McKensie, to whom she reported.

One morning, she was surprised to find in her email inbox a communication from Paul asking her to come for a chat about a challenging opportunity that he felt might be of interest to her. Alice was not one to get excited but, with all the hard work she had put in over the previous two years, she felt confident that this was the lead that she had been waiting for and that promotion was now in the bag!

She entered Paul's office and he greeted her with a smile. Paul was an amiable person and she got on well with him. She sat in the chair next to him and, thinking of promotion, smiled too. Paul started a conversation.

Paul: Hi Alice, thank you for coming to see me. It is always nice to see you. How are you getting on in customer services?

Alice: I'm getting on really well, thanks. I've just finished the Netherlands project and really enjoyed working with Antoine and Freddie on improving our customer care, particularly after the recent crisis in our service delivery. I think we are on the right path now.

Paul: That's great! Antoine has told me some great things about you, and he is very pleased with the work that you have done. It's for this reason that I have called you to see me today.

Alice: I'm intrigued. But I'm sure you will fill me in.

Paul: Alice, this is a time in your career when you will need a much broader picture of the company and its operations particularly on a global scale. I'm very excited about the recent opportunities that have opened up in Hong Kong and the possibility of breaking into the Chinese market. I'd like to offer you an international assignment to manage our customer care services in Hong Kong. This will be a great opportunity for you as I know you are already fluent in three languages, including Chinese. We will of course offer you an excellent reward package with all the benefits you presently get and a considerable enhancement to your salary to compensate for any hardship you may incur. What do you think about that?

Paul placed a piece of paper on the desk that outlined her present salary before and after tax, her flexible benefits package and health and social insurance arrangements. Alongside this were further financial details labelled 'Hong Kong' that included the following:
- assignment allowance
- housing allowance
- cost-of-living adjustment
- host-country percentage component
- parent-country percentage component
- host-country health and social insurance arrangements
- host-country tax
- net salary in host country. (This was highlighted and in bold type.)

Alice stared at the last figure and thought about the offer, before commenting.

Alice: Well, I'm a little shocked if I'm honest. I did not expect to be going abroad at this time as I felt I still had a lot to contribute to the work here.

Paul: I can understand your initial reluctance but I'm sure when you think of it more clearly, you will see what a great opportunity this is. Not only to live in a new country with all the excitement that brings but to do so in style. Hong Kong is a vibrant city. Antoine worked there for three years and he totally enjoyed the lifestyle. I know the work will be challenging at first but we would not have chosen you if we did not think you were ready for the job.

Alice: Three years!

Paul: Yes, that is the norm. I can see that you will need some time to think about this and I am sure that when you have thought this through that you will rise to the challenge and do a good job.

Alice: It's not the money. I have recently become engaged. My partner and I have to arrange the wedding and we're about to purchase a new house.

Paul: How wonderful! You can of course take your partner with you and we will make all the arrangements for your housing both here and there.

Don't worry about a thing; we have an agency to take care of this sort of thing.

Case study questions

1. Undertake research to find out as much information as possible about the details of Hong Kong's standard of living, as listed in the offer Alice received in the scenario. How does it compare with your own country? (If you are based in Hong Kong, choose another region or country of your choice.)
2. Identify which expatriate reward approach Alice's offer exemplifies, and discuss its advantages and disadvantages.
3. Explain why Alice was reluctant to go to Hong Kong, based on the reward research and practice you have learnt about in this chapter.
4. If you were the HR manager advising Paul, what reward solutions would you recommend to help him persuade Alice to accept the role?

» ACTIVITY

Role-play

Objective

This role-play for groups of three students explores the question of whether the balance-sheet approach is the most efficient choice for MNCs selecting an international reward management approach.

Roles

- Chief executive officer (CEO)
- HR director
- Reward consultant

Scenario

A North American–owned international hotel chain wishes to develop its international standing by entering the Indian market, and the company's CEO is exploring the available reward options. The HR director makes some recommendations on how to reward international employees in India, adopting the imperial position. The reward consultant then makes counterarguments from the federal position. The CEO discusses the strategic criteria (e.g. cost, quality) that will underpin his or her decision in this matter, and decides which reward approach to use, before explaining his or her choice.

■ Online resources

- For instructors: answers to activities; long media article with questions; additional questions and answers.
- For students: further reading; answers to case study; IHRM in practice.

■ References

Adler, N.J. and Ghadar, F. (1990), Strategic human resource management: A global perspective. In Pieper, R. (ed.), *Human resource management: An international comparison*, 235–60. Berlin: De Gruyter.

Almond, P., Colling, T., Edwards, T. and Ferner, A. (2006). Conclusions. In Almond, P. and Ferner, A., *American multinationals in Europe: Managing employment relations across national borders*, 271–90. Oxford: Oxford University Press.

Altman, Y. and Shortland, S. (2008). Women and international assignments: Taking stock – A 25-year review, *Human Resource Management*, 47(2):199–216.

Armstrong, M. and Murlis, H. (2007). *Reward management: A handbook of remuneration strategy and practice*, 5th edition. London: Kogan Page.

Björkman, I. and Furu, P. (2000). Determinants of variable pay for top managers of foreign subsidiaries in Finland, *International Journal of Human Resource Management*, 11(4): 698–713.

Bloom, M., Milkovich, G. and Mitra, A. (2003). International compensation: Learning from how managers respond to variations in local host contexts, *International Journal of Human Resource Management*, 8: 1350–67.

Bonache, J. (2005). Job satisfaction among expatriates, repatriates and domestic employees: The perceived impact of international assignments on work-related variables, *Personnel Review*, 34(1): 110–24.

Bonache, J. and Fernandez, Z. (2005). International compensation: Costs and benefits of international assignments. In Scullion, H. and Linehan, M. (eds), *International human resource management*, 114–30. Basingstoke, Hampshire: Palgrave Macmillan.

Boxall, P. (1995). Building the theory of comparative HRM, *Human Resource Management Journal*, 5(5): 5–17.

Brewster, C. and Suutari, V. (2005). Global HRM: Aspects of a research agenda, *Personnel Review*, 34(1): 5–21.

Corby, S., Palmer, S. and Lindop, E. (2009). Trends and tensions: An overview. In S. Corby, S., Palmer, S. and Lindop, E. (eds), *Rethinking reward*. Basingstoke, Hampshire: Palgrave Macmillan.

Dowling, P., Welch, D. and Schuler, R. (2004). *International human resource management*. Cincinnati: South-Western College Publishing.

Ferner, A. (1997). Country of origin effects and HRM in multinational companies, *Human Resource Management Journal*, 7(1): 19–37.

Gunkel, M., Lust, E. and Wolff, B. (2009). Country-compatible incentive design, *Schmalenbach Business Review*, 61(3): 290–309.

Harzing, A. W. (2001). Who's in charge?: An empirical study, *Human Resource Management*, 40(2): 139–59.

Harzing, A. W. and Christensen, C. (2004). Expatriate failure: Time to abandon the concept?, *Career Development International*, 9(6/7): 616–26.

Heenan, D. and Perlmutter, H. (1979). *Multinational organisational development*. Reading, MA: Addison-Wesley.

Heery, E. (2000). The new pay: Risk and representation at work. In Winstanley, D. and Woodall, J. (eds), *Ethical issues in contemporary human resource management*. Basingstoke, Hampshire: Palgrave Macmillan.

Hocking, J. B., Brown, M. and Harzing, A. (2007) Balancing global and local strategic contexts: Expatriate knowledge transfer, applications and learning within a transnational organization, *Human Resource Management*, 46(4): 513–33.

Johnson, L. (2005). Measuring international assignment return on investment, *Compensation and Benefits Review*, 37(2): 50–4.

Kelly, J. (2001), The role of the personnel/HR function in multinational companies, *Employee Relations*, 23(6): 536–57.

Kessler, I. (1994). Performance pay. In Sisson, K. (ed.), *Personnel management*, 465–94. Oxford: Blackwell.

Kessler, I. (2007). Reward choices: Strategy and equity. In Storey, J., *Human resource management: A critical text*, 159–76. London: Thomson Learning.

Konopaske, R. and Werner, S. (2005). US managers' willingness to accept a global assignment: Do expatriate benefits and assignment length make a difference?, *International Journal of Human Resource Management*, 16(7): 1159–75.

KPMG (2012). *Global assignment policies and practices survey*, www.kpmg.com. Retrieved 23 November 2012.

Lawler, E. (1984). The strategic design of reward systems. In Fombrun, C., Tichy, N. and Devanna, M. (eds), *Strategic human resource management*. New York: John Wiley.

Lawler, E. (1990). *Strategic pay: Aligning organisational strategies and pay systems*. San Francisco, CA: Jossey-Bass.

Lawler, E. (1995). The new pay: A strategic approach, *Compensation and Benefits Review*, 44: 14–22.

Legge, K. (2005). *Human resource management: Rhetorics and realities*. Basingstoke, Hampshire: Palgrave Macmillan.

Lewis, P. (2000). Exploring Lawler's new pay theory through the case of Finbank's reward strategy for managers, *Personnel Review*, 29(1): 10–32.

Loveridge, R. (1983). Centralism versus Federalism: Corporate models in industrial relations. In Thurley, K. and Wood, S. (eds), *Industrial relations and management strategy*, 170–93. Cambridge: Cambridge University Press.

Lovewell, D. (2010). International benefits: Global benefits, *Corporate Adviser*, 36: n.p.

Lowe, K., Milliman, J., De Cieri, H. and Dowling, P. (2002). International compensation practices: A ten-country comparative analysis, *Human Resource Management*, 41(1): 45–66.

Mahajan, A. (2011). Host country national's reactions to expatriate pay policies: Making a case for a cultural alignment model, *International Journal of Human Resource Management*, 22 (1): 121–37.

Mayrhofer, W., Kuhlmann, T. and Stahl, G. (2005). *Internationales Personalmanagement: Anspruch und Wirklichkeit*. In Stahl, G., Mayrhofer, W. and Kuhlmann, T. (eds), *Internationales personalmanagement neue aufgaben, neue lo sungen*, 1–24. Munich: Rainer Hampp.

McKenna, S. and Richardson, J. (2007). The increasing complexity of the internationally mobile professional: Issues for research and practice, *Cross Cultural Management*, 14(4): 307–20.

McNulty, Y. and Tharenou, P. (2004). Expatriate return on investment, *International Studies of Management and Organization*, 34(3): 68–95.

Mercer Human Resource Consulting (2007), surveys. www.mercer.com/surveys. Retrieved 22 January 2013.

Milkovich, G. and Newman, J. (2008). *Compensation*. New York: McGraw-Hill.

Morgan, G. and Kristensen, P. H. (2006). The contested space of multinationals: Varieties of institutionalism, varieties of capitalism, *Human Relations*, 59(11): 1467–90.

Parker, G. and Janush, E. (2001). Developing expatriate remuneration packages, *Employee Benefits Journal*, 26(2): 3–5.

Perkins, S. J. and Shortland, S. M. (2006). *Strategic international human resource management*. London: Kogan Page.

Perkins, S. J. and White, G. (2011) *Reward management: Alternatives, consequences and contexts*, 2nd edition. London: Chartered Institute of Personnel and Development.

Perlmutter, H. (1969). The tortuous evolution of the multinational corporation. *Columbia Journal of World Business*, 9–18.

Pfeffer, J. (1998). *The human equation*. Boston: Houghton Mifflin.

Phillips, L. and Fox, M. (2003). Compensation strategy in transnational corporations, *Management Decision*, 41(5/6): 465–76.

Sayım, K. Z. (2010). Pushed or pulled? Transfer of reward management policies in MNCs, *International Journal of Human Resource Management*, 21(14): 2631–58.

Schuster, J. and Zingheim, P. (1992). *The new pay: Linking employee and organisational performance*. New York: Lexington.

Scullion, H. and Starkey, K. (2000). The changing role of the corporate human resource function in the international firm, *International Journal of Human Resource Management*, 11: 1061–81.

Servais, J. (2009). *International labour law: International labour standards*, 2nd edition. Alphen aan den Rijn, Netherlands: Kluwer Law International.

Shaffer, M. H. and Ferzandi, L. (2006). You can take it with you: individual differences and expatriate effectiveness, *Journal of Applied Psychology*, 91(1): 109–25.

Sparrow, P. (2006) *International recruitment, selection and assessment*. London: Chartered Institute of Personnel and Development.

Stanek, M. (2000). The need for global managers: a business necessity, *Management Decision*, 38(4): 232–42.

Tahvanainen, M. and Suutari, V. (2005). Expatriate performance management in MNCs. In H. Scullion and M. Linehan, *International Human Resource Management: A critical text*, 91–113. Basingstoke, Hampshire: Palgrave Macmillan.

Taylor, S., Beechler, S. and Mapier, N. (1996). Toward an integrative model of strategic international human resource management, *Academy of Management Review*, 37: 125–44.

Thompson, P. (2002). *Total reward*. London: Chartered Institute of Personnel and Development.

Trevor, J. (2009). Can pay be strategic? In Corby, S., Palmer, S. and Lindop, E. (eds), *Rethinking reward*, 21–40. Basingstoke, Hampshire: Palgrave Macmillan.

Warneke, D. and Schneider, M. (2011). Expatriate compensation packages: What do employees prefer?, *Cross Cultural Management*, 18(2): 236–56.

Watson, B. W. and Singh, G. (2005). Global pay systems: Compensation in support of a multinational strategy, *Compensation and Benefits Review*, 37(1): 33–6.

Westerman, J., Beekun, R. I., Daly, J. and Vanka, S. (2009). Personality and national culture: Predictors of compensation strategy preferences in the United States of America and India, *Management Research News*, 32(8): 767–81.

WorldatWork. (2008). *Global compensation practices survey*, www.worldatwork.org/pub/globalsurvey04.pdf. Retrieved 22 January 2013.

Yan, A., Zhu, G. and Hall, D. (2002). International assignments for career building: A model of agency relationships and psychological contract, *Academy of Management Review*, 7(3): 373–91.

7 Employee retention

Maria Balta

■ Learning objectives

- To identify the importance of employee retention for the organisation.
- To define and identify ways to manage employee retention.
- To explain how job satisfaction can affect organisational commitment and employee retention.
- To identify strategies for employee retention, including remuneration and benefits, work environment, training and career development opportunities as well as inpatriation and repatriation.

■ Learning outcomes

After reading this chapter, students will be able to:
- identify the benefits of retention for the employees and for the organisation
- understand the role of job satisfaction and organisational commitment on employee retention
- identify the key strategies that enhance employee retention.

Introduction

Organisations are increasingly adopting HR practices, with two main benefits: increased organisational effectiveness and the fulfilment of employees' needs. Organisations are operating in an increasingly competitive environment due to global competition, cost leadership strategies, employee turnover and global skills shortages. These pressures have made the **recruitment** and **retention** of talented employees a top priority for all organisations, particularly those who are operating internationally. To survive in the long term and achieve competitive advantage in the global economy, the retention of valuable employees is a critical strategy for HR managers and organisational leaders (Reiche, 2007). Senior executive selection and retention are becoming even more important because these executives are responsible for the overall direction and scope of business activities, set organisational goals and shape its strategy and culture. Some executives have a clear vision and articulate it throughout the organisation, including at board of directors, top management and senior executive levels.

> **recruitment and training** A talent management system that attracts, retains, develops and utilises employees in ways that create competitive advantage for an organisation.

Employee retention

The retention of valuable employees is a global challenge. Organisations seek to become sustainable by attracting talented people and keeping them satisfied and productive. Their aim is to employ exceptional people who add value and help the organisation create a culture that cannot be copied (Jackson & Schuler, 2003). The retention of intellectual capital is of growing strategic importance (Tymon, Stump & Doh, 2010) and as a result the retention of qualified employees has attracted growing interest among organisations, practitioners and academics (Scullion, Collings & Gunnigle, 2007). As McKinsey & Company consultants highlight, there is 'a war for talent' mainly in recruitment for multinational firms, where leaders have a key role in the success of the company (Chambers et al., 1998). Employee retention has been a major issue for many companies across the world, but Asian countries such as South Korea, Malaysia, Singapore, Taiwan and China have faced particular difficulties, despite the economic growth of the region in recent years (Barnett, 1995; Chang, 1996; MacLachlan, 1996; Syrett, 1994).

> **employee retention** The ability to keep valuable employees by maintaining a working environment that supports staff.

Effective employee retention is a systematic effort by employers to create and foster an environment that encourages current employees to stay with the company by putting in place policies and practices that address their individual needs. Organisations are focusing on employee retention by encouraging employees to remain in the organisation as long as possible. So, HR managers must know what factors motivate their employees to stay in the field or cause them to leave. Employee retention refers to the ability of the organisation to keep its valuable employees through various strategies, including making available training and career development opportunities (see chapter 5) and **job satisfaction**, motivation and competitive remuneration packages (see chapter 6). Employee retention is beneficial for the organisation as well as the employee because organisational performance is a product of individual performance (Pfeffer & Sutton, 2006). As a result, companies provide training and mentoring to their top employees and strive to retain them by helping them to broaden their skills and competences (Groysberg, Nanda & Nohria, 2004).

The retention of key employees is critical to the long-term survival and success of any organisation. We know that employee retention is associated with customer satisfaction, increases in product sales, satisfaction among colleagues and staff, effective succession planning and deeply embedded organisational knowledge and learning. Organisations that enjoy lower staff turnover than close competitors benefit in two ways: first, by reducing their costs and second, by improving productivity. Cost reductions associated with employee turnover include the expense of recruitment efforts to fill empty positions, the risk of recruiting inexperienced staff and the need to invest in new recruits' training. Productivity is also improved when customer and client-effective employees remain in the organisation, bringing their knowledge and expertise in contact with the business.

job satisfaction A pleasurable or positive emotional state resulting from a person's appraisal of his or her job or job experiences.

Retention management is a strategic, coherent process that starts with an examination of the reasons employees join an organisation (Davies, 2001; Solomon, 1999). Organisations that are effective at retention have identified the key hard and soft skills they require. Salary is an important issue that often causes employee dissatisfaction, particularly for some professionals, such as medical practitioners and engineers, who have long-term tenure in a specialist field. In both professions, there is a mismatch between a person's remuneration and their occupation (Allen & Van Der Velden, 2001). Sloane and Williams (2000) and Nguyen, Taylor and Bradley (2003) claim that remuneration determines whether an employee is satisfied or dissatisfied. Therefore, managers need to retain their experienced, skilled employees; high employee turnover may have an impact on effective service delivery.

Salary and wages Rewards based on financial recompense.

Teamwork is another important means of retaining workers. According to Nel et al. (2002), teamwork allows greater employee participation and increases the organisation's performance and, as a consequence, influences the motivation and satisfaction of employees. Studies have shown that employees who participate in different forms of communication networks in organisations are more satisfied with their jobs and more committed to the organisation compared to those who do not participate. Another important means of retaining employees is ensuring that each person knows his or her responsibilities. By creating a culture of responsibility, employers can improve the morale and productivity of employees and enhance retention in the organisation, so reducing turnover costs.

Employers can also retain qualified staff by identifying and accommodating their individual needs. Luecke (2002) mentions a series of factors that encourage people to stay in the organisation including job security, work–life balance, job recognition and flexible working hours. Increasingly, employees want to contribute to a society that reflects their values, choosing to work for organisations that hold similar values to their own; employees tend to enjoy working for organisations where they feel they can 'make a difference'. This is critical for organisations: greater alignment between company and employee values will cause employees to engage.

■ Recruiting and retaining valuable staff

The purpose of a successful talent management system is to attract, retain, develop and utilise employees in ways that create competitiveness, staff engagement and commitment, lower external sourcing costs and lower loss rates of knowledge and experience (Smilansky, 2007). In an international context, it is challenging for a multinational company (MNC) to retain talented staff, and a firm should examine determinants of staff turnover and adopt specific retention-oriented HR practices. The retention of talented employees has become a key challenge for large MNCs (Stahl et al., 2007; Stahl et al., 2012) but also for small-to-medium sized firms that have recently experienced rapid internationalisation (Scullion & Brewster, 2001; Festing, 2007). As the workforce becomes more mobile, MNCs must coordinate globally to create a strong, shared corporate culture and harmonise their activities across the countries in which they operate (Brewster et al. 2011). Employee retention helps to build a workforce with unique skills that employees of other organisations do not have. The retention of employees provides a competitive advantage to the organisation that develops a loyal workforce and enhances its ability to deliver to customer demands. This helps the organisation to produce products and services that competitors cannot easily imitate, reduces recruiting expenses and helps employees feel secure with their jobs even when they receive comparatively low salaries. The rapid growth of knowledge-based economies has resulted in the growing need for companies to hire and retain high-value workers in demanding roles and responsibilities; workers' growing knowledge is valuable (CIPD, 2007).

The recruitment and retention of managerial talent also require the implementation of specific strategies (Scullion & Brewster, 2001). For example, where a firm is located in a remote area, the recruitment effort can be smoothed by offering to hire the spouse or partner of a prospective employee as well as the candidate. In this way, the organisation reduces recruiting and relocation costs by creating a unique incentive for the employee to accept the job relocation, at the same time reducing the risk of their accepting an offer from a rival firm. However, MNCs can also lose staff this way, when a spouse or partner leaves his or her job to accept such an offer. Therefore, it is crucial for organisations to recruit employees who can fit with the organisational culture because they are likely to stay longer in the company. The retention of high-calibre employees remains a key issue among HR departments in both local and multinational firms. The retention of local employees is important because they are the main source of knowledge, skills and social networks available for leveraging the business (Novicevic & Harvey, 2001). MNCs adopt a pluralist approach to international staffing decisions between headquarters and subsidiaries (Bartlett & Ghoshal, 1998; Novicevic & Harvey, 2001). This helps individuals with their career commitment and long-term membership in the organisation (Reiche, 2007). Employees who are happy with their work environment have fewer reasons to quit their jobs; so, managers should prevent employee turnover by focusing on their employees' job satisfaction, motivation, remuneration and training and development opportunities.

■ Job satisfaction

Job satisfaction has been treated as both a global concept referring to overall satisfaction and as a facet-specific concept referring to various aspects of work, including pay, supervision and workload. A number of researchers (Cook et al., 1981; Anderson et al., 2001) have stated that job satisfaction is widely relevant in industrial and organisational psychology. Brayfield and Crockett (1955) argue that an employee who is satisfied at work is more productive. Therefore, managers should ensure that employees remain enthused with their work. Locke (1976: 1304) defines job satisfaction as 'a pleasurable or positive emotional state resulting from the appraisal of one's job or job experiences'. Greenberg and Baron (2003: 148) define job satisfaction as 'positive and negative attitudes held by individuals toward their jobs'. People are motivated to fulfil certain goals that lead to satisfaction and productivity. Job satisfaction is a psychological variable at micro-level and represents an effective response to specific aspects of the job; it is an attitudinal, affective and cognitive construct (Porter et al., 1974). Job satisfaction derives from motivational factors such as autonomy, responsibility for tasks, clear job expectations, organisational policies, professional interactions and perceived job status (Luthans, 1995). It is very important for employees to have autonomy and authority that allows them to participate in the decision-making process when it comes to their work because this increases motivation to continue to work for the organisation, fulfil responsibilities to others in the workplace and complete tasks. Employee participation influences performance and increases the satisfaction and productivity of employees (Pfeffer, 1994). Employee participative work systems enhance employee motivation and lead to greater quality of work and productivity. For employees to stay with the organisation, they need to feel satisfied with their job and commited to the organisation. Other factors that help employees remain satisfied with their jobs include pay, recognition, good relationships with co-workers, working conditions, opportunities for personal growth through training and development and challenge in their roles.

job status and recognition Interpersonal employee rewards that generate job satisfaction.

autonomy Jobs that provide individuals with freedom to make decisions and operate without close supervision.

personal growth Expansion of individual capabilities.

completion The ability to start and finish a project or job.

■ Defining job satisfaction

Various theories and investigations have tried to clarify job satisfaction at work. Maslow (1943) explained that human beings have five sets of needs: psychology, safety, love, esteem and self-actualisation. He visualised these needs in a hierarchy or pyramid, in which one need must be satisfied before the next can be satisfied. Herzberg, Maunser and Snyderman (1959) later concluded that job satisfaction consists of hygiene factors and motivators. Hygiene factors include company policy and administration, supervision, salary, interpersonal relations and working conditions. Motivators influence the individual's determination and productivity and include responsibility, advancement, achievement, recognition and the nature of the work itself. Hackman and Oldham (1976) added further dimensions to the concept of job satisfaction, such as task identity, task significance, skill variety, autonomy and feedback. They focused on the importance of these job characteristics in the achievement of workers' satisfaction and motivation.

Achievement A self-administered reward that is derived when a person reaches a challenging goal.

Smith, Kendall and Hulin (1969) developed the Job descriptive Index (JDI), a measure of job satisfaction that consists of five aspects of work:

1. pay
2. promotion
3. supervision
4. co-workers
5. the work itself.

JDI is the most frequently used measurement for satisfaction at work (Kinicki et al., 2002), and various researchers and managers have used it to assess employee attitudes. The JDI's validity as an instrument for measuring job satisfaction is proven (Roznowski, 1989), and it remains without doubt 'the most carefully constructed measure of job satisfaction in existence today' (Vroom, 1964: 100).

Pay is the amount of money that a worker receives in return for their services (see chapter 6 for more discussion of different forms of reward). Price & Mueller, (1981) and Lum and colleagues (1998) suggest that it is a significant facet of job satisfaction. Herzberg, Maunser and Snyderman (1959) consider pay as a hygiene factor that leads to job satisfaction. The discrepancy theory of satisfaction argues that satisfaction depends on what the job involves and what the employee expects from it (Porter & Steers, 1973). So, an employee is satisfied with pay only if it meets their expectations of what they need to be paid (Schwab & Wallace, 1974).

Promotion is the advancement of a worker to a higher position in an organisation (Price & Mueller 1981), and it is something that any employee who is determined to advance his or her career seriously considers. Company training programs enable employees to advance to higher

promotion A promotion reward decision based on performance and seniority.

positions as they provide a means for them to develop their skills through an investment by the organisation in their human capital. Hulin (1968) suggests that employees are dissatisfied when they are stuck in a job that does not have promotional opportunity, which reinforces the importance for the organisation of signalling to their employees that they are investing in their future careers by enrolling them in development programs. In short, demonstrable opportunities for employee advancement have a positive effect on job satisfaction and reduce employees' turnover intention.

Supervisors and co-workers are also capable of ensuring employee job satisfaction, according to Babin and Boles (1996). An employee who enjoys good relationships with his or her co-workers is more likely to remain in an organisation and cooperate with others to achieve company objectives. If a worker does not have a good relationship with his or her supervisor, however, it is likely they he or she will not be satisfied with multiple facets of his or her job. It is therefore important that supervisors establish a healthy relationship with workers and promote collegiality between workers to ensure that individuals in their team are satisfied with their jobs (Babin & Boles, 1996). Finally, the work itself plays a key role in job satisfaction. Results have shown that employees who are enjoying their work, are satisfied and less likely to leave the organisation (Porter et al., 1974).

Price and Mueller (1981) developed a causal model for turnover with in which job satisfaction and some of its determinants are said to influence turnover. In the model there are seven determinants that influence turnover indirectly through job satisfaction:
1. routinisation
2. participation
3. instrumental communication
4. integration
5. pay
6. distributive justice
7. promotional opportunity.

■ Organisational commitment

Organisational commitment is associated with issues that influence the entire organisation, while job satisfaction is concerned with job aspects of an employee. According to Williams and Hazer (1986), organisational commitment is the extent to which individuals are associated with the activities of the organisation in which they work. Porter et al. (1974) suggest the following three factors promote organisational commitment:

organisational commitment The extent to which individuals associate themselves with the activities of the organisation for which they work.

1. a strong belief in and acceptance of organisational goals and values
2. a willingness to exert considerable effort on behalf of the organisation
3. a definite desire to maintain organisational membership.

Employees who are committed to the organisation should understand its objectives and should work hard towards achieving those objectives. Moreover, Meyer and Allen (1991) argue that organisational commitment consists of three components which indicate a desire (affective commitment), a need (continuance commitment) and an obligation (normative commitment) to remain in an organisation. This model explains that employees with affective commitment remain in the company simply because they choose to, those with continuance commitment remain because it is essential for them to, and those with normative commitment remain because they feel obliged to do so. Therefore, to understand an employee commitment to an organisation, we must examine these psychological states; they may help to characterise the employee's relationship with the organisation and predict whether he or she is likely to remain with the organisation (Meyer, Allen & Smith, 1993).

Satisfied workers are more likely to remain with an organisation and participate in the organisation's activities than are dissatisfied workers (Locke & Latham, 2006). Evidence from various studies has suggested a strong relationship between job satisfaction and organisational commitment (Lee & Mowday, 1987; Williams & Hazer, 1986; Rayton, 2006). However, other studies (Bateman & Strasser, 1984; Vandenberg & Lance, 1992) suggest that, to the contrary, organisational commitment determines satisfaction. Further studies suggest that there is no correlation between satisfaction and organisational commitment (Currivan, 1999; Curry et al., 1986; Rayton, 2006), attributing the lack of a demonstrable relationship between job satisfaction and organisational commitment to a likely 'spurious relationship' between those two factors (Rayton, 2006: 124).

■ Employee turnover intention

Employee turnover is a serious matter in any organisation as it costs a company two of its most important resources: time (to hire new employees or find another person to perform the tasks) and money (the cost in hiring and training new workers) (Singh & Loncar, 2010). Early studies (Brayfield & Crockett, 1955; Herzberg, Maunser & Snyderman, 1957; Vroom, 1964) concluded that an employee is more likely to leave when he or she is not satisfied at work. Since then, most studies have concentrated on job satisfaction as the main factor that influences employee turnover. Although organisations have studied the reasons for employee turnover, it is a persistent problem for many (Porter et al., 1974). As the costs of employee turnover increase, organisations must inevitably examine the factors that contribute to employees' turnover intention (Koch & Steers, 1978).

Hulin (1968) examined the effect of job satisfaction on turnover. Job satisfaction aspects such as pay and promotional opportunities predict any decrease in turnover rates among employees. However, macro-level aspects, such as changes in the labour market and unemployment rates may also raise or lower turnover intention. Studies have focused on employee turnover intentions, since information on workers who leave their jobs by choice has proven tough to obtain (Currivan, 1999). It is suggested that external factors influence actual turnover (Shore & Martin, 1989), and so managers must develop a better understanding of turnover intentions from both internal and external perspectives to keep employee turnover to a minimum.

Mobley (1977) explains that several steps occur before an individual decides to quit a job with which he or she is dissatisfied. Dissatisfaction leads him or her to think of quitting and searching for another job. Further, a study by Mobley, Horner and Hollingsworth (1978) concludes that job dissatisfaction has a greater effect on the thought of quitting and the intention to quit than on turnover. Tett and Meyer (1993) suggest that satisfaction is closely related to turnover intentions, while organisational commitment is closely related to actual turnover. However, according to Michaels and Spector (1982), job satisfaction has a small but significant effect on turnover in comparison to the effect of organisational commitment.

Strategies for employee retention

Working environment and conditions

The working environment is considered one of the most important factors in employee retention (Zeytinoglu & Denton, 2006). The work environment in industrial work-places may cause employees to be exposed to noise or toxic substances and manual handling risks (e.g. heavy lifting work). Yet the work environment is equally important in consumer and client-facing sectors such as service industries (Normann, 1986). Here, the interaction between employees and clients is more psychological than phys-ical because it creates trust between the client and the vendor, which contributes to the client's purchasing intention. The psychological work environment consists of work-load, decision, support, latitude and decision-making. It is crucial for managers to understand that employees need a good work environment where they feel valued and can make a difference to the organisation. Important aspects from the psycholog-ical point of view are job content, job-switching, opportunities for personal and pro-fessional development, opportunity for continuous training, ability to use personal knowledge and experience, opportunities to influence the personal work situation and contacts with colleagues and management. Managers should recognise the emerg-ing needs of employees and provide a healthy and safe environment for employees to ensure they remain committed to the organisation; good working conditions will motivate employees to stay in an organisation. Employees tend to stay in corporations that provide them with a positive work environment where they feel that there is trust, open communication, team spirit and a good physical environment, and that they are valued and make a difference. In particular, the physical work environment plays a pivotal role in employees' decision to leave or remain, and it is considered a major factor in employee retention.

working environment and conditions
Conditions that contribute to the creation of a healthy, safe and enjoyable workplace.

We can increase employee retention levels by improving the work–life balance of employees. Flexible working hours policies (such as flexible rosters, compressed working weeks, part-time and job-sharing arrangements, working from home and teleworking arrangements) can improve the working conditions of employees with children. Employees grow more loyal when they can identify themselves in a group and contribute to the performance of a group (Van Knippenberg, 2000). Therefore, managers should focus on team performance and on helping the individual to feel part of the group. Managers can promote teamwork by determining the key requirements for team working through knowledge, skills and abilities of employees. This can be achieved through conducting job selection in a team-based environment, training employees in teamwork and including performance indicators of team-based work in appraisals (Stevens & Campion, 1994). In Australian organisations, flexible working time arrangements reduce turnover for managers, professionals and technicians as well as skilled workers (Smith, Oczkowski & Smith, 2011). Such policies sit within a range of factors to consider in improving employee retention, including job security and recognition, training and development, supervisor support culture, good work environment, work–life balance and organisational justice (Stein, 2000; Beck, 2001; Clarke, 2001).

■ Remuneration and benefits

Remuneration and **benefits** play a key role in retaining good employees, particularly those who perform exceptionally or have indispensable, unique skills. A competitive remuneration package demonstrates the company's strong commitment to its employees and builds strong employee commitment in turn. Compensation is the most popular retention strategy (Horwitz, Heng & Quazi, 2003) and organisations that offer high compensation packages attract a large number of candidates and usually enjoy a low turnover rate, at least in the short term. Organisations may seek to attract and retain talented employees by offering attractive reward packages that include stock options, special pay, retention pay, gain share pay, performance base pay and bonuses. However, as Smith (2001) argues, such remuneration may encourage high-calibre applicants to join an organisation but is not sufficient to retain them in the long term.

remuneration Intrinsic rewards (e.g. variety, challenge and autonomy) and extrinsic rewards (e.g. recognition, cash bonuses, awards or free trips).
benefits Rewards that an employee receives on top of cash pay.

It is important to distinguish between standard compensation, such as salary, wages and benefits and what is normally referred to as pay for performance (see chapter 6 for more discussion of pay for performance). Reward is the offer an organisation makes to its employees for their contribution and encouraging them to do well in the future. Reward can be **intrinsic** (i.e. cash) or **extrinsic** (e.g. cash bonuses and other **financial benefits**, professional awards, free trips or recognition); see chapter 6 for further discussion. Of the extrinsic kinds, recognition from managers, team members, co-workers and customers can enhance employee loyalty in the organisation. For example, in Japanese organisations, the employee benefit system includes healthcare, childcare support and retirement schemes, which enhance employee satisfaction and help to ensure that employees remain committed to the organisation (Yamamoto, 2011).

intrinsic rewards Rewards derived from the job itself, such as variety, challenge and autonomy.
extrinsic rewards Rewards derived from, for example, pay and fringe benefits, promotion or advancement opportunities in the organisation, the social climate and physical working conditions.
financial benefits Fringe benefits, superannuation or pension plans, healthcare cover, vacations.

MNCs have introduced compensation packages to prevent employee turnover (Tang, Kim & Tang, 2000) and may offer their expatriate assignees salary and benefits compensation comparable to another part of the organisation (e.g. another subsidiary, headquarters) to create competitive, equitable remuneration across the organisation's operations (Briscoe, Schuler & Tarique, 2012).

◼ Training and development interventions

Training and development opportunities are an important factor in employee retention. Organisations invest in the training and development of employees who can provide them with a return on that investment (Messmer, 2000). Managers of talented employees should provide a proficiency analysis, give opinions on employee interests, appraise the capabilities of employees and develop an action plan according to the needs of employees. Managers focus on workforce 'analytics' by focusing on staffing processes to analyse and optimise the whole system or improve individual aspects (Stepstone, 2005). Organisations invest in human capital through training that helps employees to enhance the skills and knowledge they need to perform well in their jobs (Noe, 1999). As organisations operate in a globally competitive environment, managers should ensure that employees are equipped with the appropriate training to perform their duties now and in the future; for example, interpersonal communication, technological knowledge, problem solving and basic literacy. Large organisations tend to spend more on physical resources to retain their talent (Black & Lynch, 1996) and firms that offer more benefits tend to train their employees more by adopting innovative job practices (Frazis et al., 1998). Leading professional services companies recognise the importance of comprehensive training, skills and career development as a factor in attracting and retaining intellectual capital (Accenture, 2001).

training and development Schemes in which organisations invest to help employees improve their skills and knowledge.

A company should invest in employees' career development in order to retain intellectual capital. Career development is a formalised, organised and planned effort that considers both what the organisation requires from its employees and what the individual needs to achieve progression. As we have seen, career advancement opportunities motivate employees to stay with an organisation and organisations can strengthen the bond with the employees in this way (Steel, Griffeth & Hom, 2002). From this perspective, a company should offer training and development schemes that aim to equip its employees with skills that are valued in the labour market (Butler & Waldroop, 2001). Career development is beneficial for employees and employer alike: organisations that seek competitive advantage require talented employees with unique skills, and employees need particular skills and training to enhance and cultivate their competencies in the labour market (Prince, 2005). For example, German firms that focus on the long-term investment of human capital through employee training and development have tended to retain talent (Festing, Schäfer & Scullion, 2013); in French and Swedish firms, learning and development opportunities are also crucial for the retention of talented employees (Hytter, 2007). The Ritz-Carlton Hotel Company is a global organisation that provides intensive training to transform its newly hired employees into the kind of service providers who win awards. It focuses on specific training and asks the five best employees in each job category to deliver it.

■ Inpatriation, nationalisation and repatriation

The concept of inpatriation involves the transfer of local nationals in a MNC on a semi-permanent or permanent basis (Harvey & Buckley, 1997; Harvey, Novicevic & Speier, 2000). Inpatriation reduces the share of foreign expatriates through a localisation strategy and fosters international assignments for local staff (see chapter 3).

Nationalisation is one of the retention strategies that dictate aspects of employment practices in both the public and private sectors, encouraging and supporting the employment of local people. Nationalisation strategies are commonly used in United Arab Emirates (UAE) countries and involve mainstream strategic HR activities such as selection and recruitment, education and training, career management and the design of reward systems (Rees, Mamman & Bin Braik, 2007). In the case of UAE, nationalisation is known as 'Emiratisation' and described as the recruitment and development of UAE nationals to increase their employability and so reduce the country's dependence on an expatriate workforce (Abed, Vine & Vine, 1996; Dale, 2004; Ingo, 2008). Emiratisation is a process governmental and private sector organisations use with the aim of retaining their local workforce by providing work opportunities and career prospects to local workers.

Repatriation is a process of change and adjustment that expatriates undergo at the end of an assignment (Suutari & Brewster, 2003). Repatriating employees need support to reconstruct their identities in their home organisations (Harvey & Novicevic, 2006). This support can be provided to them through short-term assignments as assistance towards the repatriation process (Starr, 2009). Crucial aspects in the repatriation process are career management, clear repatriation policies and practices and accurate working expectations (Sánchez Vidal, Sanz Valle & Aragón, 2008). Expatriates from North American MNCs perceive the companywide appreciation of global experience and opportunities for career planning as key to the repatriation process (Lazarova & Caligiuri, 2001). The level of adjustment repatriates achieve contributes to their levels of job satisfaction and job attachment (Stevens et al., 2007). For Australian professionals, the key factors for repatriation in the home country include national identity, length of time already spent overseas and quality of life available in the home country (De Cieri et al., 2009). MNCs can achieve greater employee retention by adjusting generalisable practices from the home country to create context-specific practices that are flexible across different host environments (table 7.1 shows strategies that companies can use and gives examples of each type).

repatriation The transfer of local nationals to an MNC on a semi-permanent or permanent basis.

Table 7.1 Strategies for employee retention	
Strategy area	**Approaches**
Working environment	Health and safety issues, working conditions, relationships with co-workers and supervisors.
Remuneration	Monetary and non-monetary rewards.
Training and development	Staff development programs, development of skills and abilities, personal growth.
Inpatriation and repatriation	Inpatriation strategy aims the transfer of local nationals to the MNC's on a semi-permanent to permanent basis. Repatriation strategy aims to provide, regulate and promote employment for nationals as retention strategy.

Conclusion

In this chapter, we have explained that employee retention refers to the ability of the organisation to keep its valuable employees through various strategies, including managing job satisfaction and motivation, offering competitive remuneration packages and making training and development opportunities available. High levels of job satisfaction are the key to employee retention and arise from work-related issues such as autonomy, task requirements, organisational policies, professional interactions and perceived job status. A company can achieve good employee retention through establishing favourable working conditions; offering financial and non-financial benefits and training and development opportunities; and managing inpatriation and repatriation strategies. To retain staff, organisations need to enhance and cultivate the competencies and skills of their employees through significant investment.

Take-home messages

- It is important to understand that employee retention offers benefits for both employees and the organisation, and that HR managers need to focus on retaining staff and reducing employee turnover intentions.
- Job satisfaction, achieved through remuneration, promotion opportunities, supervision, collegiality and challenging tasks, has been found to be a sufficient reason for employees to stay with an organisation. Also, affective, continuance and normative commitment can increase employees' willingness to remain in the organisation.
- Strategies that can enhance employee retention include good working conditions, a healthy work environment, intrinsic and extrinsic rewards, on-the-job training, ongoing career development schemes and the recruitment of local employees.

■ Closing the learning loop

1. Why should HR managers be aware of employee retention issues?
2. How can employee retention provide organisations with a competitive advantage?
3. Why do job satisfaction and organisational commitment help prevent employee turnover intentions?
4. What strategies can HR managers use to retain talented employees?

CASE STUDY 7.1   BOOTS

Boots, a UK retailer, is considered by many as the market leader in the health and beauty retail industry. It was established in the 19th century and today has a huge presence in the UK, operating more than 1500 stores. Boots employs more than 62 000 people and is considered a major employer, with staff working in roles across distribution, logistics and support. The Boots brand is highly valuable as customers associate it with trust and expertise given the company's reputation for high-quality customer care. The company is always looking to its future by consistently hiring exceptional young people, mostly graduates, to become part of the Boots heritage, a dedication to development that pays dividends in terms of employee retention: more than half of the current Boots workforce (32 000 people) has been with the company for 5 years or longer.

Employee development

Boots has consistently focused on the development of its employees and continues to do so. This is evident not only in the company's record of winning industry awards, but also in its framework for employee development. Employees are encouraged to reach their full potential through programs such as the award-winning Work Inspiration program, which offers young people

opportunities to gain work experience, and its apprenticeship scheme for school leavers. Further, the graduate program converts young professionals into future store leaders and is a vital part of Boots' company culture.

Career development

Career development is important to Boots and the company continually invests in its people through a range of internal masterclass and coaching opportunities. A dedicated program is also available for employees interested in managerial roles, and this training support is available at all levels, from first-time line managers to the senior leadership team. As high-quality customer care is one of the hallmarks of Boots, the main focus in-store is to deliver excellent customer care. To that end, employees are trained to address customers' needs and to find personalised solutions to people's health problems. Constant training and support are available through the company's internal eLearning system and through professional development days.

Workplace health

Boots is committed to the health of its employees. Employees have the option to assess their health and monitor their weight and diet through online health assessments, modifying their lifestyle where needed. Further, comprehensive information is available on the company intranet and public website, to help its managers and employees cope with health conditions and lead healthy lives. In recognition of the company's efforts, Boots' Occupational Health Service was granted Safe Effective Quality Occupational Health Services (SEQOHS) accreditation in 2011.

Case study questions

1. Which career development strategies have been adopted by Boots?
2. In what ways do Boots' programs enhance the career development of its employees?
3. Describe the benefits of the workplace health programs Boots provides to its employees?
4. How effective do you think Boots' strategies may be in terms of preventing absenteeism and enhancing employee retention, and why?

» ACTIVITIES

Individual activity

Imagine that you are the chief executive of an MNC in an industry that interests you. You are preparing a discussion paper in which you explain why employee retention is crucial for your organisation. In your paper, discuss the main strategies your organisation has used to retain its valuable staff and explain why they did or did not work.

Researching employee retention

Using the internet, locate and research a company that offers exceptional employee support in one or more of the following aspects:
- working conditions
- reward and incentive systems
- training and development.

Why do you think this firm has decided on this approach to the financial and/or non-financial benefits it offers?

■ Online resources

- For instructors: answers to activities; long media article with questions.
- For students: further reading; answers to case study; IHRM in practice.

■ References

Abed, I., Vine, P. and Vine, P. (1996). *The United Arab Emirates handbook: 1996–1997*. London: Trident Press.

Accenture (2001). The high performance workforce: separating the digital economy's winners from losers in the battle for retention, study by Accenture, 1–5.

Allen, J. and Van Der Velden, R. (2001). Educational mismatches versus skill mismatches: Effects on wages, job satisfaction, and on-the-job search, *Oxford Economic Papers*, 53: 434–52.

Anderson, N., Ones, D. S., Sinangil, H. K. and Viswesvaran, C. (eds) (2001). *Handbook of industrial, work and organizational psychology*. Vol. 2. London: Sage.

Babin, B. J. and Boles, J. S. (1996). The effects of perceived co-worker involvement and supervisor support on service provider role stress, performance and job satisfaction, *Journal of Retailing*, 72(1): 57–75.

Barnett, R. (1995). Flexible benefits: Communication is the key, *Benefits and Compensation International*, 24(6): 25–8.

Bartlett, C. A. and Ghoshal, S. (1998). *Managing across borders: The transnational solution*, 2nd edition. Boston: Harvard Business School Press.

Bateman, T. S. and Strasser, S. (1984). A longitudinal analysis of the antecedents of organizational commitment, *Academy of Management Journal*, 27(1): 95–112.

Beck, S. (2001). Why associates leave and strategies to keep them, *American Lawyer Media*, 5(2): 23–7.

Black, S. E. and Lynch, L. M. (1996). Human capital investments and productivity, *American Economic Review*, 86(2): 263–7.

Brayfield, A. H. and Crockett, W. H. (1955). Employee attitudes and employee performance, *Psychological bulletin*, 52(5): 396–424.

Brewster, C. Sparrow, P., Vernon, G. and Houldsworth, E. (2011). *International human resource management*, 3rd edition. London: Chartered Institute of Personnel and Development.

Briscoe, D., Schuler, R. and Tarique, I. (2012). *International human resource management*. 4th edition. New York: Routledge.

Butler, T. and Waldroop, J. (2001). *Job sculpting: The art of retaining your best people*, Boston: Harvard Business Press Books.

Chambers, E. et al. (1998). The war for talent, *McKinsey Quarterly*, 3: 44–57.

Chang, H. (1996). In Singapore, the dreams are getting bigger, *Business Week*, 23 September.

Chartered Institute of Personnel and Development (CIPD) (2007). *Annual survey report 2007: Recruitment, retention and turnover*, London: Chartered Institute of Personnel and Development.

Clarke, K. F. (2001). What businesses are doing to attract and retain employees: becoming an employer of choice, *Employee Benefits Journal*, 3(1): 34–7.

Cook, J., Hepworth, S., Wall, T. and Warr, P. (1981). *The experience of work*. New York: Academic Press.

Currivan, D. B. (1999). The causal order of job satisfaction and organizational commitment in models of employee turnover, *Human Resource Management Review*, 9(4): 495–524.

Curry, J. P., Wakefield, D. S., Price, J. L. and Mueller, C. W. (1986). On the causal ordering of job satisfaction and organizational commitment, *Academy of Management Journal*, 29(4): 847–58.

Dale, B. (2004). *Legal issues related to doing business in the United Arab Emirates*. Dubai: American Business Council of Dubai and the Northern Emirates.

Davies, R. (2001). How to boost staff retention, *People Management* 7(8): 54–6.

De Cieri, H., Sheehan, C., Costa, C., Fenwick, M. and Cooper, B. (2009). International talent flow and intention to repatriate: an identity explanation, *Human Resource Development International*, 12(3): 243–61.

Festing, M. (2007). Globalization of SMEs and implications for international human resource management, *International Journal of Globalisation and Small Business*, 2: 5–18.

Festing, M., Schäfer, L. and Scullion, H. (2013). Talent management in medium-sized German companies: An explorative study and agenda for future research, *International Journal of Human Resource Management*, 24(9): 1872–93.

Frazis, H., Gittleman, M., Horrigan, M. and Joyce, M. (1998). Results from the 1995 survey of employer provided training, *Monthly Labour Review*, 21(6): 3–14.

Greenberg, J. and Baron, R. A. (2003). *Behaviour in organisations*, 8th edition. Upper Saddle River, NJ: Prentice Hall.

Groysberg, B., Nanda, A. and Nohria, N. (2004). The risky business of hiring stars, *Harvard Business Review*, 1 (May): 1–10.

Hackman, J. R. and Oldham, G. R. (1976). Motivation through the design of work: Test of a theory, *Organizational behavior and human performance*, 16(2): 250–79.

Harvey, M. and Buckley, M. R. (1997). Managing inpatriates: Building a global core competency, *Journal of World Business*, 32: 35–52.

Harvey, M. and Novicevic, M. (2006). The evolution from repatriation of managers in MNE's to 'repatriation' in global organisations. In Stahl, G. and Björkman, I. (eds), *Handbook of research in international human resource management*. Cheltenham, Gloucestershire: Edward Elgar.

Harvey, M., Novicevic, M. M. and Speier, C. (2000). Strategic global human resource management: The role of inpatriate managers, *Human Resource Management Review*, 10: 153–75.

Herzberg, F., Maunser, B. and Snyderman, B. (1959). *The motivation to work*, New York: John Wiley.

Horwitz, F., Heng, C. and Quazi, H. (2003). Finders, keepers? Attracting, motivating and retaining knowledge workers, *Human Resource Management Journal*, 13(4): 23–44.

Hulin, C. L. (1968). Effects of changes in job-satisfaction levels on employee turnover, *Journal of Applied Psychology*, 52(2): 122–6.

Hytter, A. (2007). Retention strategies in France and Sweden, *Irish Journal of Management*, 28(1): 59–79.

Ingo, F. (2008). Workforce nationalization in the UAE: Image versus integration, *Education, Business and Society: Contemporary Middle Eastern Issues*, 1(2): 82–91.

Jackson, S. and Schuler, R. (2003). *Managing human resources through strategic partnerships*, 8th edition. United Kingdom: Thomson SouthWestern.

Kinicki, A. J., McKee-Ryan, F., Schriesheim, C. A. and Carson, K. P. (2002). Assessing the construct validity of the Job Descriptive Index: A review and meta-analysis, *Journal of Applied Psychology*, 87(1): 14–32.

Koch, J. L. and Steers, R. M. (1978). Job attachment, satisfaction, and turnover among public sector employees, *Journal of Vocational Behavior*, 12(1): 119–28.

Lazarova, M. and Caligiuri, P. (2001). Retaining repatriates: The role of organisational support practices, *Journal of World Business*, 36(4): 389–401.

Lee, T. W. and Mowday, R. T. (1987). Voluntarily leaving an organization: An empirical investigation of Steers and Mowday's model of turnover, *Academy of Management Journal*, 30(4): 721–43.

Locke, E. A. (1976). The nature and causes of job satisfaction. In Dunnette, M. D. (ed.), *Handbook of industrial and organizational psychology*, 1297–349. Chicago: Rand McNally.

Locke, E. A. and Latham, P. G. (2006). Current directions in psychological science: New directions in goal-setting theory, *Current Directions in Psychological Science*, 15(5): 265–8.

Luecke, R. (2002). *Hiring and keeping the best people*. Boston: Harvard Business School Publishing.

Lum, L., Kervin, J., Clark, K., Reid, F. and Sirola, W. (1998). Explaining nursing turnover intent: Job satisfaction, pay satisfaction, or organizational commitment? *Journal of Organizational Behavior*, 19(3): 305–20.

Luthans, F. (1995). *Organizational behavior*, 7th edition. New York: McGraw-Hill.

MacLachlan, R. (1996). Job-hopping or 'industrial espionage', *Personnel Management*, 2(14): 15–16.

Maslow, A. H. (1943). A theory of human motivation, *Psychological Review*, 50(4): 370–96.

Messmer, M. (2000). Orientations programs can be key to employee retention, *Strategic Finance*, 81(8): 12–15.

Meyer, J. and Allen, N. (1991). A three-component conceptualization of organisational commitment, *Human Resource Management Review*, 1(1): 61–89.

Meyer, J. and Allen, N. (1997). *Commitment in the workplace*. Thousand Oaks, CA: Sage.

Meyer, J. P., Allen, N. J. and Smith, C., (1993). Commitment to organizations and occupations: Extension and test of a three-component conceptualization, *Journal of Applied Psychology*, 78: 538–51.

Michaels, C. E. and Spector, P. E. (1982). Causes of employee turnover: A test of the Mobley, Griffeth, Hand and Meglino model, *Journal of Applied Psychology*, 67(1): 53–9.

Mobley, W. H. (1977). Intermediate linkages in the relationship between job satisfaction and employee turnover, *Journal of Applied Psychology*, 62(2): 237–40.

Mobley, W. H., Horner, S. O. and Hollingsworth, A. T. (1978). An evaluation of precursors of hospital employee turnover, *Journal of Applied Psychology*, 63(4): 408–14.

Nel, P. S., Gerber, P. D., Van Dyk, P. S., Haasbroek, G. D., Schultz, H. B., Sono, T. and Werner, A. (2002). *Human resource management*, 5th edition. Cape Town: Oxford University Press.

Nguyen, A., Taylor, J. and Bradley, S. (2003). Relative pay and job satisfaction: Some new evidence, *Munich Personal RePEc Archive*, 1382: 1–24.

Noe, R. A. (1999). *Employee training and development*. New York: Irwin McGraw-Hill.

Normann, R. (1986). *Service management: Strategy and leadership in service business*. Chichester, West Sussex: Wiley.

Novicevic, M. M. and Harvey, M. G. (2001). The emergence of the pluralism construct and the inpatriation process, *International Journal of Human Resource Management*, 12: 333–56.

Pfeffer, J. (1994). *Competitive advantage through people: Unleashing the power of the workforce*. Boston: Harvard Business School Press.

Pfeffer, J. and Sutton, R. (2006). *Hard facts, dangerous half-truths, and total nonsense: Profiting from evidence-based management*. Boston: Harvard Business School Press.

Porter, L. W. and Steers, R. M. (1973). Organizational, work, and personal factors in employee turnover and absenteeism, *Psychological bulletin*, 80(2): 151–76.

Porter, L. W., Steers, R. M., Mowday, R. T. and Boulian, P. V. (1974). Organizational commitment, job satisfaction, and turnover among psychiatric technicians, *Journal of Applied Psychology*, 59(5): 603–9.

Price, J. L. and Mueller, C. W. (1981). A causal model of turnover for nurses. *Academy of Management Journal*, 24(3): 543–65.

Prince, B. J. (2005). Career-focused employee transfer processes, *Career Development International*, 10(4): 293–309.

Rayton, B. A. (2006). Examining the interconnection of job satisfaction and organizational commitment: an application of the bivariate probit model. *International Journal of Human Resource Management*, 17(1): 139–54.

Rees, C., Mamman, A., and Bin Braik, A. (2007). Emiratization as a strategic HRM change initiative: Case study evidence from a UAE petroleum company. *International Journal of Human Resource Management*, 18(1): 33–53.

Reiche, S. (2007). The effect of international staffing practices on subsidiary staff retention in multinational corporations, *International Journal of Human Resource Management*, 18(4): 523–36.

Roznowski, M. (1989). Examination of the measurement properties of the Job Descriptive Index with experimental items, *Journal of Applied Psychology*, 4(5): 805–14.

Sánchez Vidal, Ma E., Sanz Valle, R. and Arágon, I. (2008). International workers' satisfaction with the repatriation process, *International Journal of Human Resource Management*, 19(9): 1683–702.

Schwab, D. P. and Wallace Jr., M. J. (1974). Correlates of employee satisfaction with pay, *Industrial Relations*, 13(1): 78–89.

Scullion, H. and Brewster, C. (2001). Managing expatriates: Message from Europe, *Journal of World Business*, 36: 346–65.

Scullion, H., Collings, D. G., and Gunnigle, P. (2007). International human resource management in the 21st century: Emerging themes and contemporary debates, *Human Resource Management Journal*, 17(4): 309–19.

Shore, L. M. and Martin, H. J. (1989). Job satisfaction and organizational commitment in relation to work performance and turnover intentions, *Human Relations*, 42(7): 625–38.

Singh, P. and Loncar, N. (2010). Pay satisfaction, job satisfaction and turnover intent, *Industrial Relations*, 65(3): 470–90.

Sloane, P. J., and Williams, H. (2000). Job satisfaction, comparison earning and gender, *Labour*, 14: 473–502.

Smilansky, J. (2007). *Developing executive talent: Best practices from global leaders*. Chichester: John Wiley.

Smith, A., Oczkowski, E. and Smith, C. (2011). To have and to hold: Modeling the drivers of employee turnover and skill retention in Australian organisations, *International Journal of Human Resource Management*, 22(2): 395–416.

Smith, M. K. (2001). Young people, informal education and association, www.infed.org/youth work/ypandassoc.htm.

Smith, P. C., Kendall, L. and Hulin, C. L. (1969). *The measurement of satisfaction in work and retirement*. Chicago: Rand McNally.

Solomon, C. (1999). Brace for change. *Workforce*, 78(1): 6–11.

Stahl, G. K., Bjorkman, I., Farndale, E., Morris, S. S., Stiles, P., Trevor, J. and Wright, P. M. (2007). *Global talent management: How leading multinationals build and sustain their talent pipeline*, Faculty and Research Working Paper. Fontainebleau, France: INSEAD.

Stahl, G. K., Bjorkman, I., Farndale, E., Morris, S. S., Paauwe, J., Stiles, P., Trevor, J., and Wright, P. (2012). Six principles of effective global talent management, *MIT Sloan Management Review*, 53: 25–32.

Starr, T. (2009) Repatriation and short-term assignments: an exploration into expectations, change and dilemmas, *International Journal of Human Resource Management*, 20(2): 286–300.

Steel, R. P., Griffeth, R. W., and Hom, P. W. (2002). Practical retention policy for the practical manager, *Academy of Management Executive*, 18(2): 149–69.

Stein, N. (2000). Winning the war to keep top talent: Yes! You can make your workplace invincible, *Fortune*, 141(11): 132–8.

Stepstone. (2005). Stepstone and Hire.com, www.stepstone.com/solutions/hire.htm. Retrieved 10 October 2005.

Stevens, M. and Campion, M. (1994). The knowledge, skill and ability requirements for teamwork: Implications for human resource management, *Journal of Management*, 20(2): 503–30.

Stevens, M., Oddou, G., Furuya, N., Bird, A. and Mendenhall, M. (2007). HR factors affecting repatriate job satisfaction and job attachment for Japanese managers, *International Journal of Human Resource Management*, 17(5): 831–41.

Suutari, V. and Brewster, C. (2003). Repatriation: Empirical evidence from a longitudinal study of careers and expectations among Finnish expatriates, *International Journal of Human Resource Management*, 14: 1132–51.

Syrett, M. (1994). Through thick and thin, *Asian Business*, 30(12): 26–30.

Tang, T., Kim, J. and Tang, D. (2000). Does attitude towards money moderate the relationship between intrinsic job satisfaction and voluntary turnover, *Human Relations*, 53(2): 213–45.

Tett, R. P. and Meyer, J. P. (1993). Job satisfaction, organizational commitment, turnover intention, and turnover: Path analyses based on meta-analytical findings, *Personnel Psychology*, 46(2): 259–93.

Tymon, W., Stump, S. and Doh, J. (2010). Exploring talent management in India: The neglected role of intrinsic rewards, *Journal of World Business*, 45: 109–21.

Van Knippenberg, D. (2000). Work motivation and performance: A social identity perspective, *Applied Psychology: An International Review*, 49: 357–71.

Vandenberg, R. J. and Lance, C. E. (1992). Examining the causal order of job satisfaction and organizational commitment, *Journal of Management*, 18(1): 153–67.

Vroom, V. H. (1964). *Work and motivation*. New York: Wiley.

Westover, J. H., Westover, A. R. and Westover, L. (2010). Enhancing long-term worker productivity and performance. The connection of key work domains to job satisfaction and organizational commitment, *International Journal of Productivity and Performance Management*, 59(4): 372–87.

Williams, L. J. and Hazer, J. T. (1986). Antecedents and consequences of satisfaction and commitment in turnover models: A reanalysis using latent variable structural equation methods, *Journal of Applied Psychology*, 71(2): 219–31.

Yamamoto, H. (2011). The relationship between employee benefit management and employee retention, *The International Journal of Human Resource Management*, 22(17): 3550–64.

Zeytinoglu, I. U. and Denton, M. (2006), Satisfied workers, retained workers: Effects of work and work environment on homecare workers' job satisfaction, stress, physical health and retention, *Social and Economic Dimensions of an Aging Population Research Papers*, SEDAP Research Paper 166.

8

International labour relations

Mustafa F. Özbilgin

■ Learning objectives

- To introduce and define the concept of international labour relations.
- To explain the historical transformation of labour relations in the international context.
- To define international labour standards and explain why they are sometimes controversial.
- To present a multilevel model of international labour relations and explore how macro-, meso- and micro-level actors and stakeholders contribute to the crafting, transposition, implementation and monitoring of international labour relations and standards.
- To explain why nation states and multinational companies choose to adopt international labour relations.
- To present two case studies that illustrate the complexity of adopting international labour standards at national level.

■ Learning outcomes

After reading this chapter, students will be able to:
- understand international labour relations, their key stakeholders and processes
- appreciate the historical transformation of labour relations in the international context
- define international labour standards and debate sources of and controversies surrounding international labour standards
- identify the macro-, meso- and micro-level actors and stakeholders in international labour relations and appreciate their respective roles in the crafting, transposition, implementation and monitoring of international labour relations and standards
- explain why nation states and multinational companies may choose to adopt international labour relations
- account for the complexity of adoption of international labour standards at national level.

◾ Introduction

The field of research known as **international labour relations** (ILR) examines how institutional stakeholders (such as international organisations, supranational bodies, trade unions, the state, society and industry) shape the conditions, standards and relations of labour. ILR is different from domestic labour relations because it allows us to consider multiple national settings. As such, to understand ILR we need an appreciation of both various economic, social, political and institutional arrangements (Lipietz, 1997) at the domestic level and the relationships between institutional actors in two or more national settings. It is important to note that, although ILR policies and discussions may take place internationally, labour relations practice remains firmly localised. As the policy and practice of labour relations span international treaties, national regulation and local practices, this chapter's structure reflects the multilevel nature of labour relations, taking into account macro-, meso- and micro-levels (that is, labour relations at international, national and organisational levels).

> **international labour relations** A field of research that examines how institutional stakeholders, such as international organisations, supranational bodies, trade unions, the state, the society and the industry, shape the conditions, standards and relations of labour.

The chapter approaches the subject from four angles. First, we examine the contemporary context of labour relations, putting the transformation of labour relations in its historical setting; such context helps us to understand how and why ILR is practised today and how ILR connects with IHRM. Second, we assess the range of labour standards (e.g. wages and conditions) on which ILR activities focus in the international arena. The achievement of labour standards remains a distant dream and yet setting and maintaining labour standards are important mechanisms in protecting workers' rights. Third, we examine the key stakeholders (e.g. trade unions) with which international assignees and international HR managers must negotiate and agree labour standards. This section offers a political reading of the ILR and assesses the influence of its varied institutional actors. Fourth, we explain the three reasons for adoption of international labour standards – the principled stance, solidarity and voluntarism – exploring the implications of each rationale. At the end of the chapter, we offer two case studies, from Turkey and South Africa, that highlight the complexity of adopting and implementing ILS at national level.

◾ Contemporary ILR: the historical context

To understand the history of ILR, we need to understand the drivers that propelled key institutional actors such as nation states, trade unions and international organisations to engage with the terms and conditions of labour. The emergence of large global firms as dominant stakeholders in the field of ILR has alarmed the labour unions in nation states, which are concerned that the operations of global firms may effectively lower the international standards, terms and conditions of labour (Marginson et al., 1995). For example, global firms can cause social and economic dumping, pulling down wages and damaging workers' terms and conditions, as they relocate their business functions to countries and regions that offer cheap labour and weaker terms and conditions of labour.

In response to the challenge that global firms pose to labour standards, trade unions formed international alliances that have sectoral and global reach. However, these alliances did not find it easy to counterbalance the force of international firms in influencing ILS. The emergence of resistance against the imbalanced transformation of labour relations in favour of international firms and to the detriment of labour took multiple forms such as trade union alliances and work-council formations (Pries & Seeliger, 2013). Collaboration between trade unions can often be complex, due to differences in structure, function and substance in worker collectives (e.g. trade unions) across countries. Nation states, similarly to worker collectives, have developed alliances with other nations, based on common values and shared understanding of labour relations, to more effectively influence ILR. International collaboration between nation states on labour standards has also been complicated due to differences in national priorities between states.

Therefore, it would be an understatement to suggest that ILR has been subject to fundamental challenges and transformation. Labour relations have not transformed to the same degree or in the same form across countries and sectors, due to divergence of national interests. However, the transformation of labour relations does have some core themes that have been commonly studied. First, scholars in the field of ILR have been concerned with the withdrawal of the state from a regulatory role for labour in industrialised countries. The practical implication of this transformation has been that state interests have become more closely aligned with those of international firms, and less so with the interests of workers and worker collectives (Purcell, 1993). Second, the power of worker representation and trade unions has declined in the traditional tripartite relationship between workers, employers and the state (Dundon et al. 2004), with power now skewed towards employer and corporate interests. Third, in this new order, notions of individualism and voluntarism (Jonsen et al., 2013; Özbilgin and Tatli, 2011) are now seen as fundamental values of labour relations and popular recipes for the effective management of labour relations.

This altered international setting presents a relatively hostile context for the collective representation of worker interests and the setting of international standards for labour relations. In response to change, workers have transformed their traditional mechanisms (such as solidarity, collective bargaining, negotiations, strikes) for counterbalancing the interests of employers, as in the case of Latin American unions (Anner, 2011). There is some continuity, in terms of the forms of collective action that are available to trade unions, but as Townsend, Wilkinson and Burgess (forthcoming) explain, new forms of employment relations have emerged in response to individualisation and de-unionisation, which have emphasised collaboration rather than conflict between interests of workers and employers.

■ Labour standards in the international context

International labour standards (ILS) may be defined using a range of norms about the terms (e.g. working time), conditions (e.g. equality), and experiences (e.g. wellbeing) of workers – a dynamically debated set of economic, social, and moral considerations. Labour standards vary markedly from nation to nation; as individual countries often take different economic, social and political paths, they develop their own norms and standards of labour. ILS are aspirational standards that are agreed and enshrined in international, supranational and regional conventions, which seek to reconcile areas of divergence between terms and conditions of labour in different nations; they represent a movement towards common standards, based on shared economic, social and ethical concerns. ILS remain a distant dream, among the most contested issues in international trade and politics.

international labour standards Aspirational standards agreed and enshrined in international, supranational and regional conventions, which seek to reconcile areas of divergence between terms and conditions of labour in different nations. ILS represent a movement towards common labour standards, based on shared economic, social and ethical concerns.

Many institutional actors have an interest in shaping the debate on ILS, including international and supranational organisations. The former include the International Labour Organization (ILO), World Trade Organization (WTO) and United Nations (UN) and the latter include the Association of Southeast Asian Nations (ASEAN), European Union (EU), international trade unions, international identity networks and social and political lobbies. These actors have joined a wide-ranging debate on labour standards, discussing matters such as freedom of association among workers, working time arrangements, the use of forced labour and slavery, child labour, health and safety at work, minimum pay, discrimination at work and labour migration.

EXERCISE

What roles do the ILO and WTO play in shaping the debate on ILS? How do their agendas converge and diverge? Check out the organisations' websites for relevant information about ILS.

Although the subject of ILS appears innocuous at first sight, the matter of setting and complying with standards is controversial, since some countries experience disproportionate economic and social effects when they adopt labour standards. For example, there is widespread legal protections against workplace gender discrimination, but fewer countries yet offer legal protection against workplace discrimination based on sexual orientation. There remain significant differences in implementation and monitoring of standards, and in the penalties imposed for non-compliance, among countries that offer gender equality legislation. Here, it is critical to understand the underlying reasons for each country's local methods in managing labour relations, which range from disparities of economic power and differences in historical context to contrasting social norms and ethical approaches. Therefore, it is important to question what the creation of a single set of standards means for different countries (see Charnovitz, 1987 for a detailed historical overview of ILS), as their adoption is likely to create strongly disproportionate impacts in each country that takes part. If ILS are to be set, it is critically important to ask whose labour standards should be adopted as ILS; in answering this question, we highlight power disparities between countries that assert the importance of ILS and other nations.

If disparities between national conditions and systems render adoption of international standards difficult, why do countries ratify and adopt these standards? In a recent study, Baccini and Koenig-Archibugi (2012) offer two theory-based responses. First, the **sociological institutional approach** suggests that countries choose to ratify ILS agreements to conform to the normative expectations of allied countries in their regional or supranational networks (e.g. European laws against different forms of discrimination encourage nation states to converge on equality standards). Second, the **rational institutional approach** posits that countries ratify such agreements to remain competitive in a global market in which non-compliance may lead to the loss of trade opportunities (e.g. barriers to trade imposed because of a country's acceptance of child labour).

sociological institutional approach The proposition that countries choose to ratify ILS agreements to conform to the normative expectations of allied countries in their regional or supranational networks.

rational institutional approach The proposition that countries ratify ILS agreements to remain competitive in a global market in which non-compliance may lead to the loss of trade opportunities.

■ A multilevel model of ILR

Multiple layers of stakeholders shape the field of ILR: our model encompasses the macro-, meso- and micro-levels (that is, international, national and organisational levels). At the macro-level, organisations such as the ILO, WTO and sector, industry and interest-specific international bodies uphold ILS. At the meso-level, national actors such trade unions, employers' associations, works councils, the state and social, political and economic pressure groups shape the national interpretation of international standards. At the micro-level, stakeholders such as organisational leaders, line managers and opinion and change agents in organisations assume the responsibility of promoting, monitoring and managing the implementation of international standards. The chain of responsibility after a nation ratifies an ILS is diffuse and complicated by layers of influence at all three levels. It is therefore important to study ILR as a phenomenon in the context of this complex set of influences.

■ *Macro-level stakeholders*

The international field of labour relations is replete with interest groups and lobbies that represent nation states, regional alliances and the collective interests of global organisations, multinational companies (MNCs) and international confederations of trade unions. In this section, we look at the key players at the macro-level. The ILO is the premier reference organisation, as it sets ILS through international conventions among its member countries. Each member country is represented in the ILO not only by its national government but also by its worker and employer representatives. The ILO was established in 1919 as part of the Treaty of Versailles at the end of the First World War.

> **macro-level stakeholders** Actors at the international level, including international agencies, supranational organisations, regional blocks, global and international firms and international trade unions.

Today, it boasts 182 member countries, more than 120 of which are signatories to the eight core standards, based on four principles that shape ILO's work:

1. the right to collective bargaining
2. the right to freedom of association
3. the abolition of child labour and forced labour
4. the fight against discrimination at work.

The ILO's key aim is to foster peace in the world by promoting better conditions of work and life for everyone. The ILO uses international agreements and conventions as a way to seek agreement for common standards that nations can agree on and ratify at meso-level. Member states do not only adopt and ratify as law the conventions on which they have agreed; they must also report regularly on their progress in implementing the standards.

WTO members uphold certain principles set out in the core ILO conventions: freedom of association, the elimination of forced and child labour, and the fight against discrimination at work. Given these shared principles, the WTO plays a complementary role to the ILO. There are other regional and supranational alliances among nation states, such as the EU, North American Free Trade Association (NAFTA), ASEAN, the Arab League and the African Union (AU), among others. Such supranational alliances also have a range of perspectives on the setting of international standards. Some of the powerful nation states that participate in supranational alliances also assert their own agendas for labour standards through unilateral arrangements in the international arena, which has a considerable impact.

Multinational, international and global firms exert influence on the ILS debate both in their own right and as part of strategic alliances. Commercial enterprises have as much coercive power as nation states, which clamour to attract global firms in an effort to foster economic growth and reduce unemployment and poverty. Therefore, the interests of MNCs are also represented through their political influence on nation states (Rodriguez et al., 2006).

The International Trade Union Confederation (ITUC) is an important stakeholder in the international arena of labour relations. Representing trade unions and affiliated organisations from 156 countries, ITUC represents the labour relations interests of 125 million workers. ITUC asserts influence in negotiating terms and conditions of labour at the international level, and seeks to combat the negative consequences of international trade for workers. Such negative consequences may include a loss of jobs due to offshoring, the denigration of workers' rights and a decline in terms and conditions of employment (www.ituc-csi.org). ITUC collaborates with Global Unions (www.global-unions.org), an international trade unions organisation that upholds the ideals and priorities of the trade union movement. ITUC and Global Unions organise to defend human rights and labour standards across the world.

Other organisations are also instrumental in generating data for monitoring, studying and effectively managing labour relations. One prominent example is the International Labour and Employment Relations Association (ILERA), founded in 1966, which focuses on scientific studies of labour and employment relations in the international context by fostering the development of national industrial relations specialists; enabling knowledge transfer and sharing through research and education in labour relations; hosting global congresses; and fostering international studies of aspects of labour relations.

EXERCISE

What roles do the ILO and WTO play in setting international labour standards? What are the differences and similarities in their respective approaches and responsibilities? Check out the websites of both institutions for more information about their goals and activities.

■ Meso-level stakeholders

Although ILR refers to the rules, resources and relations of labour in the international context, the terms of internationally agreed standards and actions are always subject to renegotiation and wide interpretation at meso-level (that is, nationally or locally). Here, the conditions, terms, rules and resources of labour relations are negotiated among national actors, which may include a configuration of the state, trade unions, employers' associations and other economic, political and social lobbies. Nation states must ratify ILS in order to adopt them as national standards and so ILS themselves are subject to local reinterpretation; this process allows for the divergence of interests across nation states and among **meso-level stakeholders** in each nation state. Therefore, a range of nation states may interpret a single set of standards in multiple ways and the unique institutional setting in each country may affect the form of the ratified standards.

meso-level stakeholders Actors at the national level, including workers' collectives, the state, employers' associations, lobbies, interest groups and society.

Further, many institutions, networks and interest groups seek to influence and shape the policy and practice of ILR not only at the meso-level but also at macro- and micro-levels. Some national contexts offer plentiful opportunities for institutional actors such as employers' unions, trade unions, lobbies and interest groups to speak to the international arena.

EXERCISE

Identify a country and search for labour standards agencies including the state regulator, trade unions, employers' associations and other stakeholders and discuss their effectiveness in their ability to enforce and/or oppose ILS at the national level.

◼ Micro-level stakeholders

Multinational, international and global organisations are sites in which ILR are practised and ILS are implemented; at the micro-level, the terms and conditions of those labour relations and standards are played out. **Micro-level stakeholders**, including organisational leaders and gatekeepers, can interpret, promote or resist standards, depending on their local tradition and institutional customs. Studying micro-level practices is essential to identifying potential gaps between ILS and organisational practices and to locating disparities in how different regions, sectors and branches in organisations are implementing standards.

micro-level stakeholders Actors at the organisational level, including managers, workers, employers, pressure groups, shareholders, society and interest groups.

Organisations operate in a relational context, in which they interact with other significant labour relations institutions such as trade unions, works councils and the state; with external stakeholders such as society and the overlapping institutions of education, employment, justice, health and safety; and with social institutions of family, religion, tradition and customs. Therefore, any attempt to implement labour standards at the organisational level should consider the interplay between organisational processes and these institutional and individual actors inside and outside the organisation. Civil Society Organisations (CSOs) are a remarkable example of emergent stakeholders, with their advocacy of identity-based standards (Fransen & Burgoon, 2013); one such organisation, the International Lesbian, Gay, Bisexual, Trans and Intersex Association (ILGA) promotes the equality of sexual orientation at work. Organisations on either the international stage (e.g. Amnesty International) or the local scene can address specific or broad concerns on labour relations. They can launch campaigns and effect changes by galvanising support for a range of causes through social and political action.

In summary, Table 8.1 shows the multilevel model of ILS and lists the key stakeholders for each level. It also presents the main focus of ILS activities at each level.

Table 8.1 Multilevel models of international labour relations – stakeholders and focus		
Level	Key stakeholders	Focus
Macro	Nation states Global, multinational and international organisations Trade unions and employers unions Regulators of international and supranational conventions	International negotiations on political, economic, social and ethical terms and conditions for labour relations.
Meso	The state Trade unions Employer associations Social, economic and political lobbies	Interpretation of the international standards at the national level among key actors. Definition and interpretation of terms and conditions, drawing on local interests.
Micro	Internal and external organisational actors Leaders in the organisation	Interpretation of standards through institutional strategic lenses and implementation at the level of practice.

■ Reasons for meso- and micro-level adoption of ILS

To understand ILR, we must explore the reasons why nation states (at meso-level) and MNCs (at micro-level) adopt labour standards (Brown, 2000). There are three distinctly different political processes for the adoption of labour standards in the international arena. These are the principled, solidarity and voluntary approaches, which overlap to cover the spectrum of reasons for the adoption of labour standards.

■ *The principled approach*

First, nation states and multinationals may choose to adopt labour standards unilaterally based on a principled stance. For example, they can use trade sanctions (e.g. suspension

of trade relations) to enforce compliance to certain standards of a political, economic and social nature, including
labour standards. In the 1980s, a number of countries introduced principled trade sanctions to force the South African
government to abolish its apartheid regime. Unilateral trade
sanctions are often saved for severe cases of non-compliance
with, or breach of expectations of, a nation state. The **principled approach** may draw on rationales drawn from eco-
nomic thought (Palley, 2004) or from political or social philosophy (Brown, 2000) to
support the unilateral imposition of labour standards. Some countries also choose to
adopt a principled stance against certain standards when they clash with the dominant
economic, social, or political choices and customs of the country.

principled approach A nation state or MNC's
unilateral imposition of trade restrictions on a
country that does not comply with a set of
agreed labour standards to which the nation or
MNC agrees.

EXERCISE

Search online for 'trade restrictions' and 'labour standards' plus a country (or regional block) of your choice.
Identify sources that illustrate how the country you have chosen imposed trade restrictions on another
country that did not comply with its labour standards. Prepare a class presentation based on the information
you found.

■ *The solidarity approach*

Solidarity or alliance behaviour (commonly known as a
'multilateral enforcement model') among countries and
organisations is the second approach nations and MNCs
may adopt in aiming to enforce labour standards. In this
model, a group of countries and organisations forms a
multilateral alliance to enforce compliance with an agreed
set of labour standards. The EU is one such solidarity
model, as the member states agree on standards of labour

solidarity approach A nation state or MNC's
multilateral alliance, formed with the aim of
enforcing compliance to an agreed set of labour
standards; also known as the multilateral
enforcement model.

EXERCISE

Choose a sector and a country. Search online for alliances that unions in your chosen sector have formed to
promote labour standards in their home country and/or internationally. Have the unions formed an
international coalition? What are their core labour standards and to what extent do the standards converge
with the ILO conventions?

including terms, conditions and mobility and enforce them within the EU. Another prominent example is NAFTA, a trade agreement between the United States, Canada and Mexico; although it seeks to enforce common standards of labour, NAFTA takes a less coercive approach to imposing common labour standards than does the EU.

■ *The voluntary approach*

Voluntary adoption of labour standards is the third approach nation states and MNCs may adopt. Using this approach, organisations choose to adopt ILS on their own initiative without the need for coercive measures (e.g. litigation). The voluntary model involves a spectrum of activities at the organisational level, including championing of labour standards by leaders in the organisation, which allows labour standards to 'cascade' down the organisational hierarchy to the level of individual practice. Organisations can choose to apply for approval under certain labour standards schemes: for example, the SA 8000 standards. The granting body for these standards, Social Accountability International (www.sa-intl.org), is a multi-stakeholder non-governmental organisation (NGO) that aims to advance the human rights of workers internationally. A company with SA 8000 certification is indicating to concerned customers that it has voluntarily complied with a set of labour standards (Gilbert & Rasche, 2007). Although companies do act voluntarily, we find that the term 'voluntarism' does not sufficiently acknowledge the coercive power of customers and other stakeholders in encouraging organisations to adopt measures to meet labour standards.

voluntary approach A nation state or MNC's adoption of ILS on their own initiative, without the threat of coercive measures such as litigation.

EXERCISE

Identify an organisation which adopts SA 8000 and locate its annual report, in which you may find a comment on its implementation. What barriers to implementation has the organisation encountered? To what extent do its targeted activities converge with the core standards of the ILO?

■ Implications of ILS for international assignees

Variations in labour standards require that international assignees must acquaint themselves with labour standards in countries to which they are assigned. They need to understand the legal context, institutional arrangements and labour relations practices in their destination country. Yet such understanding is not sufficient to be able to operate effectively in a new national setting. International assignees also need to develop competencies for influencing, shaping and engaging with labour relations in a host country.

■ Implications for international HR managers

It is important to note that the home-country tradition of MNCs, in terms of union recognition, use of child labour and management of equality, diversity and inclusion, can affect the transposition and local adoption of labour standards in other countries. However, the debate on this issue is multifaceted. Hamill (1983, 1984) illustrated that United States firms had a weaker propensity to recognise trade unions than did the United Kingdom and Europe with their traditionally stronger industrial relations controls. US and European MNCs may still adopt different strategies for implementing labour standards in their branch networks. However, Muller (1998) identified that even in the case of Germany, which has a highly regulated employment relations system, the presence of a home-country tradition or perspective does not necessarily block the transposition of labour relations strategies.

HR managers in MNCs need to recognise international regulation, national discussions and local practices in terms of labour relations. Differences in economic, political and legal systems across countries require local interpretation and implementation of ILS. As a result, MNCs cannot offer a single, unified strategy in this area, nor can they delegate these matters to national branches, as localised labour standards may generate negative stakeholder reactions when they jar with international standards. MNCs, with their global recognition, often operate in a volatile environment in terms of labour relations disputes. As a result, they are more likely engage with debates on the ILS as a strategic priority.

■ Conclusion

In this chapter, we have explored the field of ILR, an area of research and business practice that explores how stakeholders, such as international organisations, supranational bodies, trade unions, the state, society and industry, seek to shape the conditions, standards and relations of labour. We saw that a number of patterns underpin the transformation of international industrial relations, including the withdrawal of the state from labour regulation and the diminution of the collective power of worker representation in the traditional tripartite relationship between workers, employers and the state, as the power balance has become skewed towards the interests of employers and corporations.

Next, we examined ILS, aspirational standards that are agreed on and enshrined in international, supranational and regional conventions. Such conventions seek to reconcile differences in national terms and conditions of labour and to converge on common standards based on shared economic, social and ethical concerns. However, ILS remain controversial and debates about their interpretation and implementation indicate a gap between the aspirational standards set out in conventions and what is achieved in practice. There are also issues of the affordability of ILS, as economically stronger countries tend to perform better in terms of their compliance with standards. International, national and organisational stakeholders play varied roles in shaping, agreeing, interpreting and implementing ILR and ILS. While international actors shape, set and monitor the debate on ILS, national stakeholders are required to interpret and devolve responsibility to the level of practice using effective campaigns and regulations. Organisations are where labour standards are practised and experienced. Therefore, the organisational stakeholders are important at the level of effective implementation. We set out broad and interrelated reasons why nation states and MNCs choose to adopt ILR. First, they can adopt a principled stance and impose trade restrictions on countries that do not comply with labour standards the nation or firm has adopted. Second, solidarity among nation states and organisations in terms of alliances may lead others to comply with certain standards. Finally, countries and organisations may adopt ILS on a voluntary basis without the need for coercive measures.

▪ Take-home messages

- International labour relations take place in multi-actor, multilevel contexts.
- The historical transformation of labour relations in the international context reveals the significance of struggles for power and influence over standards of labour, and terms and conditions of work.
- International labour standards are often defined globally but it is at the local level that people receive and respond to them. As such, ILS remain aspirational and are highly contested.
- There are macro-, meso- and micro-level actors in ILR and their respective roles and influence is highly variable in crafting, transposing, implementing and monitoring ILR and ILS.
- There are three different approaches to adoption of ILS: principled, solidaristic and voluntary approach.

▪ Closing the learning loop

1. What are international labour relations?
2. Why do countries have different stances on labour standards?
3. What or who are the key stakeholders in international labour relations, and what roles do they play?
4. Why do nation states and organisations choose to adopt international labour standards?
5. In what ways are international labour relations complex, and how does this complexity affect the implementation of standards?

CASE STUDIES 8.1 AND 8.2

The following case studies illustrate that, although individual countries may be signatories of one or more standard, there is often a gap between the aspirations ILS set out and the workplace practices that companies use. The case studies help to identify complex, multilevel reasons for the existence of this gap. Case study 8.1 concerns the death of a 13-year-old boy, Ahmet Yildiz, in an industrial 'accident' in Turkey. Case study 8.2 discusses a wildcat miners' strike in Marikana district, South Africa, and its violent consequences.

Case study 8.1   The death of Ahmet Yildiz

Ahmet Yildiz was a 13-year-old Turkish boy from the southern Mediterranean city of Adana. He was the youngest child of a family of seven children. He was attending school and was working in a plastics manufacturing firm after school, to pay for his school expenses. He earned 100 YTL (approximately AU$35) per week from his job at the factory. His family thought that he was making tea and cleaning in the factory.

One day, a manager from the factory took an injured Ahmet to hospital, where Ahmet died. Although the boss claimed Ahmet's injuries were the result of a traffic accident, doctors identified that heavy blows to both sides of his head were the cause of death. The suspicious doctors passed the case to police, who discovered that Ahmet had been operating a pressing machine in the plant when there was an industrial accident, and detained the factory owner.

The case of Ahmet Yildaz highlights that, although Turkey has ratified international agreements that abolish child labour, companies there continue to use child labour; several national and international reports have also underlined Turkey's problem in this area, including one remarkable report by the ILO.

This case was an urgent reminder that a comprehensive strategy to tackle child labour must consider multiple stakeholders, including businesspeople, employers, families, government agencies (education, healthcare, police) and trade unions.

Case study 8.2   The Marikana massacre

In 2012, wildcat strikes at a Lonmin-owned mine in Marikana district, South Africa, culminated in violent outbursts between the national police service and miners, drawing widespread international attention. The clashes killed 47 people and injured many workers.

This was a very complex case. The violent clashes involved four parties, each with a different agenda: the leadership of the National Union of Mineworkers (NUM), the striking members of the NUM, Lonmin company security forces and the South African police force. It was reported that the clashes began with an inter-union rivalry between leadership and members of the union, when NUM leadership fired shots at the NUM members who had launched the wildcat strike. The violence grew and many workers, policy and security personnel were killed or injured, leading the media to call it the 'Marikana massacre'.

After rounds of mediation, the wildcat strikers accepted a deal to return to work: a 22 per cent pay rise and a one-off payment. As commentators have observed, the miners' unrest had arisen from poor economic conditions, a high unemployment rate and the lack of local affordable accommodation for workers. The absence of a tradition of collective bargaining in the South African mining sector and the poor economic climate that platinum mines faced at the time also influenced the poor terms and conditions at Marikana.

The Marikana case involved a complex set of circumstances and in such cases we would expect the solution to be correspondingly complex. It would be likely to include development activities in the organisation, among corporate leaders, union leadership and members, the community and workers at all levels. The international community would also need to play a role, as it would set, enforce and broker labour standards.

Case study questions

After reading case studies 8.1 and 8.2, conduct independent web research into the incidents they describe, and answer the following questions.

1. Which macro-, meso- and micro-level stakeholders may need to be involved in responding to:
   - an individual incident such as those described in the case studies
   - systemic problems that come to light as a result of an incident?
2. If you were a national regulator of labour standards, how would you deal with an incident such as those described in the case studies? Explain your response, considering the principled, solidarity and voluntary approaches to adoption of international standards.

» ACTIVITIES

Web research and presentation

Download a comparative table from the International Labour Organization web-site (www.ilo.org), showing countries' compliance with ILS. Using the internet, research reasons for differences between countries and potential solutions to resistance and non-compliance. Present your research to the class.

Group discussion

Form groups. Each student in the group should choose one of the stakeholders shown below and talk about the particular interests of that stakeholder in labour relations. Next, the group should discuss what each of the selected stakeholders would need to do to ensure compliance with labour standards, based on the two case studies in this chapter.

Stakeholders

- Business owners
- Consumers in a country that buys products
- Consumers in the home country

- Education sector
- Employers
- Employers' associations
- Families
- Health sector
- Local community
- Non-union workers
- Police service
- State regulator for labour relations
- Trade union leadership
- Trade union members

Online resources

- For instructors: answers to activities; long media article with questions; additional questions and answers.
- For students: further reading; answers to case studies; IHRM in practice.

References

Anner, M. S. (2011). *Solidarity transformed*. Ithaca, NY: Cornell University Press.

Baccini, L. and Koenig-Archibugi, M. (2012). Why do states commit to international labor standards? The importance of 'rivalry' and 'friendship', *LSE Working Papers Series*. 23 August.

Brown, D. K. (2000). International trade and core labour standards: A survey of the recent literature, *OECD Labour Market and Social Policy Occasional Papers*, 43. Paris: OECD Publishing.

Charnovitz, S. (1987). Influence of international labour standards on the world trading regime: A historical overview, *International Labour Review*, 126: 565.

Dundon, T., Wilkinson, A., Marchington, M. and Ackers, P. (2004). The meanings and purpose of employee voice, *International Journal of Human Resource Management*, 15(6): 1149–70.

Fransen, L. and Burgoon, B. (2013), Global labour-standards advocacy by European civil society organizations: Trends and developments, *British Journal of Industrial Relations*. doi: 10.1111/bjir.12017.

Gilbert, D. U. and Rasche, A. (2007). Discourse ethics and social accountability: The ethics of SA 8000, *Business Ethics Quarterly*, 17(2): 187–216.

Hamill, J. (1983). The labour relations practices of foreign-owned and indigenous firms, *Employee Relations*, 5(1): 14–16.

Hamill, J. (1984), Labour relations decision making within multinational corporations, *Industrial Relations Journal*, 15: 30–4.

Jonsen, K., Tatli, A., Özbilgin, M. F. and Bell, M. P. (2013). The tragedy of the uncommons: Reframing workforce diversity, *Human Relations*, 66(2): 271–94.

Lipietz, A. (1997). The post-Fordist world: Labour relations, international hierarchy and global ecology, *Review of International Political Economy*, 4(1): 1–41.

Marginson, P., Armstrong, P., Edwards, P. K. and Purcell, J. (1995). Extending beyond borders: Multinational companies and the international management of labour, *International Journal of Human Resource Management*, 6(3): 702–19.

Muller, M. (1998). Human resource and industrial relations practices of UK and US multinationals in Germany, *International Journal of Human Resource Management*, 9(4): 732–49.

Özbilgin, M. and Tatli, A. (2011). Mapping out the field of equality and diversity: Rise of individualism and voluntarism, *Human Relations*, 64(9): 1229–53.

Palley, T. I. (2004). The economic case for international labour standards, *Cambridge Journal of Economics*, 28(1): 21–36.

Pries, L. and Seeliger, M. (2013). Work and employment relations in a globalized world: The emerging texture of transnational labour regulation, *Global Labour Journal*, 4(1): 26–47.

Purcell, J. (1993). The challenge of human resource management for industrial relations research and practice, *International Journal of Human Resource Management*, 4(3): 511–27.

Rodriguez, P., Siegel, D. S., Hillman, A. and Eden, L. (2006). Three lenses on the multinational enterprise: Politics, corruption, and corporate social responsibility, *Journal of International Business Studies*, 37(6): 733–46.

Townsend, K., Wilkinson, A. and Burgess, J. (forthcoming). Routes to partial success: Collaborative employment relations and employee engagement, *International Journal of Human Resource Management*, 1–16.

9

Reputation in the international context

William S. Harvey

■ Learning objectives

- To introduce the concept of corporate reputation.
- To highlight the importance of reputation for organisations as well as for cities and countries.
- To underscore the connection between reputation and IHRM.
- To emphasise the significance of scale when measuring reputation.
- To provide an overview of reputation and its significance for different stakeholders.
- To demonstrate how and why reputation is important for talent, international assignees and skilled migrants.

■ Learning outcomes

After reading this chapter, students will be able to:
- understand the concept of corporate reputation
- acknowledge how reputations can benefit and damage organisations acknowledge that reputation is closely linked to IHRM
- explain why reputation is important for potential, existing and former employees, and how they can shape corporate reputations
- recognise that international assignees and skilled migrants move to countries, cities and companies because of their reputations, and that they can both create and destroy such reputations.

■ Introduction

Reputation is a collective assessment of a country, institution, organisation, group or even individual. Hence, it can be applied at different levels of analysis, including the macro (e.g. countries, regions and cities), meso (e.g. institutions and organisations) and micro (e.g. groups and individuals). Reputation is a 'collective assessment' because many dimensions are judged. For example, in the context of an organisation, these elements might include the quality of the product or service or the calibre of the

corporate reputation The collective assessment of a company made by particular stakeholders in relation to its competitors.

employees (Fombrun, 2012). This '**corporate reputation**' also depends on a specific group of stakeholders such as investors, customers and employees. Finally, it is judged in relation to a reference group. The reputation of the Coca-Cola Company, for example, is benchmarked against its major competitors, such as PepsiCo; in the same way, the tennis player Roger Federer's reputation may be positioned in relation to the reputation of his long-term rival, Rafael Nadal.

Context is an important starting point for reputation because we need to understand which stakeholders are forming perceptions (e.g. employees, customers or competitors), the location of those stakeholders (e.g. in China, the United States or the UK) and the time frame in which the perceptions form (e.g. 2011, 2012 or 2013). This is particularly significant in the context of IHRM because people in organisations have very specific and also different contexts, which will shape their own individual reputations and those of their organisations as well as the regions and countries in which they reside. Once we have an understanding of the contexts, we can begin to examine individual perceptions. This is intricately linked to HRM because people are at the centre of how reputation is judged (perception); as people shape the perceptions of others, we can measure corporate reputation through them. A female employee of McDonald's, for instance, may hold personal perceptions of the quality of customer service at the company. In addition, her own behaviour as an employee of McDonald's will shape the perceptions of others about the quality of customer service the company offers. Countries and companies are gaining greater visibility internationally and people are increasingly moving across the world for professional and lifestyle opportunities, and so reputation is no longer a local, but a global phenomenon.

The macro-, meso- and micro-levels are all relevant to an understanding of reputation. Geography, for example, may be considered at multiple levels, from macro- and meso-levels (international and national) to micro-level (local community). Similarly, time can be considered at any scale ranging from a broad time frame (a decade or year) to a narrow one (a month, day, hour or minute). The use of scales has practical importance because we can analyse different results at different scales; for example, the reputation of the Government of the People's Republic of China in 2013 may be quite different to its reputation in May 2013 or on 15 May 2013. When we combine different scales, such as time frame and geography, the measurement becomes more complex because the reputation of the Government of the People's Republic of China in Shanghai on 15 May 2013 may not match its reputation in Beijing on 15 May 2013. Scale is not only relevant to contexts, but also to perceptions. We could ask, for example, residents of Shanghai and Beijing what perceptions they hold about the People's Republic of China (macro), the Central Politburo Standing Committee of the Communist Party of China (meso) or the President of the People's Republic of China (micro). Again, these perceptions are highly likely to vary. In short, it is vital to understand different scales because they determine the types of reputation we are measuring. Of course, there is no right or wrong scale for measuring reputation and each has advantages and disadvantages. Whichever scale we use, we should be transparent about exactly what kind of reputation we are measuring.

Measuring reputation at different scales is highly relevant in the context of IHRM because the results affect the mobility decisions of organisations as well as individuals. For example, positive country, regional and city reputations will arguably make organisations more likely to deploy their talent in such places and increase the propensity of talented people to want to move there, while negative country, regional and city reputations are likely to have the opposite effect.

The importance of reputation

Reputation is also significant for IHRM because companies that have positive reputations are able to attract talented employees, while companies that have negative reputations find it difficult to attract high-quality workers. Many organisations now operate on an international scale, which means that they have global reputations, enabling them to attract workers from multiple countries. Companies with positive global reputations can tap into a much larger pool of labour than companies with negative global reputations. Reputable organisations are also better able to retain existing employees than less reputable organisations (labour market reputation is discussed in more detail below). This is important because the cost of replacing talented workers is expensive. According to the Australian Human Resource Institute (AHRI, 2008), the cost of turnover for organisations for an average employee salary of $55 660.80 is 75 per cent of that salary, which is considered a conservative estimate.

Reputation is vital for organisations because it is an 'intangible asset'. It is intangible because it is not physical in nature (e.g. an iPad), and it is an asset because it can hold tremendous value for organisations, particularly global ones (e.g. Apple Inc.). Reputation is valuable for organisations because customers assume that companies with good reputations sell high-quality products and services; if a potential customer has no prior experience with the company but it is reputable, they are more likely to buy its products and services because they feel confident that its products and services are reliable and of a high quality (Roberts & Dowling, 2002). In the same way, the more difficult it is for new customers to assess the quality of products and services, the more likely they are to rely on signals of quality such as reputation (Rindova et al., 2005). Existing customers are also more likely to repeat-buy the products and services of a reputable company, particularly if the reputation is consistent with their positive experience of a product or service. Apple, for example, has gained a reputation for both producing high-quality products and for having a loyal customer base.

In summary, companies with positive reputations in consumer and client markets hold a competitive advantage over companies with weaker reputations because they are in a better position to sell products and services (Fombrun, 1996). An additional bonus for companies with positive reputations is they are able to charge premium prices for products and services. McKinsey & Company, for example, arguably holds the strongest reputation among global management consulting companies and also reputedly charges the highest prices to its clients. Of course, customers and clients do not *want* to pay a premium, but they are *willing* to do so if they perceive the product or service to be higher quality than other options; reputation provides them with some indication of likely quality outcomes (Pfarrer, Pollock & Rindova, 2010). This is particularly important in certain industries, such as professional services, because potential clients cannot assess the quality of a service before they purchase it. An engineering company seeking a law firm to represent it during a merger and acquisition, for example, does not know what quality of service the available firms will provide and so may well select the firm with the best reputation.

While there are many positive consequences for organisations that hold good reputations, the opposite is also true for organisations who hold negative reputations (see table 9.1). The London Stock Exchange share price of the oil and gas company British Petroleum (BP) was £639.70 on 19 April 2010, a day before the Deepwater Horizon oil spill in the Gulf of Mexico. On 31 June, its share price had fallen to just £304.60. In other words, the valuation of BP had more than halved in light of the disaster. During this period, BP received unprecedented criticism from the federal and state governments in the United States, the global media, non-government organisations and interest groups and competitor organisations, which distanced themselves from the company. This is an extreme example of how negative reputation can have major negative financial, legal and social repercussions for organisations.

Table 9.1 Consequences of positive and negative reputations

Consequences of a positive reputation	Consequences of a negative reputation
A company experiences increased sales and investments.	A company experiences decreased sales and investments.
Customers assume high quality.	Customers assume low quality.
A company may charge premium prices.	A company must charge lower prices.
A company can attract and retain workers.	A company may lose potential and existing workers.
A company can create media and public attention.	A company is subject to media and public scrutiny.
A company may overemphasise leadership quality.	Customers may lose faith in leadership quality.

Organisations that build a consistent reputation over the long term tend to become more prominent (that is, a greater range of stakeholders are familiar with their products, services and activities) and enjoy enhanced **status** (the ranking and prestige assigned to organisations). If organisations continue to build their prominence and status then they will likely become '**celebrity firms**'. Celebrity firms are those that receive a large degree of attention from the media and the general public because they serve as examples of organisations adopting bold or unusual action in a given industry (Rindova, Pollock & Hayward, 2006). Google, for example, has been consistently ranked by *Fortune* magazine as one of the most admired companies and in part this is a function of its long-term commitment to bold initiatives, in line with the following mission statement: 'Google's mission is to organise the world's information and make it universally accessible and useful' (Google, 2013). Although celebrity firms can greatly benefit from their high-profile status, they can also suffer from it. The automobile company, Toyota, for example, has historically held a reputation for reliability (Ahrens, 2010), but in light of a number of reports of problems with the acceleration pedal in some of its vehicles in 2009 and 2010 it has had to recall several million vehicles and has suffered a tarnished reputation as well as significant financial losses (Madslien, 2010).

> **status** Prestige and ranking assigned to an organisation, relative to similar organisations.
>
> **celebrity firms** Companies that receive high levels of media and public attention because of their distinctive actions, cultures, identities and leadership styles.

Organisations can also benefit and suffer when their chief executive officer is a **celebrity CEO**; that is, when journalists attribute the outcomes of organisations, such as their financial performance, to the actions of their leaders (Hayward, Rindova & Pollock, 2004). In other words, the media gives the behaviour and influence of a CEO disproportionate weight in assessing an organisation's positive or negative performance. This is particularly the case with leaders who have founded companies that have subsequently become celebrity firms. Sir Richard Branson, for example, has become synonymous with Virgin, the international investment group he founded. The same is also true of former leaders of organisations. Hayward, Rindova and Pollock (2004) cite the example of Jack Welch, former chairman and CEO of General Electric, revered by the business press for his transformation of the company's fortunes between 1981 and 2001. Yet much of the business press vehemently criticised Welch for implying that White House employment figures released during the 2012 presidential election campaign had been tampered with. The different responses of the media, which could equally be applied to other celebrity CEOs such as Warren Buffett of Berkshire Hathaway, illustrate how celebrity leaders can both create and harm an organisation's reputation. Sanders and Hambrick (2007) use a baseball analogy to describe how celebrity status can enable organisations to 'hit home runs' and to 'strike out'. This is highly relevant to IHRM because attracting and retaining high profile and internationally recognised talent can be both an asset and a burden.

> **celebrity CEO** A chief executive officer who receives high levels of media and public attention and who is credited with the actions and performance of the organisation.

▪ Reputation and talent

The reputation of organisations is closely aligned with IHRM. The literature on the 'war for talent', for example, emphasises the importance for organisations of attracting, retaining and developing employees (Chambers et al., 1998; Michaels, Handfield-Jones & Axelrod, 2001). The primary argument is that the skills of talented individuals are a source of competitive advantage for organisations and that this source is now global in nature (Beechler & Woodward, 2009). Therefore, organisations need to use innovative strategies to attract the best workers, providing good workplace environments to positively engage potential and existing employees and creating career development initiatives so that high-potential employees have the opportunity to thrive in the workplace. This is particularly true today because the service sector has come to dominate many national economies and the quality of employees is the unique selling point of organisations in that sector. There has been some criticism of the war for talent. Pfeffer (2001), for example, argues that an overemphasis on talent can suppress teamwork and discourage people from listening and learning; Gladwell (2002) suggests that too much focus is placed on individual intelligence, rather than on systems, processes and communication. Such debates are important to IHRM because they influence, both locally and globally, organisations' abilities to attract, recruit, select, train, develop and measure talented employees.

Despite reservations about the overemphasis on talent, the academic evidence shows that potential employees are attracted to companies with higher reputations (Hannon & Milkovich, 1996). Research with the Careers Service and Student Union at the University of Oxford, for example, found that an organisation's reputation played an important role in determining whether undergraduate and postgraduate students applied for a position there, with students showing a much stronger tendency to apply for celebrity firms than for less well-known companies (Harvey, 2011a). The findings showed not only that potential employees' perceptions about organisations influenced their decisions about applications, but also that the perceptions of family members, peers and careers advisers also contributed. In short, reputation in different guises played a significant role in shaping where potential employees applied for jobs.

Existing employees also shape reputations because they act as ambassadors for their organisations, which is known as **labour market reputation** (Harvey & Morris, 2012). Gray and Balmer (1998) argue that a positive reputation among employees is important because it improves morale and productivity, which then influences the impressions of people outside the company. For example, if employees feel disengaged and unhappy with their organisation and they are asked to attend a university careers fair on behalf of their employer, it is likely that potential employees will sense their discontent; this will influence both their impression of the organisation and their decision whether or not to apply for a job at the company. The academic evidence suggests that employees are becoming increasingly demanding of employers and that they care more about

labour market reputation Reputations of organisations that are shaped by employees.

working for companies that hold strong reputations than receiving higher salaries or better professional development opportunities (Pruzan, 2001).

The role of reputation among employees is likely to become more important for organisations as the transfer of information online accelerates. With greater use of mobile devices such as smart phones and tablet computers, the growth of information-sharing websites and the rise of online media, it is becoming easier and faster for people to share and learn about the activities of organisations. In an example of how quickly a company's reputation can change, in 2009 two employees of Domino's Pizza filmed and shared on YouTube footage of one of them preparing sandwiches for delivery while putting cheese up his nose and nasal mucus on the sandwiches. In two days, more than one million people had viewed the video and the company faced a public relations disaster, with one YouGov poll suggesting that the perception of its quality among consumers had rapidly changed from positive to negative (Clifford, 2009). Although this is an extreme example of how employees can affect a company's reputation, it serves to show that modern forms of online information sharing enable employees to shape the reputations of their employers proactively rather than reactively.

Employees are also increasingly tending to work for multiple employers in the course of their careers rather than for one career-long employer; Arthur and Rousseau (1996) use the term '**boundaryless career**' to describe this tendency. This has important implications in terms of reputation because former employees can also shape the reputations of their former employers. Greg Smith, a former executive director of the investment bank, Goldman Sachs, for example, wrote the following about his former

> **boundaryless career** A career built by working for multiple employers rather than through a career-long role with one employer.

employer in the *New York Times*: 'I can honestly say that the environment now is as toxic and destructive as I have ever seen it' (Smith, 2012). Similarly, Michael Woodford, a former CEO and president of the Japanese camera company, Olympus, not only blew the whistle on systemic accountancy fraud in the company in 2012, but also suggested that such problems were entrenched in Japanese business culture (Woodford, 2012). The evidence from the business media as well as from academia suggests that senior employees, whether current or former members of organisations, have greater clout in shaping corporate reputation than junior members, although the latter are still highly significant and should not be underestimated (Harvey & Morris, 2012).

■ Reputation, international assignees and skilled migrants

Organisations are not the only ones sourcing talented workers from abroad as part of their competitive strategies; employees are also seeking out opportunities to work for multiple employers in different countries throughout their careers. Although there are many types of migrant with varying skills levels, we focus here

international assignees People who are transferred abroad to another job post through their existing organisation

skilled migrants A well-educated individual who moves from one country to another for work.

on **international assignees** and **skilled migrants** (SMs) – that is, migrants who hold a tertiary level qualification or equivalent training and at least three years of paid or unpaid employment since qualification or completion of training (Harvey & Groutsis, 2012). International assignees are transferred abroad through their organisations and SMs move abroad either to work for a new employer or independently. Both groups are significant in terms of reputation because they make a major contribution to the economies in their host and home countries (Saxenian, 2006; Harvey, 2011b). They are influenced by the reputation of countries as well as organisations when making decisions about where they live and work, and they also influence the reputations that other people hold towards the same countries and organisations. Gaining experience of working in other countries is also expected by many global employers and considered an important means of climbing the career ladder, particularly in certain fields such as professional services (Beaverstock, 2002). With countries and companies becoming more integrated into the global economy, it is likely that the role of international assignees and SMs will grow in the future.

In his 'theory of migration', Lee (1966) suggested that people move because of a combination of **push** and **pull factors**. Push factors are created when people feel dissatisfied with their current location, causing them to wish to leave, while pull factors are created when people are attracted to other appealing work locations, causing them to wish to move. Employees interested in working overseas are pulled to countries and companies whose reputations appeal to them. The actions of governments and organisations shape such reputations: for example, the Singaporean Prime Minister, Lee Hsien Loong, has actively promoted Singapore's wish to attract and retain foreign workers and has stressed their importance to the country's economy. Such actions have led to many foreign workers moving to Singapore, which now has a strong reputation for welcoming skilled and ambitious professionals from overseas (Ong, 2007). Another example is Start-Up Chile, an initiative started in 2010 by a Chilean businessman, Nicholás Shea, who has pulled technology talent from abroad by offering promising young firms $40 000 and a year's visa to work on their ideas in Chile. To date, 500 companies and 900 entrepreneurs from 37 countries have participated in this initiative, presumably because the country has gained a reputation for being easy to work in and for offering a good lifestyle (Economist, 2012a).

push/pull factors Factors that encourage (pull) or compel (push) people to move from one location to another.

SMs are not only interested in workplace factors, but also attracted to the glamour of working abroad for reputable companies. In South Korea, for instance, many Indian IT professionals have moved to the country because they wish to work abroad for a celebrity company, such as Samsung (Kim & Lee, 2012). SMs are also attracted to countries, and particularly cities, that have a reputation for a good lifestyle and quality of life (Harvey, 2011b, 2011c). *The Economist*'s (2012b) Liveability Ranking and Mercer's Quality of Living Survey (2012) are two examples of popular rankings that shape the reputations of world cities among SMs. In short, the reputations of countries, cities and organisations play a critical role in people's decisions about where to live and work.

International assignees and SMs can also actively shape the reputations of countries, regions and organisations. Saxenian (2006), for example, argues that Chinese, Taiwanese, Indian and Israeli engineers and scientists have been instrumental in building the success and reputation of Silicon Valley in the United States as the world's leading high-technology cluster. Over many decades, these engineers and scientists have also helped to build the reputations of their home countries as producers of highly skilled graduates in IT and engineering. A number of these professionals have returned to their home countries to start up companies, which has facilitated the growth of the area's reputation. Chinese returnees, for example, have helped to develop Zhongguancun as a very reputable high-technology region in Beijing (Chen, 2008). Similarly, returning Indian entrepreneurs have played a critical role in building Bangalore's reputation as a leading information technology cluster (Saxenian, 2006). Although returning SMs have been instrumental in building the reputations of their home and host countries, they are able to build the reputations of both places no matter which of them they currently work in, because of the value of their transnational social networks. These networks create cross-border business opportunities that would not be possible if the SMs did not have the business and cultural experience of living and working in both countries (Harvey, 2008, 2012). For example, a Chinese scientist who has experience of working in the United States has the advantage of knowing the business and cultural climate in both countries, which can help foster transnational business networks and opportunities between the two.

Finally, reputation can be built through various intermediaries who broker meso- and micro-level knowledge. In terms of country reputation, there are a number of intermediaries such as governments, migration agents, online forums and media organisations, who shape the perceptions of potential migrants about other countries. In the context of British expatriates, for example, the BBC (2012) produced a series of television program in 2012 called *Wanted Down Under*, in which British families were given the opportunity to live in Australia for a week before deciding whether they would emigrate. This is an example of an **intermediary** (the BBC) shaping how other people (the viewing audience) form perceptions of other countries, through the production, editing and presentation of the program. In terms of corporate reputation, there are many labour market intermediaries who shape the impressions of potential and existing employees. Vault (2013), for example, is an organisation that seeks to provide high-potential professionals with insider information and advice about the best employer organisations. Such rankings have an important bearing on whether potential and existing employees apply for, and accept, positions at particular organisations.

> **intermediary** A person or group who acts as an agent between two people or groups.

■ Conclusion

In this chapter, we have examined reputation as a collective assessment related to a particular group made with reference to an organisation's competitors. While reputation is an intangible asset, it provides organisations with tangible results, both positive and negative, and is closely related to the key concepts of IHRM, such as the attraction and retention of global workers. Advantages and disadvantages to companies arise from the presence of certain individuals, such as celebrity CEOs, and organisations, such as celebrity firms. At an individual level, potential and existing employees are becoming more interested in reputation and more actively engaged in shaping it. At the same time, employees are now less bounded to organisations and have become powerful actors in the creation and destruction of reputations. At a global scale, too, countries and organisations are experiencing more workers moving across the world, and international assignees and skilled migrants are an important part of this trend. Talented workers are influenced to move by not only corporate reputations, but also city and country reputations. International assignees, SMs and intermediaries are therefore important agents in shaping country and corporate reputations. Finally, this chapter has demonstrated that reputation is multifaceted, becoming more widespread and more significant for individuals, organisations, cities, regions and countries.

■ Take-home messages

- Reputation is a collective assessment of an organisation in relation to its competitors, based on the judgements of a particular group.
- Reputation is a vital intangible asset for companies and can provide positive and negative returns.
- Reputation can be measured at the macro-, meso- and micro-levels.
- Much attention has been paid to the effect of reputation on organisations, but reputation also plays an important role for individuals, cities, regions and countries.
- Reputation can change rapidly, both positively and negatively, through new forms of technology and communication.
- A range of intermediaries can shape country and corporate reputation.

■ Closing the learning loop

1. What do you understand by the term 'corporate reputation'?
2. Give one example of a celebrity firm and one example of a celebrity CEO.
3. What is meant by a 'boundaryless career', and how does this concept relate to corporate reputation?
4. How are employees becoming more important in shaping corporate reputation?
5. In what ways does reputation influence international assignees and skilled migrants, and vice versa?

CASE STUDY 9.1   MINERAL MINING IN A DEVELOPING COUNTRY

A global mining company located mineral deposits in a coastal region of a developing country in Africa, following exploration work. The area where the mineral deposits were found was one of the largest biodiversity hotspots in the world, rich in flora and fauna. The region was very poor, with few job opportunities and a degraded infrastructure; some villagers lived in the rural area adjacent to the proposed mining area, the majority of whom earned less than AU$2 per day. The mining company proposed to invest heavily in local infrastructure and services, including building roads, a new port, schools and hospitals and accommodation for employees.

The company recognised that it needed to respect local biodiversity as well as respond sensitively to the needs of regulators, local communities, investors, non-governmental organisations and employees. It entered a joint partnership with the national government that constituted one of the largest investments in the country for many years.

Now, the mining project has been approved, with an expected duration of approximately 50 years. At the end of the contract, the mine and the entire local infrastructure will belong wholly to the national government. International conservation groups have become aware of the company's plans and are campaigning against them, despite the support of the local community, including local village leaders, for the project.

Case study questions

1. What are the reputational risks for the mining company described in this case study?
2. Which stakeholders should the company prioritise in managing its reputation?
3. Why is communication important in the company's management of its reputation?
4. What role should the company take in environmental protection for the area in which it plans to mine?
5. Which do you think should take priority: conservation or development?

» ACTIVITIES

Group or individual tasks

The following questions may be discussed as a group in class or assigned to students as written tasks.

1. The American business magnate Warren Buffett said: 'It takes 20 years to build a reputation and five minutes to ruin it. If you think about that, you'll do things differently.' Discuss the implications of this statement for corporate reputation.

2. How far do you agree that leaders receive too much praise and criticism when it comes to their companies' reputations?
3. 'Today's employees are obsessed by corporate reputation.' Discuss this statement.
4. Assess the effects of reputation on skilled migrants. Are they greater or lesser than the influence of skilled migrants on reputation?

Online resources

- For instructors: answers to activities; long media atricle with questions; additional questions and answers.
- For students: further reading; answers to case study; IHRM in practice.

References

Ahrens, F. (2010). Toyota's shares slide as its reputation loses steam, *Washington Post*, 4 February, www.washingtonpost.com/wp-dyn/content/article/2010/02/03/AR20100203 02109.html. Retrieved 2 January 2012.

Australian Human Resource Institute (AHRI) (2008). Love 'em don't lose 'em: Identifying retention strategies that work, *HR pulse research report*, www.ahri.com.au/ MMSdocuments/profdevelopment/research/research_papers/0803_pulse_vol2_no1_lo-ve_em_don't_lose_em_web.pdf. Retrieved 15 April 2013.

Arthur, M. B. and Rousseau, D. M. (1996). *The boundaryless career: A new employment principle for a new organizational era*, Oxford: Oxford University Press.

Beaverstock, J. V. (2002). Transnational elites in global cities: British expatriates in Singapore's financial district, *Geoforum*, 33(4): 525–38.

Beechler, S. and Woodward, I. C. (2009). The global 'war for talent', *Journal of International Management*, 15(3): 273–85.

Chambers, E. G., Foulon, M., Handfield-Jones, H., Hankin, S. M. and Michaels, E. G. (1998). The war for talent, *McKinsey Quarterly*, 1(3): 44–57.

Chen, Y.-C. (2008) The limits of brain circulation: Chinese returnees and technological development in Beijing, *Pacific Affairs*, 81(2): 195–215.

Clifford, S. (2009). Video prank at Domino's taints brand, *New York Times*, 15 April, www.nytimes.com/2009/04/16/business/media/16dominos.html?_r=0. Retrieved 2nd January 2013.

Economist (2012a). Entrepreneurs in Latin America: The lure of Chilecon Valley, *Economist*, 13 October, www.economist.com/node/21564589. Retrieved 3 January 2013.

Economist (2012b). Liveability ranking: Australian gold, *Economist*, 14 August, www.economist.com/blogs/gulliver/2012/08/liveability-ranking. Retrieved 3 January 2013.

Fombrun, C. J. (1996). *Reputation: Realizing value from the corporate image*. Boston: Harvard Business School Press.

Fombrun, C. J. (2012). The building blocks of corporate reputation: Definitions, antecedents, consequences. In Barnett, M. L. and Pollock, T. G. (eds), *Oxford Handbook of Corporate Reputation*, 94–113. Oxford: Oxford University Press.

Gladwell, M. (2002). The talent myth, *New Yorker*, 22 July, 28–33.

Google (2013). Company website, www.google.com/about/company/. Retrieved 2 January, 2013.

Gray, E. R. and Balmer, J. M. (1998). Managing corporate image and corporate reputation, *Long Range Planning*, 31(5): 695–702.

Hannon, J. M. and Milkovich, G. T. (1996). The effect of human resource reputation signals on share prices: An event study, *Human Resource Management*, 35(3): 405–24.

Harvey, W. S. (2008). Brain circulation? British and Indian scientists in Boston, Massachusetts, USA, *Asian Population Studies*, 4(3): 293–309.

Harvey, W. S. (2011a). How University of Oxford students assess corporate reputations of companies, *Regional Insights*, 2(1): 12–13.

Harvey, W. S. (2011b). British and Indian scientists moving to the US, *Work and Occupations*, 38(1): 68–100.

Harvey, W. S. (2011c). Immigration and emigration decisions among highly skilled British expatriates in Vancouver. In Nicolopoulou, K., Karatas-Özkan, M., Tatli, A. and Taylor, J. (eds), *Global knowledge workers: Diversity and relational perspectives*. Cheltenham, Gloucestershire: Edward Elgar.

Harvey, W. S. (2012). Brain circulation to the UK? Knowledge and investment flows from highly skilled British expatriates in Vancouver, *Journal of Management Development*, 31(2): 173–86.

Harvey, W. S. and Groutsis, D. (2012). Skilled migrants in the Middle East: Definitions, mobility and integration, *International Journal of Business and Globalisation*, 8(4): 438–53.

Harvey, W. S. and Morris, T. (2012). A labor of love? Understanding the influence of corporate reputation in the labor market. In Barnett, M. L. and Pollock, T. G. (eds), *Oxford handbook of corporate reputation*, 341–60. Oxford: Oxford University Press.

Hayward, M. L., Rindova, V. P. and Pollock, T. G. (2004). Believing one's own press: The causes and consequences of CEO celebrity, *Strategic Management Journal*, 25(7): 637–53.

Kim Y-H and J. A. Lee (2012) To outdo rivals in mobile software, Samsung turns to outside talent, *Wall Street Journal*, http://online.wsj.com/article/SB10001424052702303877 604577381601758850814.html. Retrieved 3 January 2013.

Lee, E. S. (1966). A theory of migration, *Demography*, 3(1): 47–57.

Madslien, J. (2010). Toyota's reputation could be tarnished for years, BBC News website, http://news.bbc.co.uk/2/hi/business/8498036.stm. Retrieved 2 January 2012.

Mercer (2012). *Worldwide quality of living survey*. New York: Mercer LLC.

Michaels E., Handfield-Jones, H. and Axelrod, B. (2001). *The war for talent*. Boston: Harvard Business School Press.

Ong, A. (2007). Please stay: Pied-a-terre subjects in the megacity, *Citizenship Studies*, 11(1): 83–93.

Pfarrer, M. D., Pollock, T. G. and Rindova, V. P. (2010). A tale of two assets: The effects of firm reputation and celebrity on earnings surprises and investors' reactions, *Academy of Management Journal*, 53(5): 1131–52.

Pfeffer J. (2001) Fighting the war for talent is hazardous to your organization's health, *Organizational Dynamics*, 29(4): 248–59.

Pruzan, P. (2001). Corporate reputation: Image and identity, *Corporate Reputation Review*, 4(1): 50–64.

Rindova, V. P., Pollock, T. G., Hayward, M. L. A. (2006). Celebrity firms: The social construction of market popularity, *Academy of Management Review*, 31(1): 50–71.

Rindova, V. P., Williamson, I. O., Petkova, A. P. and Sever, J. M. (2005). Being good or being known: An empirical examination of the dimensions, antecedents, and consequences of organizational reputation, *Academy of Management Journal*, 48(6): 1033–49.

Roberts, P. W. and Dowling, G. R. (2002). Corporate reputation and sustained superior financial performance, *Strategic Management Journal*, 23: 1077–93.

Sanders, W. G. and Hambrick, D. C. (2007). Swinging for the fences: The effects of CEO stock options on company risk taking and performance, *Academy of Management Journal*, 50(5): 1055–78.

Saxenian A (2006) *The New Argonauts: Regional advantage in a global economy*. Cambridge: Harvard University Press.

Smith, G. (2012). Why I am leaving Goldman Sachs, *New York Times*, www.nytimes.com/2012/03/14/opinion/why-i-am-leaving-goldman-sachs.html?pagewanted=all&_r=0. Retrieved 3 January 2013.

Vault (2013). About us, www.vault.com/wps/portal/usa/aboutvault/About-Vault?id=1. Retrieved 15 April 2013.

Woodford, M. (2012). *Exposure: Inside the Olympus scandal – How I went from CEO to whistle-blower*. London: Portfolio Penguin.

Expatriation and repatriation in the Asia–Pacific region

Valerie Caven, Susan Kirk
and Cindy Wang-Cowham

■ Learning objectives

- To explore the theoretical and empirical issues in expatriation and repatriation in the Asia–Pacific region that inform the development and management of global mobility policy and practice.
- To examine the contextual facilitators of, and constraints on, management of globally mobile talent in the region.
- To critically evaluate the issues inherent in the management of global talent.
- To show how the impact of sociopolitical, economic and cultural factors in the region can inform approaches to global talent mobility.

■ Learning outcomes

After reading this chapter, students will be able to:
- identify issues that affect expatriation and repatriation in the Asia–Pacific region
- differentiate between various contextual factors that enable and constrain the mobility of global talent in the region
- evaluate macro-, meso- and micro-level issues, tensions and contradictions associated with managing international human resources in the region
- understand a range of approaches to global mobility, taking into account the different cultural, economic and sociopolitical environments of the region.

■ Introduction

In this chapter, we look at region-specific issues that affect the **expatriation** and **repatriation** of workers around, as well as into and out of, the Asia–Pacific region. The management of globally mobile labour has become a key challenge for multinational companies (MNCs) worldwide, and particularly in parts of the Asia–Pacific, where demographic issues and the supply of skills have created difficulties in staffing businesses (Collings, Scullion & Morley, 2012). This presents particular challenges in the Asia–Pacific due to great disparities between standards of living in emerging markets (e.g. India) and more established countries (e.g. Singapore). The multitude of contexts in which to study expatriation and repatriation includes complex and diverse national cultures, institutional systems and political and economic regimes.

expatriation The process of assigning employees to international, cross-border and cross-cultural jobs.

repatriation Voluntary and self-directed efforts of employees to develop careers abroad. Repatriation, unlike expatriation, is initiated without official support from the focal company.

We restrict our discussion to countries that the World Bank (www.worldbank.org) includes in its definition of the East Asia and Pacific region: Australia, Brunei, Cambodia, China, Fiji, Hong Kong, Indonesia, Japan, North Korea, South Korea, Lao, Macau, Malaysia, Mongolia, Myanmar, New Zealand, Papua New Guinea, Philippines, Singapore, Solomon Islands, Taiwan, Thailand and Vietnam.

■ Context

At a macro-level, governments obtain competitive advantage through skill development or acquisition; thus attracting key skilled workers from outside of the country as a solution to supply-side shortages. However, success in this endeavour is dependent on how attractive the destination is perceived to be in terms of relocation. Australia, for example, is a well-developed first-world nation that offers an excellent infrastructure and abundant natural resources (APEC, 2011) whereas the Indian subcontinent is seen as a less desirable destination due to its levels of poverty and associated welfare issues. The Australian points system for acquisition of a work permit is designed to attract expatriates with scarce skills that are unavailable locally, but Australia otherwise recruits from the internal labour market. Conversely, the Vietnamese government is seeking to address skill deficits by attracting incoming foreign direct investment (FDI) and associated expatriate technical and managerial talent from neighbouring Taiwan and China (Cooke & Lin, 2012).

So, firms seeking to expand operations in the Asia–Pacific must face a number of key challenges and make important choices, which are influenced by the movement of labour in, out of and around the region. This is explored in more detail in the next section.

■ Talent flows in the Asia–Pacific

China and India face 'critical **talent flows**' (Tung, 2008; Cooke, 2008), resulting in skills shortages and intense competition for certain pools of labour (De Cieri et al., 2009). In sectors where the circulation of highly skilled individuals is constant, problems in continuity and stability are extreme. Carr, Inkson and Thorn (2005) observe how in New Zealand labour outflows (known as a **'brain drain'**) have been of concern since the 1980s. Harvey (2011) notes that this is a particular problem in certain occupations, and cites the movement of skilled scientists from India to the United States. The attitudes of Asia–Pacific talent to expatriation also influence the movement of labour; Asian expatriates tend not to consider certain 'pull' factors (such as family issues and spousal career) that would be likely to cause employees from other regions to decline an assignment (Kim & Froese, 2012). For example,

talent flows The movement of skilled labour around a region.
brain drain Net loss of skilled labour as it moves out of a region or country.

when the MNC Aglionby – this chapter's case study company – required one of its Korean employees to relocate to Indonesia for a year, he decided to leave behind his wife and children (Kirk, 2010).

In contrast, Singapore, Malaysia and Thailand rely on inbound talent flows and migration policies to facilitate economic growth (Kaur, 2010). In China, reform of the *hukou* system of work (a permit system) has eased restriction of internal migration between regions and encouraged talent flows in the country (China Daily, 2011; Huang & Zhan, 2005). At national level, the issue is how to balance flows of key skilled workers to support countries' current and future economic needs.

The macro-economic situation has an impact on organisations (meso-level), for which the challenge is balancing talent flows not only out of and into, but also around global operations. Parts of the Asia–Pacific that have experienced either 'brain drain' or **'brain gain'** when restrictions on global mobility are in place can experience **'brain circulation'** once those restrictions are eased (Tung, 2008). Brain drain occurs when a worker's home country loses skill or knowledge due to the movement of human capital to a host country; brain gain occurs in the host country that receives the human capital. These concepts have less relevance in parts of Asia–Pacific where individuals may choose to leave their home country to take advantage of economic or developmental opportunities but later return; as Tung (2008: 469) argues, this involves a 'triangular human talent flow', known as brain circulation. Brain circulation activ-

brain gain Net gain of skilled labour as it moves into a region or country.
brain circulation Flow of skilled labour and knowledge between multiple regions or countries.

ities between Silicon Valley, India and Taiwan suggest that the movement of skill and talent has multiple benefits (see the discussion of Silicon Valley in chapter 9). Saxenian (2005, 2006), for example, finds that there is significant mobility of talent and knowledge flows between these regions.

▨ Brain drain, brain gain or brain circulation?

Emerging markets such as India and China experience labour supply difficulties because they are producing insufficient numbers of graduates who have the requisite skill levels (Collings, Scullion & Morley, 2012). This is also true of more developed countries, such as Australia, where 35 per cent of posts across a range of sectors remain unfilled (ADEEWR, 2012). The Asia–Pacific region is a source of talented labour: for example, the United Kingdom's National Health Service recruits well-qualified nurses from the Philippines and India (Alonso-Garbayo & Maben, 2009). There are also talent flows into, out of and around the Asia–Pacific region. Inbound assignees to India are increasing at the fastest rate, where an overall increase is expected of 80 per cent between 2010 and 2014. China, which currently has the highest inbound expatriate rate, is predicting a 23 per cent rise in the same period (Ernst & Young, 2011).

India and China's outbound assignees are growing at the fastest rate of all the Asia–Pacific countries, with China projecting an outbound increase comparable to that of the inbound rate. In India, 75 per cent of outbound assignees are junior employees sent abroad to gain the experience necessary to ensure that the country benefits economically when they return (Ernst & Young, 2011). Other parts of the region predict a similar outflow of talent, with Australians the most willing to work abroad (Roobol & Oonk, 2011). Thus, the talent pool in the Asia–Pacific region is not static and is subject to ebbs and flows dependent on macro-, meso- and micro-level factors.

In China and India, brain circulation (a triangular human talent flow) is replacing brain drain and brain gain (Tung, 2008), as highly skilled individuals leave their country of origin to study abroad or accept senior posts in other countries and later return home. In some sectors, such as science and technology, formal networks have been established to encourage this circulation of human capital. This 'diaspora option' (Meyer & Brown, 2003) arguably overcomes problems a country or organisation experiences when it loses human and social capital through migration.

Thus, talent flows are complex and often problematic, since talent inflow does not always compensate countries and organisations for talent outflow. For example, the brain drain of educated workers from the Taiwanese electronics sector has resulted in Taiwan losing out to its competitors in Korea and China (Mishkin, 2013). Table 10.1 summarises the key factors that influence global talent flows at macro-, meso- and micro-levels in the Asia–Pacific region.

At the meso-level, in organisations and industries, HR professionals operating in the region are concerned with the recruitment, retention and mobilisation of talent. Their priorities in this environment are to develop competitive recruitment strategies; to attract available talent; to devise appropriate engagement policies (e.g. attractive reward packages); and to ensure such talent remains with the organisation. Global mobility strategy should recognise the importance of both

Table 10.1 Factors that influence global talent flows in the Asia–Pacific region

Level	Factors
Macro-level	Cross-cultural understanding and knowledge sharing encouraged by both governmental and non-governmental organisations in the region (Fee & Gray, 2013).
	Support from host country (particularly in relation to family) influences intention to repatriate (Forstenlechner, 2009).
	Cultural expectations and dominant social norms (e.g. repatriation to China) (Guo, Porschitz & Alvez, 2013).
	Differences in education systems deter or encourage talent flows in parts of the region (Cho, Hutchings & Marchant, 2012).
Meso-level	Knowledge transfer and succession planning, to encourage retention (De Cieri et al., 2009).
	Polycentric approaches to staffing, to reduce the influx of expatriates (e.g. South Korea's approach in China) (Kang & Shen, 2013).
	Expatriates replaced with local hires (Smedley, 2012).
	A lack of reintegration programs deters expatriation and/or return to the region (Newton, Hutchings & Kabanov, 2007).
	Increased social capital (Cappellen & Janssens, 2005; Dickmann & Doherty, 2008).
	Enhanced leadership skills (Mendenhall, 2001; Dickmann & Harris, 2005).
	Greater functional flexibility (Guthridge & Komm, 2008).
Micro-level	Opportunities for career capital acquisition through expatriation (McNulty, De Cieri & Hutchings, 2012; Saxenian, 2006).
	National identity and quality of life act as push/pull factors (De Cieri et al., 2007; Harvey, 2011).
	Religious and cultural influences (Cho, et al., 2012).

support throughout an employee's international assignment and reintegration once he or she has completed it.

A number of factors influence expatriation, especially strategic considerations; control and coordination; knowledge transfer; leadership development; and operational planning (e.g. launching new initiatives) to fill skills shortages and ensure career development (Dickmann & Baruch, 2011). However, a significant number of individuals decline expatriate assignments: the refusal rate is estimated at 57 per cent (Atlas, 2012). It is vital to understand both the issues that influence an individual's decision to accept an international assignment and the ways in which push/pull factors can be manipulated to encourage global mobility (Baruch, 1995; Dickmann & Baruch, 2011). Thus, an appreciation of the implications of micro-, meso- and macro-level factors is crucial in managing globally mobile talent.

▪ Push/pull forces

Baruch (1995) developed a framework for analysing people's decisions to accept or decline an international assignment. The influencing factors that exert a push or pull on the individual include:

- a person's values and needs
- organisational systems and processes
- national culture
- economic and legal issues.

push/pull factors Factors that encourage (pull) or compel (push) people to move from one location to another.

These forces operate in conflicting directions, either pulling the employee to accept the move or pushing them to reject it. Kirk (2010) has also shown that the range of macro-, meso- and micro-level elements that influence a decision is broad, which helps explain why people choose to move or to remain. Factors include:

- global economic forces (not just local or national)
- social factors (e.g. attitudes to travel, especially since the events of 9/11)
- social responsibility (e.g. employee welfare) and ethical issues (e.g. reducing carbon footprint)
- technological developments (e.g. video conferencing as an alternative to travel)
- legal issues (e.g. work permits/visas and the use of flexible contracts).

These issues may be external to the individual (e.g. legal issues such as obtaining a visa) or internal (e.g. a person's identity). They exert either a pull or push depending on the context, including the existence of perceived alternatives. For example, a pull may influence an individual whose identity includes a willingness to travel, encouraging him or her to accept opportunities; conversely, a push may arise from a person's strong sense of local family commitments or national identity, leading him or her to reject a relocation offer. In this way, the push influences without necessarily compelling a person's decision.

At micro-level, performance issues act as push factors, with managers acting as gatekeepers who constrain the mobility of the individuals they value and wish to retain. This reflects a larger debate over individual agency versus managerial control and highlights the complexities of the multiple forces and trajectories of push/pull factors. A desire to control operations may exert a push for mobility of employees but too much mobility may exert a pull to retain employees in the parent country since it can lead to communication and decision-making problems. In terms of recruitment and retention, mobility opportunities can exert a push or pull, motivating those individuals who seek mobility and deterring those who do not.

Interorganisational influences on mobility include the acquisition of social capital through networking; development of global leaders; harmonisation of global practices; and encouragement of cultural diversity, as discussed, for example, by Cooke and Lin (2012) in their study of Chinese firms with established operations in Vietnam. Figure 10.1 draws on Kirk (2010) in adapting Baruch's push/pull model to represent the range of macro-, meso- and micro-level factors that act at international, national and organisational/individual contexts. As the figure shows, these factors may act to push or pull factors for people seeking or rejecting mobility.

As discussed in chapters 3 and 4, there are many reasons to send staff on international assignments, and many actors are involved. Such assignments, of course, can help a company to gain a foothold in a host country, but they also enable staff to develop a broader perspective of how their company operates in different

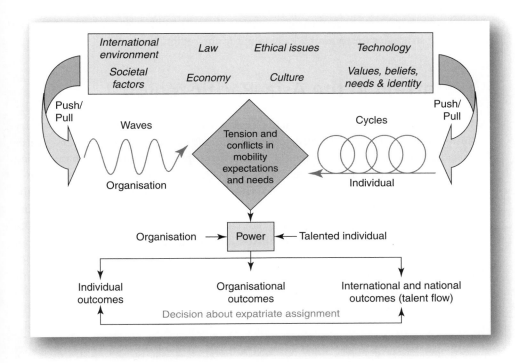

Figure 10.1 Organisational perspective on the push/pull model (adapted from Kirk, 2010)

environments, increasing their identification with the global organisation. Global networks can be developed to exchange knowledge and share ideas and skills, where international assignees may have responsibility for training local staff in specific areas of expertise. Host-country governments may require a subsidiary to recruit local staff once it is established. Thus, expatriates are utilised to train host-country nationals (HCNs) in preparation for a handover, as for instance in the case of Indonesian, Filipino and Hong Kong expatriates assigned to China to provide such development for local managers (Wang-Cowham, 2007). Incentives may be needed as pull factors to encourage employees to take up foreign assignments, as working and living conditions in the host country may differ from the home country. The most desirable Asia–Pacific locations for expatriates, in terms of quality of living and infrastructure, are Japan, Singapore, Hong Kong, Australia and New Zealand, and the least attractive location is the Indian subcontinent (Mercer, 2012). Organisations will tailor their pull factors depending on how attractive the country and region are for potential expatriates. For example, if an area is seen as less desirable or even dangerous, a company may offer an enhanced salary and safe, secure accommodation. However, the region's dependency on Western expatriates has steadily reduced in recent years (Smedley, 2012) as organisations have increasingly recruited local talent. So, organisations operating in the region may now need to focus on strategies for retaining local talent in the region.

■ Staffing in the Asia–Pacific region

Firms recruiting for the Asia–Pacific region can choose to hire parent-country nationals (PCNs), HCNs or third-country nationals (TCNs). Table 10.2 summarises the advantages and disadvantages of each staffing option. Although companies need to prevent expatriate failure (see discussion in chapter 5), there is clear evidence of a lack of concern about HR issues. Cho, Hutchings & Marchant (2013) highlight the lack of support for Korean employees relocated to Australia, citing lack of training and preparation time and poor assignee selection. The costs of expatriate failure are high both for the organisation and for the individual, not only financial terms but also in terms of damage to reputation (at macro-, meso- and micro-levels), loss of future business and emotional stress. There are also difficulties with repatriation or reintegration, although less so in some parts of the region than others, as we discuss in the next section.

Table 10.2 Staffing strategies in the Asia–Pacific region			
Staffing option	**Example**	**Advantages**	**Disadvantages**
Parent-country national	Korean companies have adopted this approach (Tung, Paikb & Bae, 2013).	Aids communication and transfer of HQ culture and policy.	Host-country staff may resent the PCN; adaptation takes time and is expensive; the PCN and HQ may lack cultural awareness.
Host-country national	Indonesian and Thai managers often lack the language skills for foreign postings (Chalré Associates, 2012).	No language barriers; cultural familiarity; no adjustment problems for assignee or family; less expensive as lower relocation costs; can be politically sensitive.	Greater language and cultural gaps between the parent and subsidiary; difficult for assignees to gain international experience; constraints on decision-making.
Third-country national	Malaysians and Filipinos adapt well to assignments (Chalré Associates, 2012).	Best for expertise and experience; promotes cooperation; eliminates the disadvantages of the other two approaches.	Immigration controls by host countries may impede transfer; need to justify employment of a TCN; expensive; longer lead times.

■ Repatriation in the Asia–Pacific

Traditionally, the term 'repatriation' has been used to describe the process of when an expatriate completes an overseas assignment and is preparing to return to their country of origin (Osman-Gani & Hyder, 2008). However, it has little relevance in some parts of the Asia–Pacific (e.g. China) where companies tend not to repatriate international assignees but instead to reassign them to a new expatriate project. This can be problematic for both the organisation, in terms of continuity and control of operations, and the individual, with regard to career capital and identity issues (Kirk, 2010). Such employees have been described as 'career nomads' (Driver, 1982; Cadin, Bailly-Bender and de Saint-Gieniez (2000), whose global mobility may be the result more of the 'fecklessness and/or marginalisation' of the individual concerned than of their proactive, self-managing career behaviour (Inkson, 2006). Kirk (2010) noted that a person's excessive number of international moves may be seen in a negative light, and used the term 'glo-pat' (**glopatriate**) to denote a serial expatriate who moves frequently between international assignments, performing poorly and therefore disenfranchising himself or herself from both superiors and colleagues.

> **glopatriates** Expatriates who have lost their identification with their home country.

The term has also been used to describe the sense of de-identification that some expatriates experience in relation to their home country after spending time away. Such expatriates may perceive re-entering their home country as more difficult (for personal or family reasons) than accepting another expatriate assignment (McPhail et al., 2012). This perception becomes stronger the longer the expatriate and their family are away from their country of origin (Suutari & Brewster, 2003). Yeoh and Huang (2011) focus on the careers of transnational elites from the Asia–Pacific region and refute the existence of 'perfect global citizens', who Salt (2008) describes as floating 'effortlessly' between cities. Citing the cases of Chinese transnationals who choose to shuttle between Hong Kong and Vancouver, while managing their businesses in Asia, rather than to relocate to Canada, Yeoh and Huang (2011) argue that we must understand such careers in the context of broader cultural–political concerns about moving and belonging to a place, and in the light of tensions between flexibility, citizenship and nationality.

The scant research that focuses on repatriation in the Asia–Pacific region reports similar problems to those found elsewhere. For example, Newton, Hutchings and Kabanof (2007: 308) note 'a lack of comprehensive and multifaceted reintegration programmes being offered in Australian organisations'. Companies are increasingly referring to reintegration in preference to repatriation (Nery-Kjerfve & McLean, 2012; Leblang, 2013), reflecting the need for policies that address employees' needs beyond mere physical resettlement, including the need for their emotional and social engagement with their new community. Yet, as Cho, Hutchings and Marchant (2013) have identified in the case of poor cultural and linguistic support for Korean expatriates returning from Australia, there is little evidence that reintegration policies are commonly adopted across the Asia–Pacific.

■ Conclusion

In this chapter, we have discussed the importance of developing an awareness of the different recruitment and redeployment strategies organisations can adopt in managing staffing for the Asia–Pacific region. We looked at the implications of the movement of talent to, from and within the Asia–Pacific region and analysed the macro-, meso- and micro-level push/pull factors that influence the management of globally mobile talent in the region. Finally, we examined major theoretical and empirical issues in relation to expatriation and repatriation in the region, before noting the need for organisations to pay further attention to employees' needs in the light of an increased emphasis on repatriation.

■ Take-home messages

- It is important to be aware of the different recruitment and redeployment strategies organisations can adopt in managing staffing for the Asia–Pacific region.
- It is essential to have a sound understanding of the macro, meso and micro-level push/pull factors that influence talent flows in and around the region.
- HR professionals should always critically evaluate the difficulties and challenges of expatriating and repatriating staff to and from the region.
- HR professionals can use a range of strategies for supporting talent flows in the region.

■ Closing the learning loop

1. What key issues should an organisation consider when it plans to:
   a) expatriate an employee between countries in the Asia–Pacific region?
   b) repatriate an employee to his or her home country in the region?
2. Which macro-, meso- and micro-level push/pull factors influence the movement of talent?
3. How might HR professionals facilitate expatriation and reintegration processes in the Asia–Pacific region?

CASE STUDY 10.1 AGLIONBY EXPANDS IN THE ASIA–PACIFIC

Aglionby is a large MNC, with a global presence in 65 countries around the world. The agricultural commodities sector, in which the company is a market leader, is volatile because of produce seasonality and other factors relevant to agricultural production (e.g. weather, pests, disease), and agricultural crop prices are inherently unstable (Haile, Kalkuhl & Von Braun, 2013). Aglionby is a diversified conglomerate that grows through acquisitions and joint ventures. Its corporate strategy relies on collaboration with other Aglionby organisational units around the world and with its external customers, as it works to create new ingredients and new food-processing methods and to manage its supply chains. Aglionby is now expanding its business operations in the Asia–Pacific region to take advantage of the expanding market for their products and plans to set up a hub in Singapore.

Case study questions

1. What staffing strategies would you suggest for Aglionby, based on the information in the case study?
2. What issues does a firm such as Aglionby need to take into account when recruiting for the Asia–Pacific region?

CASE STUDY 10.2 NO PLACE LIKE HOME?

Chengdu Construction Industry, established in 2003, is a building company that focuses on large-scale construction projects. In line with its global image, it has recruited a large number of expatriates not only from Asia but from Australia, the United Kingdom and the United States. The company has recently expanded in the Asia–Pacific region and now needs to attract enough talented managers to meet the demand of 10 forthcoming construction projects. It has offered open-ended secondment contracts to candidates for expatriate roles, which will secure their future in the company. While on assignment, each assignee will receive a localised compensation and benefits package, aligned with local managers working at the assignee's level in the region where they are working. The company has decided not to develop a repatriation policy, in the belief that it is unnecessary because all expatriates will be assigned to new locations on completion rather than repatriating.

Case study questions

1. To what extent may a company's 'nomadic' (Inkson, 2006) global mobility policy negatively affect talent management?
2. In what ways can a company benefit from employing 'glo-pats' (Kirk, 2010)?

» ACTIVITY

Group report

Read case study 10.1 and then break into teams of three or four. Imagine that you are management consultants appointed to advise Aglionby on its new venture in the Asia–Pacific. Aglionby has decided to move its Asia–Pacific operations from Singapore to Vietnam, but has no experience of operating in Vietnam, nor of moving production in the Asia–Pacific region. You must advise Aglionby on appropriate international HR considerations and processes for this situation. Working as a team, produce a report detailing how Aglionby may be able to manage the move to Vietnam. Identify potential staffing problems that the company may encounter, and offer solutions.

Discussion questions

1. What barriers may Western employees face in seeking an expatriate assignment in the Asia–Pacific region?
2. Why might gaining an expatriate assignment have become more challenging recently?
3. How can HR professionals facilitate expatriates' cultural adjustment to the Asia–Pacific region?

▪ Online resources

- For instructors: answers to activities; long media article with questions; additional questions and answers.
- For students: further reading; answers to case studies; IHRM in practice.

▪ References

Alonso-Garbayo, A. and Maben, J. (2009). Internationally recruited nurses from India and the Philippines in the United Kingdom: The decision to emigrate, *Human Resources for Health*, 7: 37.

Asia–Pacific Economic Cooperation (APEC) (2011). Guide to Investment Regimes of APEC Member Economies, 2nd revision (May), 1–296. Publication Number: APEC#211-CT-03.2.

Atlas. (2012). *Results 45: Corporate relocation survey*. Retrieved from www.atlasvanlines.com/relocation-surveys/corporate-relocation/2012.

Australian Department of Education, Employment and Workplace Relations (ADEEWR) (2012) [now Department of Employment], http://employment.gov.au/employment-research-and-statistics.

Baruch, Y. (1995). Business globalization: The human resource management aspect, *Human Systems Management*, 14: 313–26.

Cadin, L., Bailly-Bender, A. F. and de Saint-Giniez, V. (2000). Exploring boundaryless careers in the French context. In Peiperl, M. (ed.), *Career frontiers: New conceptions of working lives*. Oxford: Oxford University Press.

Cappellen, T. and Janssens, M. (2005). Career paths of global managers: Towards future research, *Journal of World Business*, 40: 348–60.

Carr, S. C., Inkson, K. and Thorn, K. (2005). From global careers to talent flow: Reinterpreting 'brain drain', *Journal of World Business*, 40: 386–98.

Chalré Associates. (2012). Sources of experienced managers, www.chalre.com/hiring_managers/manager_sources.htm.

China Daily (2011). *Hukou* limit on new graduates to direct talent, *China Daily*, www.china.org.cn.

Cho, T. Hutchings, K. and Marchant, T. (2012). Key factors influencing Korean expatriates' and spouses' perceptions of expatriation and repatriation, *International Journal of Human Resource Management*, 24(5): 1051–75.

Collings, D. G., Scullion, H. and Morley, M. J. (2012). Challenging patterns of global staffing in the multinational enterprise. In Stahl, G. K., Mendenhall, M. E. and Oddou G. R. (eds), *Readings and cases in international human resource management and organisational behaviour*, 5th edition. New York: Routledge.

Cooke, F. L. (2008). *Competition, strategy and management in China*. Basingstoke, Hampshire: Palgrave Macmillan.

Cooke, F. L. and Lin, Z. (2012). Chinese Firms in Vietnam: Investment motives, institutional environment and human resource challenges, *Asia Pacific Journal of Human Resources*, 50: 205–26.

De Cieri, H., Sheehan, C., Costa, C., Fenwick, M. and Cooper, B. (2007). International talent flow and intention to repatriate: An identity explanation, Department of Management Working Paper Series, Monash University, 10/07.

De Cieri, H., Sheehan, C., Costa, C., Fenwick, M. and Cooper, B. K. (2009). International talent flow and intention to repatriate: An identity explanation, *Human Resource Development International*, 12(3): 243–61.

Dickmann, M. and Baruch, Y. (2011). *Global careers*. New York: Routledge.

Dickmann, M. and Doherty, N. (2008). Exploring the career capital impact of international assignments within distinct organizational contexts, *Journal of Management*, 19: 145–61.

Dickmann, M. and Harris, N. (2005). Developing career capital for global careers: The role of international assignments, *Journal of World Business*, 40(4): 399–408.

Driver, M. J. (1982). *Career concepts: A new approach to career research*. Englewood Cliffs, NJ: Prentice Hall.

Ernst & Young. (2011). *Global mobility effectiveness survey 2011*, http://emergingmarkets.ey.com/global-mobility-effectiveness-survey-2011. Retrieved 7 May 2013.

Fee, A. and Gray, S. J. (2013). Transformational learning experiences of international development volunteers in the Asia–Pacific: The case of a multinational NGO, *Journal of World Business*, 48: 196–208.

Forstenlechner, I. (2009). Exploring expatriates' behavioural reaction to institutional injustice on host country level, *Personnel Review*, 39(2): 178–94.

Guo, C., Porschitz, E. T. and Alves, J. (2013). Exploring career agency during self-initiated repatriation: A study of Chinese sea turtles, *Career Development International*, 18(1): 34–55.

Guthridge, M. and Komm, A. B. (2008). Why multinationals struggle to manage talent, *McKinsey Quarterly*, May: 1–5.

Haile, M. G. Kalkuhl, M. and Von Braun, J. (2013). Short-term global crop acreage response to international food prices and implications of volatility, ZEF Discussion Papers on Development Policy, Center for Development Research, Bonn, Germany, 175.

Harvey, W. S. (2011). British and Indian scientists moving to the United States, *Work and Occupations*, 38(1): 68–100.

Huang, P. and Zhan, S. H. (2005). March. *Internal migration in China: Linking it to development*, paper presented at the Regional Conference on Migration and Development in Asia, People's Republic of China Ministry of Foreign Affairs. Lanzhou, China.

Inkson, K. (2006). Protean and boundaryless careers as metaphors, *Journal of Vocational Behaviour*, 69(1): 48–63.

Kang, H. and Shen, J. (2013). International recruitment and selection practices of South Korean Multinationals in China, *International Journal of Human Resource Management*, 24(17): 3325–42.

Kaur, A. (2010). Labour migration in Southeast Asia: Migration policies, labour exploitation and regulation, *Journal of the Asia–Pacific Economy*, 15(1): 6–19.

Kim, J. and Froese, F. J. (2012). Expatriation willingness in Asia: The importance of host-country characteristics and employees' role commitments, *International Journal of Human Resource Management*, 23(16): 3414–33.

Kirk, S. J. (2010). Global mobility choices: A study of international leaders, unpublished doctoral thesis, Nottingham Trent University, Nottingham, UK.

Leblang, D. (2013). Harnessing the diaspora: The political economy of dual citizenship, migrant remittances and return, http://personal.lse.ac.uk/RICKARD/david.pdf.

McNulty, Y, De Cieri, H. and Hutchings, K. (2012). Expatriate return on investment in the Asia–Pacific: An empirical study of individual ROI versus corporate ROI, *Journal of World Business*, 48(2): 209–21.

McPhail, R., Fisher, R., Harvey, M. and Moeller, M. (2012). Staffing the global organization: 'Cultural nomads', *Human Resource Development Quarterly*, 23(2): 259–76.

Mendenhall, M. (2001). New perspectives on expatriate adjustment and its relationship to global leadership development, in developing global business leaders. In Mendenhall, M., Kuhlmann, T. and Stahl, G. (eds), *Developing global business leaders: Policies, processes and innovations*, Westport, CT: Quorum.

Mercer (2012). *Worldwide quality of living survey*. New York: Mercer LLC.

Meyer, J. P. and Brown, M. (2003). Scientific diasporas: A new approach to the 'brain drain' in management of social transformations, UNESCO Management of Social Transformations Programme Discussion Paper, 4, www.unesco.org/most/meyer.htm.

Mishkin, S. (2013). China causes Taiwanese brain drain, *Financial Times*, March: 1–3.

Nery-Kjerfve, T. and McLean, G. N. (2012). Repatriation of expatriate employees, knowledge transfer and organizational learning: What do we know?, *European Journal of Training and Development*, 36(6): 614–29.

Newton, S., Hutchings, K. and Kabanof, B. (2007). Repatriation in Australian organizations: Effects of function and value of international assignments on program scope, *Asia Pacific Journal of Human Resources*, 45: 295–313.

Osman-Gani, A. A. M. and Hyder, A. S. (2008). Repatriation adjustment of international managers: An empirical analysis of HRD interventions, *Career Development International*, 13(5): 456–75.

Roobol, C. and Oonk, V. (2011). Global Talent Mobility Survey: What attracts the world's work-force? www.the-network.com/recruitment/recruitment-expertise/global-talent-mobility-survey/upload/GTMS_Wave3.pdf.

Salt, J. (2008). International migration and the United Kingdom: Report of the United Kingdom SOPEMI correspondent to the OECD.

Saxenian, A. (2005). From brain drain to brain circulation: Transnational communities and regional upgrading in India and China, *Studies in Comparative International Development*, 40(2): 35–61.

Saxenian, A. (2006). *The new Argonauts: Regional advantage in the global economy*. Harvard, MA: Harvard University Press.

Smedley, T. (2012). Working in East Asia: Region reduces its reliance on expatriates, *Financial Times,* June.

Suutari, V. and Brewster, C. (2003). Repatriation: Empirical evidence from a longitudinal study of careers and expectations among Finnish expatriates, *International Journal of Human Resource Management*, 14(7): 1132–51.

Tung, R. L. (2008). Human capital or talent flows: Implications for future directions in research on Asia–Pacific, *Asia Pacific Business Review*, 14(4): 469–72.

Tung, R. L., Paikb, Y. and Bae, J. (2013). Korean human resource management in the global context, *International Journal of Human Resource Management*, 24(5): 905–21.

Wang-Cowham, C. (2007). The transfer of HRM knowledge in multinational corporations in China: The perspectives of Chinese HR managers, unpublished doctoral thesis, Manchester Metropolitan University, Manchester, UK.

Yeoh, B. S. A. and Huang, S. (2011). Introduction: Fluidity and friction in talent migration, *Journal of Ethnic and Migration Studies*, 37(5): 681–90.

Balancing inflows and outflows in the European context

Joana Vassilopoulou, Barbara Samaluk and Cathrine Seierstad

■ Learning objectives

- To provide a deep understanding of international labour relations.
- To provide an overview of migration theories and their various levels of analysis.
- To illustrate forms of migratory inflows and outflows and their consequences for IHRM.
- To highlight that understanding the migratory experience and agency of immigrants is crucial in developing IHRM theories and practices.
- To demonstrate the role of employment agencies in sourcing and supplying migrant workers from Accession 8 countries to the UK and to explain its consequences for IHRM in organisations.

■ Learning outcomes

After reading this chapter, students will be able to:

- understand the relevance to IHRM of migratory inflows and outflows to and from multinational companies
- discuss how the globalised labour market is changing and explore the challenges and relevance of such change for IHRM
- explain why comprehensive and ethical IHRM strategies are needed in relation to migration
- understand the need to explore migration from multiple levels and through a combination of different theories of IHRM
- understand the impact that migratory inflows and outflows can have on local labour markets and migration policies, with reference to a case study from the European context.

■ Introduction

The effective international management of HR is a key element of success and failure in international business. Changes in the labour market – the result of globalisation, multiculturalism and altered **migration** patterns – present important opportunities and challenges for IHRM in organisations, particularly for multinational companies (MNCs), in the light of skilled labour shortages. Comprehensive and adaptive IHRM strategies and practices that consider, for example, the implications of employing migrant labour, are essential for the success of international business. This is true of a variety of areas of HR practice, such as recruitment and selection, training and development, cross-cultural management, HR planning and diversity management. To develop such IHRM strategies and practices, HR practitioners must first understand the multifaceted nature of migratory inflows and outflows and how it can influence their work. For example, the shortage of skilled labour has become an increasing problem for MNCs, and so HR practitioners need to develop innovative strategies for identifying and managing the supply of labour. To do this well, HR practitioners need to understand internationalised labour relations and labour mobility and grasp how IHRM links with law, society, unions, culture, migration patterns and migratory inflows and outflows of labour. Any HR practitioner who aims to utilise migration as a workforce planning tool needs this understanding.

> **migration** The movement of people.

In this chapter, we focus mainly on skilled labour, providing a deep understanding of internationalised labour relations and migratory inflows and outflows, which we link to labour mobility and supply. We also explain how HRM practices are changing in organisations that employ migrant workers. The chapter starts with an overview of migration theories, which offer a range of levels of migration analysis. This is important because HR practitioners need to understand influences on the mobility of workers: for example, factors that influence individuals to move from one country to another (see also chapter 10). A description of different forms of migration follows. We then explore the impact of migration theories at **macro-**, **meso-** and **micro-** levels, recognising that migration at all levels is embedded in, and influences, organisations.

At the macro-level, we illustrate some difficulties that organisations, governments and HR practitioners may face as a result of skills shortages. We also show how govern-ments try to resolve such shortages by altering their migra-tion policies, as in, for example, the United Kingdom's inclusion of European Union **Accession 8** (A8) labour in its migration policy (the A8 countries are the eight post-socialist Central and Eastern European countries that joined the EU in 2004 – Czech Republic, Estonia, Hungary, Latvia,

> **macro-level migration theories** International perspectives and global perspectives on migration, such as analysis of global labour trends.
>
> **meso-level migration theories** National and local perspectives on migration, such as analysis of how communities and households influence migration.
>
> **micro-level migration theories** Individual perspectives on migration, such as analysis of individual agency in people's migration decision-making.

Accession 8 The eight post-socialist Central and Eastern European countries that joined the European Union in 2004 (Czech Republic, Estonia, Hungary, Latvia, Lithuania, Poland, Slovakia and Slovenia).

Lithuania, Poland, Slovakia and Slovenia). At the meso-level, we explore how the transformation of labour markets and migration affects the nature of IHRM in the organisational context. At the micro-level, we discuss the migratory experience of individuals, an understanding of which is crucial to the development of HR practices. In conclusion, we offer a case study from Europe, which explores the role of employment agencies in sourcing and supplying migrant workers from A8 countries to organisations in the UK. The case study highlights some of the difficulties organisations can face when employing migrant labour without considering the migratory experience of migrant individuals.

■ Migration theory

To understand the mobility and supply of labour and the complex nature of migratory inflows and outflows, we must understand why people move. A number of academic disciplines research migration, from geography to economics and sociology and, as a result, the field of migration research is spread across disciplinary boundaries. Different disciplines often approach migration research from diverse perspectives, each trying to understand aspects of migration (for example the causes of migration) relevant from its own perspective. In doing so, they use a range of theoretical models and frames, developed in isolation from the other disciplines (Massey et al., 1993). Further, such theoretical approaches offer different levels of analysis. Macro-level theories aim to explore migration in its broadest sense, for example, through study of global labour trends. Meso-level explanations focus on social aspects; for example, through study of how communities and households influence migration. Micro-level theories focus on individual agency; for example, through study of how people make their migration decisions. Some theories also combine these levels of analysis. Below, we provide an overview of different migration theories.

At the turn of the 20th century, an English geographer named Ernest Ravenstein, now widely regarded as the earliest migration theorist, used census data from England and Wales to develop his 'Laws of Migration' (1889). The main argument of his theory was that migration is based on what he called a **push/pull** process. Unfavourable conditions in one place, such as oppressive laws or high unemployment rates, push people out; conversely, favourable conditions, such as better economic opportunities in an external location, pull them in.

push/pull factors Factors that encourage (pull) or compel (push) people to move from one location to another.

Analysis of the push/pull process enables a focus on macro-level causes of migration. For example, internal migration in the EU has changed due to the current economic and financial crisis. The crisis has particularly hit countries such as Greece, Italy, Portugal and Spain, all of which are experiencing high unemployment, particularly among young people and immigrants. As a result, we can now see increased immigration from countries such as Spain and Greece to countries such as the UK and Germany, which the economic crisis has affected less. In terms of the push/pull theory, this example illustrates how high unemployment in a country pushes individuals to seek work in other countries that enjoy more favourable labour market conditions. Considering this example, we can see that Ravenstein's theory has some explanatory power, although his theory has been criticised for being an out-dated commentary on 19th-century British migration, which fails to cover the complexities of contemporary migration (Pooley & Turnbull, 2005). Indeed, the theory has some short-comings, since it bases its explanations solely on macro-level causes, leaving out individual factors, for example. However, Ravenstein's findings inspired other scholars to amend and build on his theories, resulting in an enormous body of work. Lee (1966) draws on Ravenstein's theory but emphasises micro-level analysis of the push factors. He points out that dimensions such as age, gender and social class influence people's choices in the migration process. In his view, such dimensions affect how people respond not only to push/pull factors, but also to difficul-ties they experience in the course of migration.

Further variants of the push/pull theory, which set out to explain international migration patterns, include **neoclass-ical economic theory** (Sjaastad, 1962; Todaro, 1969), cur-rently the dominant theory explaining the causes of migration. Neoclassical theory investigates migration by elaborating macro-level causes of migration, and focuses on wage and income differentials. This theory understands international migration as depending on the global supply and demand for labour. Nations facing skills shortages will have high wages. The high wages are seen as the pull factor, pulling immigrants in from nations that have a surplus of labour.

Other recent macro-level migration theories are the **segmented labour market theory** and the **world systems theory**. The first (Piore, 1981) suggests that developed economies are dualistic. Developed economies are seg-mented in a primary market of secure, well-paid work and a secondary segment of low-paid work. Immigrants are then recruited to fill the low-paid segment, which the native-born population avoids. The world systems theory (Sassen, 1988) views international migration as a byprod-uct of global capitalism. The current direction of interna-tional migration patterns is from poor to rich nations, due to industrial development in developed economies, which

micro-level analysis of push/pull A reading of the push/pull process that emphasises that dimensions such as age, gender and social class influence people's choices in the migration process. Such dimensions affect how people respond to not only push/pull factors but also difficulties they experience in the course of migration.

neoclassical economic theory A migration theory that sees migration as depending on the global demand and supply for labour. Countries that face skills shortages offer high wages, which pull immigrants from nations that have a surplus of labour.

segmented labour market theory A migration theory that sees developed economies as segmented into two markets. In developed economies, the home-country population is attracted to a primary market of secure, well-paid work, while immigrants are recruited to a secondary market of low-paid work.

world systems theory A migration theory that sees international migration as a byproduct of global capitalism. The direction of migration is from poor to rich nations, due to the industrial development in developed economies, which individuals in developing economies see as a push factor.

individuals in developing economies see as a push factor. Again, this theory does not account for meso- and micro-level causes of migration.

However, not all macro-level migration theories try to explain migration patterns and causes based only on macro-level aspects. For example, neoclassical economic macro-level theory has been transferred to the micro-level of analysis, looking also at individual choices of migrants (Todaro, 1969). In this theory, known as the **human capital theory**, sociodemographic characteristics of individuals, such as age, gender, occupation and educational background, influence the migration decision and outcome of migration (Sjaadstad, 1962). Such characteristics influence people's decision-making about their migration and choice of receiving country: for example, individuals from the same country may choose different receiving countries depending on their own occupation and skills. The central concept here is that individuals move in order to maximise profits. Hoffmann-Nowotny (1981) has introduced another micro-level theory of migration, which particularly takes into account what happens to migrants in the receiving country. He argues that individuals migrate in order to achieve a higher status in the receiving country than they held in their home country. However, migrants often take on the lowest positions in the receiving country, so they do not achieve an improved status and may even experience a lower status. For instance, in Germany the degrees of highly **skilled migrants** (SMs) are often not recognised; this applies in particular to migrants whose home countries are outside the EU. As a result, trained doctors sometimes work as taxi drivers in Germany. However, in the light of skills shortages across various sectors, including the medical sector, Germany has now introduced a law to ensure that the degrees of migrants are recognised (Mechan-Schmidt, 2013).

The major meso-level migration approach, **social capital theory**, highlights the importance of social capital, institutions and networks in encouraging or hindering people's migration decisions (Faist, 2000). Social capital is a resource that is acquired through different kinds of relationships (Bourdieu & Wacquant, 1992); that is, social networks and social capital in households, neighbourhoods, communities and more formal organisations can help individuals in the migration decision process.

human capital theory A theory that recognises that sociodemographic characteristics, such as age, gender, occupation and educational background, influence the migration decision and the outcome of migration.

social systems theory A theory that sees migration as the result of tension between structural (power) questions and anominal (prestige) questions. Individuals migrate with the aim of achieving a better status.

skilled migrant A well-educated individual who moves from a developing to a developed country for work.

social capital theory A theory based on the idea that social networks and social capital in, for example, households, neighbourhoods, communities and formal organisations can help or hinder individuals in decision-making about migration.

Finally, a recent contribution to the area of international mobility is the study of **transnational migration** and **transnationalism** (Portes, Guarnizo & Landolt, 1999; Vertovec, 2001). Transnationalism refers to the phenomenon according to which 'increasing numbers of people move and live in a transnational space, and which assumes that belonging to a nation state has been loosened' (European Commission 2008: 33). According to Portes, Guarnizo and Landolt (1999: 1–2), transnational migrants are those who 'live dual lives: speaking two languages, having homes in two countries and making a living through continuous regular contact across national borders'. Due to globalisation, a new social field of transnational migration is emerging (Basch, Glick Schiller & Szanton-Blanc, 1994; Smith & Guarnizo, 1998).

As these theories demonstrate, much theoretical work has focused on a single level of analysis, whether macro, meso or micro. However, in contemporary migration scholarship there are increasing calls to overcome disciplinary boundaries and to engage with the complexity of migration research by combining multiple levels of analysis and theoretical approaches (Healy & Oikelome 2011, Samaluk, forthcoming-a).

> **transnational migrant** A person who works in two nations, making continuous and regular contact across national borders.
>
> **transnationalism** A trend towards people living and working in a transnational space, accompanied by a weaker sense of belonging to a nation state.

▪ Types of migration and implications for IHRM

The concept of migration refers to the movement of people. With changes in migration, employers can draw from a broader and more diverse labour market, with a larger potential candidate pool. Most IHRM literature focuses on two categories of migrants: traditional expatriates whose company assigns them abroad, and **self-initiated expatriates** (SIEs) who do not have an organisational assignment. The literature often ignores migrant individuals from less developed countries. We know that people decide to move for a number of different reasons and not always because an organisation assigns them. Each migrant's circumstances and motivations are different, ranging from poverty to adventure, calculation and desperation. For example, **economic migration** commonly occurs when people move to find work, but can also happen among people who are refugees and those seeking lifestyle changes. Migration includes movement both between countries (**international migration**) and within countries (**domestic migration**), and so has spatial dimensions.

> **self-initiated expatriate** A person who moves abroad for work on their own initiative.
>
> **economic migration** Migration that occurs when people move to find work.
>
> **international migration** The movement of people between countries.
>
> **domestic migration** The movement of people within a country, as in the movement of people from rural areas to big cities.
>
> **spatial dimensions of migration** Migration is spatial because it includes movement both between and within countries.

Domestic migration takes place within a country, as in the movement of people from rural areas to big cities (Heery & Noon 2007). International migration is a growing feature of the global economy and important in terms of labour supply in the business environment. International migration increased dramatically during the 20th century, becoming more significant for most countries. In 2000, as few as 11 out of 187 countries globally had around zero in **net migration** (also known as the 'balance of migration') in comparison with the 1950 and 1960s, when the balance of inflows (**immigration**) and outflows (**emigration**) of international

net migration The balance of migration.
immigration Inflows of migrants or returning locals to a country.
emigration Outflows of migrants and locals from a country.

migrants was around zero in 53 countries (UNPD, 2000). In 2005, 191 million people lived outside of their home country, in comparison with 75 million in 1960 (Heery & Noon, 2007).

Migration can be permanent or temporary. In fact, a large and growing share of migration is temporary. Heery and Noon (2007) describe several types of temporary migration:

- circulatory – migration between the host and home country (often connected with seasonal work)
- transient – migration between several host countries, after which the migrant settles in one of them
- contract – migration to a host country for a fixed period, often determined by a residence permit or job contract
- return – migration back to a migrant's own country, often after a considerable period spent working in a host country.

HR practitioners should understand the types of temporary migration, and particularly the time restrictions on groups of migrants, for workforce planning purposes. Humphries, Brugha and McGee (2012) argue that in the case of Ireland 'the assumption that international nurse recruitment had "solved" the nursing shortage was short lived and the current presumption that nurse migration (both emigration and immigration) will always "work" for Ireland overplays the reliability of migration as a health workforce planning tool' (p. 44). Moreover, temporary migration is widespread among highly skilled migrants from, for example, Asia, Eastern and Western Europe and the United States (Mayr & Peri, 2008). Again, an HR manager can use this knowledge to determine the reliability of using migrant labour as a workforce planning tool.

Migration can further be classified into two types: emigration and immigration. The term 'immigration' describes inflows of migrants or returning locals to a country and the term 'emigration' describes outflows of migrants or locals from a country. This chapter focuses for the most part on different aspects of immigration, as noted in the end-of-chapter case study.

Migratory outflows are often discussed in relation to the **brain drain** phenomenon. This is widely debated in the light of the loss of skilled labour from sending countries, which are predominantly emerging economies. There are particular concerns about the emigration of highly skilled workers from developing countries and the associated 'exodus of talent' in many regions. The brain drain is a challenge for national governments (Tatli, Vassilopoulou & Özbilgin, 2013), some of which have reacted by promoting better alignment between their education provisions and employment practices.

brain drain Net loss of skilled labour away from a region or country.

Brain drain causes labour shortages in many vital industries, such as the Central and Eastern European Region, since developed countries continue to poach talented and skilled staff from this region. As a result of brain drain, there is a severe shortage of skilled managers in all sectors within the former socialist bloc countries (Ellerman, 2006). Poland has experienced a brain drain after its accession to the EU, for example, borne out by the number of Polish emigrants. Although most people migrating have vocational education, the proportion of university graduates has risen significantly. In particular, the United Kingdom attracts Polish university graduates, who commonly seek employment in the UK straight after graduation (Fihel & Okolski, 2009). Such knowledge can be very useful and interesting for HR managers who use migration as a workforce planning tool. An HR manager in a MNC could use the information to develop tools and measures aimed for the attraction of talent; for example, by recruiting Polish students through attendance at university careers fairs in that country. This shows how relevant it is for HR managers to understand and keep up with current migration patterns, inflows and outflows.

There has also been some return migration among highly skilled workers in recent times. The IHRM literature calls this '**brain gain**'. Mayr and Peri (2008: 3) argue that highly skilled migrants are more likely to return than the less skilled. However, this is not the case for poorer countries and cannot yet be described as a dominant trend (World Economic Forum, 2010). The development is interesting for HR managers in MNCs, however, in relation to strategic workforce planning. HR practitioners need to develop measures and practices to support the return of talent, in particular to countries facing severe skills shortages.

Migratory inflows and outflows remain a major challenge for national governments, organisations and multiple stakeholders at work. Multinational and national firms must be more proactive in transcending national regulatory and institutional arrangements and identifying competitive practices. This means that organisations and HR managers have to put serious thought into how to attract, retain and develop talent. IHRM policies are needed to successfully address brain drain. The development of comprehensive training and talent manage-ment strategies can be one way to avoid the loss of valuable talent.

brain gain Net gain of skilled labour into a region or country.

Macro-level implications of United Kingdom migration policy on A8 labour

In this section, we examine the inclusion of A8 labour into the UK's migration policy, which forms an important part of the macro-level background for our end-of-chapter case study. Organisations are influenced by, and embedded in, the external business environment. While economic and political influences are important, the legal busi-ness environment also directly affects organisations; that is, the legal framework of rules and regulations that affect migration inflows and outflows at national, European and broader international scales. A company's failure to respond to national and international legal requirements can have severe consequences, and its workforce planning depends highly on the legal framework in each country where it operates, since the legal framework sets many conditions, for example, regarding working visas for highly skilled migrants. Organisations, and HR managers in particular, must be familiar with laws related to migration. For example, the rights and regulations that affect international migrants are considerably different from those of domestic migrants. It is important to acknowledge that international agreements, national legislation and the relationship between home and host country also affect the handling of international migrants. National regulation varies dramatically from country to country, shaped by the unique historical context of each country and by global labour market developments (Vassilopoulou, 2011; Tatli et al., 2012). International HR managers should be particularly aware of such variations in migration law. International regulations, such as those set within the EU, often guide national migration policies. The importance of the EU's legislative role in regulating migration means that IHRM practitioners must know EU regulations to operate in a country in the region.

An important regulation in the EU and the single market is that of the 'four freedoms' – the free movement of people, goods, services and capital. Although the four freedoms in principle give individuals from an EU country the right to reside and work in another member state, transitional measures restricted the movement of A8 workers. Transitional measures finally resulted in four different regimes being put in place in the EU 15 member states (Vaughan-Whitehead, 2003).

Since 2004, organisations in the UK rely heavily on migrant labour coming from the A8 member states to perform services and work at the lower end of the economy (Wills et al., 2010). The UK opened its borders to workers from A8 countries to gain economic benefits from the enlargement and address national labour shortages (Lippert et al., 2001). Trade unions and employers' organisations welcomed the wider pool of potential employees, which supported the government's decision (Heyes, 2009). The government emphasised the economic benefits of free movement, based on arguments that workers from new member states would help to fill job vacancies, work legally and therefore pay taxes (Home Office, 2009). In this context, the government adopted the Worker Registration Scheme (WRS) to allow A8 nationals to work in the UK. This policy change aligned with government plans to limit non-EU/European Economic Area (EEA) labour migration, which was first achieved through the UK-managed migration scheme and then extended through the introduction of stricter transitional measures for nationals from the Accession 2 (A2) countries that joined the EU in 2007 (Bulgaria and Romania) and additional limits on non-EU/EEA country nationals (UKBA, 2010; Anderson, Clark & Parutis, 2006). The restriction of low-skilled workers from A2 and non-EU/EEA countries was based on the government's rationale that the continuing flow of A8 workers would be sufficient to satisfy demand for workers in low-skilled jobs in sectors that were experiencing labour shortages (Anderson, Clark & Parutis, 2006). Ciupijus (2011) argues that the UK's migration policy was not about enabling people to exercise EU citizenship rights of free movement but 'about filling the low-pay, low-status niche in the UK labour market'. For example, although a large proportion of Polish workers in the UK are highly qualified and skilled, they tend to fill jobs in

low-skilled migrant A migrant who does not possess work experience or tertiary education.

low-skilled and low-paid jobs (Coleman, 2010). This indicates that their talent is underused, which could be seen as a result of badly planned and implemented strategic workforce planning.

This can also be seen as a result of the fact that migration policy, the tabloid press and employers have heavily stereotyped A8 workers as originating from 'poor' and 'less developed' countries and being suitable for, and willing to take up, low-skilled and low-paid jobs (Fox & Morosanu, 2012). Such stereotypes have detrimental effects on A8 workers, particularly the highly skilled, whose skills are often devalued and who often receive lower pay than others in the UK labour market (Currie, 2008; Samaluk, forthcoming-b). However, this also indicates an unnecessary loss of talent for MNCs. Moreover, A8 workers are more likely given temporary work and are less likely to be on a standard employment contract, which means that they may not receive important employment rights (McKay, 2009). This has been further intensified in the post–Global Financial Crisis period.

So, it is crucial to take into account how internationalised policies and markets affect migrant workers, organisations and their IHRM practices. We will explore these issues further in the end-of-chapter case study.

■ Meso-level implications of the transformation of labour markets and migration

The significant transformations in the labour market over recent decades have affected the nature of HRM. Transnational production, labour outsourcing and international migration (associated with growing multiculturalism in organisations) characterise today's contemporary, globalised economy (Vassilopoulou et al., 2013). These changes have produced new challenges for managerial practices in organisations that are characterised by a mobile and diverse workforce, as well as challenges for individuals in organisations. Skills shortages (that is, when the demand for a particular skill outstrips supply) are a global phenomenon. However, the trend is felt in different ways across the Asia–Pacific, Americas, Europe and the Middle East (ManpowerGroup, 2008). A number of Western European countries are facing increasing labour shortages (Esping-Andersen, 2001) due to demographic change (Healy & Schwarz-Woelzl, 2007). For instance, in the UK and Germany, demographics are changing, in particular in terms of an ageing population. Skill shortages are a concern for various countries as well as IHRM in organisations. In the near future, it will become more difficult for HR professionals to fill vacancies with local workers. Migrant labour will be one means to address the skills shortage and will provide HR practitioners with a useful workforce planning tool. HR practitioners will need a deeper understanding of migration patterns and migratory inflows and outflows to effectively address this challenge. Several countries already rely heavily on migrant labour in order to meet skill shortages. For example, a study by Groutsis examines:

the complex and stratified nature of the health care profession in Greece, which is increasingly staffed ... by female migrants. The research explores how immigrant labour is drawn on to fill the most urgent needs in the lower end of the nursing care sector, how immigrant labour gains access to these jobs, the implications of the recruitment process and the effect of these factors on the local labour market structure (2009: 49).

Groutsis' study highlights how important it is for HR managers to focus on the recruitment of migrant labour to address labour shortages. It also shows that HR practitioners should always be informed about mobility issues, including inflows and outflows of workers, from a migration and labour perspective.

What remains consistent across these regions is that skills shortages are an ongoing challenge for employers, which are not likely to disappear in the short term. Organisations that limit their pool of talent and fail to respond to the needs of their staff are likely to face difficulties in recruiting and retaining talent. Imbalance of this kind is common in many European economies now. One of the main reasons for this is the inadequacy of both education and training systems, which has significant effects on the economy. In particular, meeting employer demand for skills is a key component for economic growth. So, a skill shortage might negatively affect the finances of an organisation or the economy of a country. In pursuit of effective ways to address the reported shortage of talent (ManpowerGroup, 2010), companies have developed various innovative practices, including outsourcing, cross-border and on-demand employment practices, and governments have made changes in educational practices and migration policies (World Economic Forum, 2010). It is acknowledged that there is an increasing need for SMs in developed countries, in particular in Europe (Al Ariss et al., 2012a; Al Ariss et al., 2012b).

Given the increased recognition of skills shortages globally, increased demand for skills internationally – often referred to as the global 'war for talent' (Michaels, Handfield-Jones & Axelrod, 2001) – means that migration is now an essential part of employers' recruitment planning. Organisations are actively sourcing workers from other countries to fill skills shortages. For instance, organisations in the UK have been using employment agencies in Poland to source workers in recent years (Currie, 2008). The use of migrant labour is quite often a result of exploitation of global inequalities between regions or nations (Albert & Standing, 2005). Host countries that experience an increase in migrant workers can benefit. For instance, in the UK, SMs 'often make a positive contribution to performance and innovation' (George et al., 2012). This is particularly the case when the SM's host country has a shortage of labour. However, there can be negative effects as well. For example, employers can exploit migrants, and an increase of migrant workers may lead to lower wages for host-national employees. Despite the obvious need for immigration to fill labour gaps, immigration remains a controversial topic in most countries.

However, it is also crucial for developing HR practices to understand the migratory experience of immigrants. It is problematic for individual workers when employers do not take into account their particular backgrounds, and this can also affect the quality of services, which is ultimately bad for organisations. Migrants may not know yet how to search for housing, access basic financial services, find local support or adopt local working practices. For instance, work-related tasks that locals often take for granted might not be as obvious to migrant workers. Their understanding of what is required might be very different from the host's views. IHRM thus demands a frame that takes into account the diversity of workers in an organisation.

◾ Micro-level: agency and the individual's migratory experience

Understanding the agency of migrants in their individual migratory experiences is crucial for developing HR theories and practices. **Agency** can be understood as the power and influence an individual holds and uses to change his or her conditions of life and work. A person's level of agency depends very much on his or her position in terms of social and economic relations (Bourdieu & Wacquant 1992). Examining the agency of migrant workers allows us to perceive how individuals shape their career choices and outcomes and how they deal with barriers, such as discrimination, that they may face in a receiving country's labour market. The end-of-chapter case study explores the situation of a UK organisation that has developed HR practices without considering the migratory experience of Polish workers who have joined the firm. Interestingly, this is not a one-off incident. Agency is more often ignored when it comes to migrants, who come from 'less developed' countries. The dominant body of literature in IHRM focuses on the traditional **expatriate** who moves to another country on an organisationally assigned expatriation for an unspecified duration. Another in the HR literature's category of migrants are SIEs, who move on their own initiative and not because of an organisational assignment. Agency is discussed in the context of these two categories of internationally mobile individuals, but less so when it comes to the 'classical' migrant. Interestingly, as Al Ariss and Crowley-Henry (2013: 80) observe:

agency The power and influence an individual holds and uses to change the conditions of his or her life and work. The level of power and influence they have depends on his or her position in terms of social and economic relations.

expatriate An employee who is assigned to an international, cross-border or cross-cultural job.

> when expatriates come from less developed countries they are most frequently labelled as 'migrants' or 'immigrants'. No rational theoretical or methodological foundation is given to explain such terminology. Instead, this terminological distinction comes to replicate and support a stereotyped image of migrants who are less advantaged in terms of their originating country and ethnic origins. The literature positions 'migrants' in stark contrast to, for example, expatriates from developed countries.

Moreover, current research in IHRM focuses largely on the barriers that migrant workers experience (Pio, 2005), such as administrative barriers in the form of visa and work permits (Syed, 2008). Other studies examine discrimination against migrants in institutional and organisational settings (Laer & Janssens, 2011) and the ways in which their education and professional experiences are discredited (Vassilopoulou, 2011; Al Ariss et al., 2012b), both of which often lead to migrant underemployment and unemployment (Carr, 2010).

Most studies do not examine the agency of, for example, SM workers in European labour markets (Al Ariss et al., 2012a; 2012b). Drawing on two field studies – one examining the career experience of highly skilled migrants in France and the other focusing on the experiences of highly skilled ethnic-minority workers in Germany – Al Ariss and colleagues (2012a; 2012b) have shown the relevance of agency to the career development of highly skilled migrants. In France, they found, discrimination and structural barriers are hindering the career development of highly skilled Lebanese migrant workers. However, these migrants used various strategies, often successfully, to overcome these barriers and further develop their careers. In the German case, the researchers found that the agency of ethnic-minority workers is much more restricted. The majority ethnic group undermines the abilities and skills of ethnic-minority workers across various job criteria. As Vassilopoulou (2011) has observed, this means that most highly skilled migrants are denied access to positions commensurate with their skills and qualifications, which limits the agency of these workers and means that organisations and HR practitioners may miss out on utilising ethnic-minority talent in Germany. That is unfortunate, given that German-based organisations face severe skills shortages across different sectors. Such studies indicate the importance of diversity management for IHRM in general and for HR practitioners in particular.

■ Employment agencies and A8 labour in the UK

Labour market intermediaries such as transnational employment agencies play an important role in sourcing and supplying migrant workers. The number of these agencies has mushroomed in A8 countries, and Poland particularly during the transition period (Currie, 2008). Employment agencies act as intermediaries, providing HRM services for employers on an international level (Ward et al., 2001) such as sourcing and supply of workers; opening offices in A8 countries; organising job fairs and advertising positions in A8 countries, online or in local media (Currie, 2008; Samaluk, forthcoming-b). Intermediaries' practices tend to make migrant workers vulnerable and can also cause problems for organisations. For example, there may be a lack of fit between organisations and agencies on the matter of how the selection and screening process of candidates should be managed to secure the right people at the right time. For example, managers in organisations are often unhappy with agencies they used, while poor agency performance directly affected the performance of workplaces (Ward et al., 2001).

As we will see in the end-of-chapter case study, HR practitioners in organisations need to be more careful when using such agencies. Quality checks of agencies and their services could be one mean to address such problems. We also highlight the fact that migrant workers need specific managerial approaches, for instance in orientating new migrants to local work processes. Organisations should not see migrants merely as assets, but rather as human beings who have specific needs, and should provide assistance to help workers achieve a smooth transition to a new country and workplace. Shifting, vague responsibilities and disregard for the migrant worker's condition are thus not only unethical and problematic for workers, but ultimately also bad for organisations. Agencies and HR practitioners must take migrant workers' specific needs into account if they wish to avoid employee dissatisfaction and lower service quality.

◼ Conclusion

In this chapter, we showed how disciplinary boundaries divide the field of migration research. Distinct disciplines deploy a range of theoretical models and frames, which offer multiple levels of analysis; the theories have often developed in isolation from each other. There are different ways of classifying migration, ranging from economic, permanent and temporary migration to migration caused by flight from persecution or natural disaster. In fact, a large proportion of migration falls into the 'temporary' category, with its variety of subgroups. The rights and regulations concerning international migration are considerably different from those for domestic migration. It is important to acknowledge that these rights and regulations also vary according to the terms of international agreements and national legislation and the nature of the relationship between home and host country. National regulation can vary dramatically from country to country and depends to a large extent on the historical context of a country, as well as on globalised labour market developments (Vassilopoulou, 2011; Tatli et al., 2012). National migration policies are often guided by international regulations, such as the EU, which is an important body in terms of regulations of migration in Europe. Skills shortages challenge many countries and organisations around the world, and migration inflows are one means of responding to such shortages.

◼ Take-home messages

- Migration can be explored from multiple levels and by combining various theoretical approaches in relation to IHRM.
- Changes in the labour market, the result of globalisation, multiculturalism and new migration patterns, present important opportunities and challenges for IHRM in organisations and particularly in MNCs, in the light of skilled labour shortages.
- Comprehensive, adaptive and ethical IHRM strategies and practices that consider, for example, the implications of employing migrant labour, are essential to success in international business.
- HR professionals must understand internationalised labour relations and labour mobility and the links between IHRM effectiveness, law, society, unions, culture, migration patterns and migratory inflows and outflows of labour. Such understanding supports HR practitioners in using migration as a workforce planning tool.
- Developing HR practices must take account of the migratory experiences of immigrants and their particular backgrounds and contexts; not to do so causes problems for migrants and can affect the quality of their services, which is bad for organisations.

■ Closing the learning loop

1. Compare and contrast the migration theories you have learnt about in this chapter.
2. What is the difference between a 'push factor' and a 'pull factor'?
3. What are the different types of temporary migration and how are they relevant to HR workforce planning?
4. What do the terms 'brain drain' and 'brain gain' mean? Why is brain drain a problem for some countries?
5. Why do you think that highly qualified Polish workers in the UK still tend to be utilised for lower skilled and paid jobs?
6. What can organisations do to address skills shortages? Give some examples.
7. What barriers may migrant workers experience in the receiving country and in particular at work?

CASE STUDY 11.1   DIGIFOR FACES LABOUR SHORTAGES

Digifor, a large telecommunications services provider in the United Kingdom, was facing labour shortages in their customer call centre. Since the company found it hard to source local workers, it decided to recruit migrant workers from Poland. In doing so, it used migration as a workforce planning tool and opted to recruit through an employment agency called Transnational Workforce. The agency selected, interviewed and brought in workers for Digifor, and was also charged with providing new migrants with accommodation on their arrival in the UK. However, when Polish workers arrived to take up their call centre roles, they discovered that the accommodation provided was substandard and had to find more suitable places to live, without the agency's help.

In the meantime, Digifor's management organised a two-week training program for the new employees. Their role was to provide customer support and advice on service problems, payment methods and new product and service information. The training consisted of general advice on how to answer customer phone calls, address customers and meet sales targets. The training was essentially the same as that provided for local Digifor employees. When the new migrant employees started work, many of them lacked familiarity with common payment methods and the local organisation of telecommunications and some did not have sufficient English language skills. This led to problems as they could not adequately respond to customers about problems or give advice or information. Digifor received several customer complaints and also faced public scrutiny over its customer services.

Case study questions

1. How can an organisation such as Digifor ensure that its recruitment of migrant workers is ethical and responsble?

2. What considerations should organisations take into account when using the services of an employment agency to recruit migrant workers?
3. How should Digifor's management have handled the selection process and ensured

the smooth transition of its Polish employees?
4. How might the company have better supported its new employees to reduce the risk of customer service problems when they started work?

» *ACTIVITY*

Group presentation

Overview

Comprehensive and adaptive IHRM strategies and practices that consider the implications of employing migrant labour are essential to international business success. This is true of a range of HR fields.

Task

Break into small groups. Each group should pick an area of IHRM, for example:
- recruitment and selection
- training and development
- cross-cultural management
- HR planning
- diversity management strategies.

Discuss the implications of employing migrant labour for the area chosen and develop recommendations for good practice. Present the results of the group discussion.

Group discussion questions

Break into small groups and discuss the following questions.

1. Why is it important to overcome disciplinary boundaries and to engage with the complexity of migration research from multiple levels? How might you combine various theoretical approaches and levels of analysis?
2. 'The United Kingdom's migration policy is more about filling the low-pay, low-status niche in its labour market than about enabling European Union citizens' rights of free movement.' Debate this statement, based on what you have learnt about A8 migration to the UK in this chapter.
3. Why is it important to examine the agency of migrant workers? Discuss with reference to the German and French examples described in this chapter.

■ Online resources

- For instructors: answers to activities; long media article with questions.
- For students: further reading; answers to case study; IHRM in practice.

■ References

Al Ariss, A. and Crowley-Henry, M. (2013) Self-initiated expatriation and migration in the management literature: Present theorizations and future research directions, *Career Development International*, 18(1): 78–96.

Al Ariss, A., Vassilopoulou, J., Groutsis, D. and Özbilgin, M. F. (2012b). A multilevel understanding of the careers of minority ethnic elites. In Kakabadse, A. and Kakabadse, N. (eds), *Global elites: The opaque nature of transnational policy determination*, Basingstoke, Hampshire: Palgrave Macmillan.

Al Ariss, A., Vassilopoulou, J., Özbilgin, M. and Game, A. (2012a). Understanding career experiences of skilled minority ethnic workers in France and Germany, *International Journal of Human Resource Management*, 24(6): 1236–56.

Albert, J. and Standing, G. (2005). Social dumping, catch-up, or convergence? Europe in a comparative global context, *Journal of European Social Policy*, 10(2): 99–119.

Anderson, B., Clark, N. and Parutis, V. (2006). New EU members? Migrant workers' challenges and opportunities to UK trade unions: A Polish and Lithuanian case study. Report written for the Trades Union Congress.

Basch, L., Glick Schiller, N. and Szanton-Blanc, C. (1994). *Nations unbound: Transnational projects, postcolonial predicaments and deterritorialized nation-states*. New York: Gordon & Breach.

Bourdieu, P. and Wacquant, L. (1992). *Invitation to reflexive sociology*. Chicago: Chicago University Press.

Carr, S. (2010). Global mobility and local economy: It's work psychology, stupid! In Carr, S. (ed.), *The Psychology of Global Mobility*, 125–150. New York: Springer.

Centre for Population Change (CPC) (2011). *Trends in East and Central European migration to the UK during recession*. London: ESRC Centre for Population Change, Briefing 5.

Ciupijus, Z. (2011). Mobile central eastern Europeans in Britain: Successful European Union citizens and disadvantaged labour migrants?, *Work, Employment and Society*, 25(3): 540–50.

Coleman, J. (2010). *Employment of foreign workers: 2007–2009*. Office for National Statistics, UK, May.

Currie, S. (2008). *Migration, work and citizenship in the enlarged European Union*. Farnham, Surrey: Ashgate.

Ellerman, D. (2006). The dynamics of migration of the highly skilled: a survey of the literature, in Kuznetsov, Y. (ed.), *Diaspora networks and the international migration of skills: How countries can draw on their talent abroad*. Washington, DC: World Bank.

Esping-Andersen, G. (2001). *A welfare state for the 21st century*. Report to the Portuguese presidency of the European Union, http://64.233.183.132/search?q=cache:tQYBhRjJcL8J: www.nnn.se/seminar/pdf/report.pdf+A+welfare+state+for+the+21st+century&hl= de&ct=clnk&cd=1&client= firefox-a. Retrieved 12 October 2009.

European Commission (2008). Education and migration. Strategies for integrating migrant children in European schools and society. Brussels: European Commission, Directorate-General for Education and Culture.

Faist, T. (2000). *The volume and dynamics of international migration and transnational social spaces*. Oxford: Clarendon Press.

Fihel, A. and M. Okolski (2009). Dimensions and effects of labour migration to EU countries: The case of Poland. In Galgoczi, B., Leschke, J. and Watt, A. (eds), *EU labour migration since enlargement: Trends, impacts and policies*. Farnham, Surrey: Ashgate.

Fox, J. E. and Morosanu, L. (2012). The racialization of the new European migration in the UK, *Sociology*, 46(4): 680–95.

George, A., Lalani, M., Mason, G., Rolfe, H. and Rosazza Bondibene, C. (2012). *Skilled immigration and strategically important skills in the UK economy*. National Institute of Economic and Social Research, Home Office, UK.

Groutsis, D. (2009). Recruiting migrant nurses to fill the gaps: The contribution of migrant women in the nursing care sector in Greece, *Journal of International Migration and Integration /Revue de l'integration et de la migration internationale*, 10(1): 49–65.

Healy, G. and F. Oikelome (2011). *Diversity, ethnicity, migration and work: International perspectives*. Basingstoke, Hampshire: Palgrave Macmillan.

Healy, M. and Schwarz-Woelzl, M. (2007). *Recruitment policies and practices in the context of demographic change*. Vienna: Centre for Social Innovation.

Heery, E. and Noon, M. (2007). *A dictionary of human resource management*, Oxford: Oxford University Press.

Heyes, J (2009). EU labour migration: Government and social partner policies in the UK. In Galgoczi, B., Leschke, J. and Watt, A. (eds), EU labour migration since enlargement: Trends, impacts and policies. Farnham, Surrey: Ashgate.

Hoffmann-Nowotny, H. J. (1981). A sociological approach toward a general theory of migration. In Kritz, M., Lim, L. L. and Zlotnik, H. (eds), *Global trends in migration*. New York: Centre for Migration Studies.

Home Office (2009). *Accession monitoring report (May 2004–March 2009)*, London: Home Office/UK Border Agency.

Humphries, N., Brugha R. and McGee, H. (2012). Nurse migration and health workforce planning: Ireland as illustrative of international challenges, *Health Policy*, 107(1): 44–53.

Laer, K.V. and Janssens, M. (2011). Ethnic minority professionals: Experiences with subtle discrimination in the workplace, *Human Relations*, 64(9): 1203–27.

Lee, E. S. (1966). A theory of migration, *Demography*, 3: 47–57.

Lippert, B., Hughes, K., Grabbe, H. and Becker, P. (2001). *British and German interests in EU enlargement: Conflict and cooperation*. London: Continuum.

ManpowerGroup (2008). *Confronting the talent crunch: 2008. A Manpower white paper*, www.manpowergroup.com/wps/wcm/connect/manpowergroup-en/home/thought-leadership/research-insights/Talent-Sources.

ManpowerGroup (2010). *2010 talent shortage survey results: Supply/demand*, www.manpower.co.za/.../2010_Global_Shortage_Survey_Results_hi_small.pdf. Retrieved 1 July 2010.

Massey, D., Arango, J., Hugo, G., Kouaci, A., Pellegrino, A. and Taylor, E. (1993). Theories of international migration: A review and appraisal, *Population and Development Review*, 19(3): 431–66.

Mayr, K. and Peri, G. (2008). Return migration and the brain drain–brain gain debate, working paper, Center for Comparative Immigration Studies, University of California, San Diego, 166, http://ccis.ucsd.edu/wp-content/uploads/2009/10/WP_166.pdf. Retrieved 10 August 2013.

McKay, S. (2009). The dimensions and effects of EU labour migration in the UK. In Galgoczi, B., Leschke, J. and Watt, A. (eds), *EU labour migration since enlargement: Trends, impacts and policies*. Farnham, Surrey: Ashgate.

Mechan-Schmidt, F. (2013). Foreign doctors in Germany need no longer be taxi drivers, *Times Higher Education*, 2 May, www.timeshighereducation.co.uk/news/foreign-doctors-in-germany-need-no-longer-be-taxi-drivers/1/2003516.article. Retrieved 16 May 2013.

Michaels E., Handfield-Jones, H. and Axelrod, B. (2001). *The war for talent*. Boston: Harvard Business School Press.

Pio, E. (2005). Knotted strands: Working lives of Indian women migrants in New Zealand, *Human Relations*, 58(10): 1277–99.

Piore, M. (1981). *Birds of passage: Migrant labor in industrial societies*. Cambridge, Cambridge University Press.

Pooley, C. and Turnbull, J. (2005). *Migration and mobility in Britain since the 18th century*. First published 1998, London: UCL Press. Ebook edition: Taylor and Francis.

Portes, A., Guarnizo, L. and Landolt, P. (1999). The study of transnationalism: Pitfalls and promise of an emergent research field, *Ethnic and Racial Studies*, 22: 217–37.

Ravenstein, E. (1889). The laws of migration, *Journal of the Statistical Society of London*, 48 (2): 167–235.

Samaluk, B. (forthcoming-a). Whiteness, ethnic privilege and migration: A Bourdieuian framework, *Journal of Managerial Psychology*.

Samaluk, B. (forthcoming-b). Commodification of migrant labour from post-socialist Europe in marketing practices of transnational employment agencies. In Pajnik, M. and Anthias, F. (eds), *Work and the challenges of belonging: Migrants in globalizing economies*. Cambridge Scholars Publishing.

Sassen, S. (1988). *The mobility of labor and capital: A study of international investment and labor flows*. Cambridge: Cambridge University Press.

Sjaastad, L. A. (1962). The costs and returns to human migration, *Journal of Political Economy* 70 (Supplement 5, part 2): 80–93.

Smith, M.P. and Guarnizo, L.E. (eds) (1998). *Transnationalism from below: Volume 6 – Comparative urban and community research*. New Brunswick, NJ: Transaction Publishers.

Syed, J. (2008). Employment prospects for skilled migrants: A relational perspective, *Human Resource Management Review*, 18(1): 28–45.

Tatli, A., Vassilopoulou, J., Ariss, A. and Özbilgin, M. F. (2012). The role of regulatory and temporal context in the construction of diversity discourses: The case of the UK, France and Germany, *European Journal of Industrial Relations*, 18(4): 293–308.

Tatli, A., Vassilopoulou, J. and Özbilgin, M. F. (2013). An unrequited affinity between talent shortages and untapped female potential: The relevance of gender quotas for talent management in high growth potential economies of the Asia Pacific region, *International Business Review*, 22(3): 539–53.

Todaro, M. P. (1969). A model of labour migration and urban unemployment in less developed countries, *American Economic Review*, 59(1): 138–48.

United Kingdom Border Agency (UKBA). (2010). Coalition commits to impose migration limit, www.ukba.homeoffice.gov.uk/sitecontent/newsarticles/2010/268071/43-impose-migration-limit1.

United Nations Population Division (UNPD) (2000). IV international migration. In *World population prospects: The 2000 revision – Volume III. Analytical report*, www.un.org/esa/population/publications/wpp2000/chapter4.pdf. Retrieved 10 November 2012.

Vassilopoulou, J. (2011). Understanding the habitus of managing ethnic diversity: A multi-level investigation, thesis, Norwich Business School, University of East Anglia.

Vassilopoulou, J., Jonsen, K., Tatli, A. and Özbilgin, M. F. (2013). Multiculturalism in organisations. In Thomas, K. M., Plaut, V. and Tran, M. (eds), *Diversity ideologies in organisations*. New York: Taylor & Francis.

Vaughan-Whitehead, D. (2003). *EU enlargement versus social Europe? The uncertain future of the European social model*. Cheltenham, Gloucestershire: Edward Elgar.

Vertovec, S. (2001). Transnationalism and identity, *Journal of Ethnic and Migration Studies*, 27 (4): 573–82.

Ward, K., Grimshaw, D., Rubery, J. and Beynon, H. (2001). Dilemmas in the management of temporary work agency staff, *Human Resource Management Journal*, 11(4): 3–21.

Wills, J., Kavita, D., Evans, Y., Herbert, J., May, J. and McIlwaine, C. (2010). *Global cities at work: New migrant divisions of labour*. London: Pluto Press.

World Economic Forum (2010). *Talent mobility: Stimulating economies through fostering talent mobility*. Geneva: World Economic Forum.

Self-initiated expatriation: case study lessons from Africa and the United States

Ahu Tatli, Daphne Berry, Gulce Ipek and Kurt April

■ Learning objectives

- To outline the key debates on self-initiated expatriation.
- To explore the complex, multilevel dynamics of self-initiation, including the factors behind decisions to migrate.
- To examine the role of context in shaping the self-initiation process.
- To explain the diversity of career opportunities and barriers faced by self-initiated expatriates.

■ Learning outcomes

After reading this chapter, students will be able to:
- critically assess what is meant by self-initiated expatriation
- identify the dynamics of self-initiation at multiple levels, including factors that influence decisions to migrate
- discuss the complex role of context in shaping the self-initiation process
- understand the diversity of self-initiated mobility in terms of careers, opportunities and barriers.

Introduction

Organisations today generally have a more diverse workforce, in terms of country of origin, than in the past. As the capital and labour markets continue to globalise, growing numbers of people move across national boundaries to work in different parts of the world. The aim of this chapter is to introduce and explore the conditions and dynamics that characterise this **self-initiated expatriation** (also known as self-initiated migration). We start by discussing the concepts of migration and self-initiated expatriation. Next, we explore the factors affecting mobility decisions and identify the challenges of moving and working abroad. In the final part of the chapter, we offer two case studies from different national contexts: the United States and South Africa. The case studies focus attention on the perspectives and lived experiences of globally mobile workers themselves and highlight the challenges of cross-border migration and the barriers to integration both within and outside the workplace.

> **self-initiated expatriation** In international management and business studies, the concept refers to individually initiated international mobility in pursuit of cultural, personal and career development.

Definitions of self-initiated expatriation and migration

Since the mid-20th century, the globalisation of trade and production, the formation of regional supranational alliances such as the European Union (EU), the emergence of regional skill shortages and the talent needs of multinational companies (MNCs) have all contributed to the movement of labour across borders. In the literature, scholars discuss international mobility using three terms: self-initiated expatriation (Jokinen, Brewster & Suutari, 2008; Suutari & Brewster, 2001), **corporate expatriation** (Brewster & Scullion, 2007) and **international migration** (Al Ariss et al., 2012; Berry & Bell, 2012).

> **corporate expatriation** In international management and business studies, the transfer of an MNC employee to another country on a temporary work assignment.
> **international migration** In migration studies and human geography, long-term movement of people across national borders.

Each of these terms refers to the process of movement of people across international boundaries predominantly for work reasons. Berry and Bell (2012) explain that scholars in migration studies use the terms 'corporate expatriate' and 'self-initiated expatriate' interchangeably with '**economic migrant**' in referring to people who move abroad for work. Interestingly, the IHRM literature tends to draw an implicit line of distinction between migration and expatriation, focusing almost exclusively on the experiences of expatriates defined as workers whose MNC employer moves them to another country on a temporary

> **economic migrant** A person who moves abroad for work.

work assignment (Berry & Bell, 2012). As a result, management research attends to the experiences of a specific minority of a relatively privileged group of people, who make up only a fraction of the international workforce. However, migrants in less privileged class positions move across national boundaries for work too. They also contribute to the labour market of the host country and are also often employed by MNCs just as their corporate expatriate counterparts do. In a similar vein, others argue that the predominant focus of international management research on corporate expatriation left us with a gaping hole in terms of our understanding of self-initiation. The experiences of self-initiated expatriates remain almost a hidden aspect of the international labour market (Jokinen, Brewster & Suutari, 2008). Self-initiated expatriation is defined as 'long-term individually initiated travel to other countries to pursue cultural, personal and career development experiences' (Suutari & Brewster, 2001: 435).

Although a considerable number of people move to another country to work and live, studies on this group of people are limited (Suutari & Brewster, 2001). However, the self-initiated expatriation literature is criticised for drawing an artificial distinction between migrants and self-initiated expatriates (SIEs). In this literature, the term 'migrant' implicitly carries negative connotations and is often associated with individuals from ethnic-minority groups and, more importantly, groups that suffer from negative ethnic stereotypes, while SIEs are framed in more positive terms, including highly skilled, motivated individuals who interact with host-country nationals (HCNs) (Berry & Bell, 2012). In fact, a scholar's choice of terminology stems from ideological and disciplinary commitments rather than empirically substantiated differences in the processes of mobility for these supposedly different groups. In this chapter, we refer to SIEs for the sake of consistency, although we recognise that the conceptual differentiation between migrant and expatriate is largely artificial.

The chapter is designed to introduce, explore and exemplify the process of self-initiation and the experiences of SIEs. In the next section, we offer a multilevel overview of self-initiation. Then, we will look at the reasons people choose self-initiation, the role of context in self-initiation decision-making and, finally, issues related to managing a self-initiated career. Table 12.1 summarises the issues that we introduce and discuss in this chapter and underlines links to student learning outcomes.

■ Self-initiation as a multilevel phenomenon

Self-initiation is a complex process that social, organisational and individual-level dynamics shape, and that is always context-specific; in other words, each self-initiation is embedded in a certain geographical location, at a certain time in history. So, an in-depth understanding of the self-initiation process and the experiences of SIEs requires us to understand the context. The context of self-initiation is generated

Table 12.1 Summary of topics, key issues and learning outcomes

Self-initiation topic	Key issues	Link to learning outcomes
Reasons for migration	• Push/pull factors • Individual circumstances • Career aspirations	You will be able to identify the dynamics of self-initiation at multiple levels, including factors that influence decisions to migrate.
Contextual influences	• Macro-economic conditions • Governmental immigration policies • Labour market context • Industry or sector-related labour shortages • Organisational strategies on utilising and integrating migrant labour	You will be able to discuss the complex role of context in shaping the self-initiation process.
Careers	• Diversity of career expectations and outcomes • Demographic diversity of SIEs • Type of self-initiated careers, including boundaryless career paradigm	You will understand the diversity of self-initiated mobility in terms of careers, opportunities and barriers.

by influences located at multiple levels of analysis. Table 12.2 presents a multilevel frame of self-initiation.

Table 12.2 Self-initiation: a multilevel framework

Level	Issues
Macro	International issues: globalisation; regional and national immigration policies and legislation; macro-economic, social and cultural conditions in home and host countries; labour market policies; anti-discriminatory policies (e.g. Berry, 2011; Berry & Bell, 2012).
Meso	Sectoral issues: supply and demand for labour and specific skills; practices and policies of responding to self-initiation; traditions of anti-discriminatory policies and practices (e.g. Leutz, 2010; Lewin Group, 2008). Organisational issues: demand for international workforce; workforce demographics; HR policies, strategies and practices in talent utilisation, inclusion and integration of diverse workforce; equality and diversity policies and programs (e.g. Altman & Baruch, 2012; Oikelome & Healy, 2007).
Micro	Individual issues: human capital; social networks and support structures; career expectations, aspirations and outcomes; strategies to overcome structural barriers; demographic and cultural diversity (e.g. Al Ariss, 2010; Jokinen, Brewster & Suutari, 2008).

The overarching level of self-initiation is the macro-level, which refers to the macro dynamics in global, international, regional and national contexts. Macro trends such as global labour market trends, macro-economic circumstances in the home and host countries and population dynamics affect demand for and supply of international workforce in different sectors of the economy (see case study 12.2). The most influential macro-level trends on self-initiation are:

- the globalisation and internalisation of labour markets and the business environment
- macro-economic circumstances in the home and host countries (e.g. economic growth, stagnation, recession)
- conditions in the labour market (e.g. demand for and supply of labour, skills shortages)
- national legislation (e.g. laws on labour, anti-discrimination and immigration)
- governmental immigration policies and discourses
- regional and international policies, agreements, standards and guidelines with respect to the international mobility of workers.

At the meso-level, there are two sets of influences on self-initiation: sectoral and organisational. Sectoral issues that influence self-initiation patterns and processes include demand and supply for labour, skill shortages, history of working with and drawing on international workforce, practices and policies that are developed to respond to self-initiation and generic traditions of anti-discriminatory policies and practices. Organisational issues that help shape companies' response to self-initiation include demand for international workers, skill and talent gaps and shortages, demographics of and diversity in the internal workforce. The organisational benefits of employing SIEs are clear, including the widening of the talent pool and other benefits associated with having a culturally diverse workforce. However, false conceptions and discriminatory and exclusionary practices and cultures may prevent companies fully responding to IHRM challenges in retention and integration.

At the micro-level, a complex set of individual factors affect the process and outcomes of self-initiation and, as our case studies from Africa will later demonstrate, the experiences of SIEs are very diverse. A range of individual-level factors influence SIE experiences, including the SIE's individual human capital, demographic characteristics and social networks and the support structures that are available in his or her home and host countries.

Although it is possible to use therory to delineate multiple levels of influence on self-initiation, in practice the distinctions between macro-, meso- and micro-levels of analysis are not always clear cut. In fact, different levels of influence intersect with and affect each other. As we demonstrate in the remainder of the chapter, all three levels of influence are at play in shaping reasons for self-initiation, the contexts for decision-making about migration and the careers of SIEs. The three case studies we offer in the following sections illustrate key issues in each of these important topics.

■ Reasons for self-initiation

In this section, we introduce our first case study (12.1), an account of self-initiation in Africa. Movement across national boundaries has multiple triggers, including global economic needs, corporate talent management practices (such as expatriate management) and individuals' interest in navigating career and employment opportunities in different organisations and national settings (Berry & Bell, 2012). Espenshade (1995) explains international migration by referring to push/pull factors (see chapter 9 for discussion of the origins of these concepts). According to neoclassical theory, international migration is driven when there is a mismatch between demand for and supply of labour. Demand for products or services changes over time and this instability may raise concerns over job insecurity in the secondary economic sector, low wages and little prospect of upward career movement. This may lead workers to seek job opportunities abroad. Neoclassical theory suggests that individuals make migration decisions on the basis of income maximisation, in which they anticipate financial gain from moving to a new destination. This view assumes that the direction of migration is from developing to developed countries; that is, that migrants come mostly from less developed countries to developed countries to maximise their economic resources, such as pay and benefits. As a result, there are fewer studies of movements of skilled labour from developed countries to less developed countries. Further, the neoclassical model is based on a model of human decision-making, which ignores non-economic drivers for migratory movement and focuses on rational, economic factors alone.

While the immigration literature focuses on macro-level contextual issues such as brain gain, brain drain and push/pull factors (see chapters 9, 10 and 11), the literature examining self-initiated mobility tends to emphasise individual-level factors in decision-making about migration (Al Ariss & Özbilgin, 2010). However, the experiences of SIEs are very diverse, in terms of opportunities and constraints, available career paths and structural barriers. The migrant labour force is composed of men and women from diverse races, ethnicities, economic and social backgrounds. Further, MNCs, as major receivers of migrant labour, significantly influence the experiences of SIEs as migrant workers. For example, gendered and racialised organisational structures in MNCs, coupled with the uneven effect of globalisation on different segments of the labour market, generate a wide array of self-initiation experiences. SIEs access diverse opportunities and experience different degrees of exposure to advantage, disadvantage, inequality and discrimination (see the discussion of 'inequality regimes' in Acker, 2006). In this context, the self-initiation literature suffers from a number of limitations. First, in common with the traditional international migration literature, the literature focuses on movement from developing to developed countries and ignores the experiences of individuals who move from developed countries to developing countries. Second, it does not acknowledge the relationship between ethnicity and career experiences of internationally mobile individuals. Third, the literature does not discuss the barriers that internationally mobile individuals face. Finally, the literature needs to pay more attention to the interconnected nature of immigration, immigration policy and SIEs' experience of self-initiation (Al Ariss, 2010).

To summarise, there are gaps in the literature's framing of the international mobility of workers across borders. The focus of the international migration literature on macro-level factors leads to neglect of the diversity and agency of SIEs, particularly so at the meso-level of the workplace. Due to an overemphasis on structural constraints, the agency of individual SIEs is often ignored, and they are depicted as having no ability to act strategically in order to overcome the structural barriers forced on them in their home and host countries (Al Ariss et al., 2012; see also chapter 11 on agency). The literature, on the other hand, fails to address the diversity of SIEs and the equality outcomes of difference across gender, race and ethnicity lines. SIEs are seen as having the agency and ability to move across national boundaries for work and able to make career choices. A major limitation in this approach is the lack of consideration for the contextual and structural factors that frame career choices and opportunities for SIEs (Al Ariss & Özbilgin, 2010).

Hardy (1975) and Lawler (2008) remind us that, as humans, we endlessly tell stories about our lives, both to ourselves and to others, and it is through such stories that we make sense of our old and new worlds, of our old and new relationships to those worlds and of the relationship between ourselves and other people. Narratives relating to self-initiated migration tend to be context and culture-specific. Case study 12.1 demonstrates the multiplicity and diversity of SIE experiences and the complexity of the decision-making processes that lead up to a person's migration.

CASE STUDY 12.1   SELF-INITIATION IN AFRICA

A study of 120 SIEs in Africa demonstrates a diverse range of experiences and expectations among SIEs. On initial investigation, researchers were told that SIEs experience three main phases when moving into a new country in Africa:

1. Excitement, living in a new country, meeting new people, working in new jobs, around new cultures and accents: in this phase, SIEs shift from only associating with people similar to themselves to making friends in the new location.

2. Disillusionment, which takes place 12–18 months after arrival, when the SIE's initial excitement turns to disappointment: 'People weren't as nice as I thought, or at least it seemed they did not like foreigners especially those from Africa at the workplace. Basically, reality kicked in.'

3. Adaptation: 'I got used to the way of doing things, the people and the work. I was able to adapt to the environment, understand the

citizens a bit more and know how to interact with them, and enjoy myself again.'

The most obvious issues that arose in talking to research respondents were bureaucratic obstacles (e.g. work permits, landed immigrant status, visitor visas for family); the cost of living and affordability; schooling for children; technological challenges; and healthcare issues. Distant relationships with family and with spouses, girlfriends or boyfriends and partners appear to become strained. The weather seemed to be important when moving from a hot home country to a colder host country (or vice versa), or from a wet home country to a drier host country (or vice versa). Even food (e.g. food types, habits, practices) was mentioned as a challenge, with additional difficulties for migrants who required specific food types for ethical or religious reasons (e.g. kosher, vegetarian, halal).

Workplace challenges included underutilisation of SIEs' skills at their current jobs and ranks, lack of formal and informal networks and lack of opportunities to socialise with co-workers, particularly with higher ranking colleagues. Financial capital (or its lack) was also frequently mentioned in our conversations. For instance, an individual or family's available funds when they move to a new country; access to (and/or the lack of) credit and bank loans. Different educational systems are in place across Africa and so we heard of many instances where an individual's home-country qualifications were not recognised in the host country. Consequently, they had to work in low- or non-skilled jobs and experienced financial distress.

The multiple languages spoken across Africa appear to create barriers to entry or feelings of exclusion for many SIEs. Often, such language challenges exist within a country as well as regionally: for example, South Africa has 11 official languages and Nigeria has 520 documented languages spoken across its 36 states. Akin to the language differences are the cultural difference and range of diversity both within a country and across the continent. Research respondents spoke of accommodating their new identities by, for example, sometimes suppressing their old identities and cultural norms to fit in better with their new environments; they also spoke of sifting through intracultural identities, looking for bits of the new environment and cultures which they can relate to in hopes of become accepted.

A Cameroonian respondent made three claims about moving to South Africa:

1. 'I have been passed over for jobs I qualified for because I would not have been able to relate in Zulu or another local language.'
2. 'Whites have also turned me down because I did not form part of the Black Economic Empowerment government policies for local blacks.'
3. 'For the longest of time, black South African ladies wouldn't date me, because I was a foreign black guy.'

A female respondent from Botswana explained that 'not understanding the local humour kept me on the periphery, and I could not add to the banter . . . which made me feel even more marginalised'. For some who overcome the challenges, it makes them more sensitive to the needs of foreigners/others in host countries. One SIE from the Netherlands said:

I've moved to South Africa about 5 years ago, and hadn't had any logistical trouble really, because I didn't entirely leave the Netherlands in my head . . . As for the working environment, my main problem was how people seem to value polite 'nothingness' here. Asking 'How are you?' but not really being interested in the answer, as well as being offended when people read me as blunt and when I tell them the way they see things very narrowly. I've adapted quite well though and I am far less blunt or direct now . . . Socially I had no trouble accommodating, as Cape Town has an extremely friendly international crowd. Getting through to locals properly was a lot harder, especially the white community which has what we would call a 'boarding school mentality' – they only seem interested to form bonds with the people they went to kindergarten and school with.

Interestingly, the significance of challenges associated with self-initiation seem to change over time and so do SIEs' accounts of their experiences, depending both on their age as well as the time spent in the host country. As one correspondent noted:

[The v]arious challenges I faced changed with the amount of time I spent in my new country. The first few years were affected by cultural differences, financial issues and, the development of significant friendships. However, the later years were affected by my level of achievement, the effectiveness of the new contact networks and the degree of personal relationships.

As the years pass, many SIEs experience weakened or lost ties and networks in their country of origin, a transition captured in the following: 'You lose your cultural links to your old networks, as they do not understand . . . or do not want to understand, who you have become, and are still becoming.'

SIEs' family and cultural support structures in the new country vary case by case, and family-related concerns have an important impact on the migration decision as well as the quality of work and private life in the host-country context. We were informed by a Somali respondent that 'leaving one's home country by choice gets more difficult with age – as one gets older, there is more reluctance to engage new uncertainty and the unfamiliar, and there is far less flexibility on the individual's part'. A Brazilian SIE to South Africa claimed that the 'self-initiated' decision to migrate depended on the individual's psycho-social and emotional comfort in answering the following questions:

Will this be an enriching experience for my family? Will the place we are going, be interesting? Are we willing to live with the risks of the new place of settlement? (e.g. safety risks, health risks, economic risks etc.)? Will we be earning reasonable earnings to support a certain lifestyle? Will this experience give me/us more employability in the future?

It appears that an individual's ability to adapt depends largely on pre-migration resilience factors, such as the person's age, depth of his or her spirituality or sense of purpose and psycho-social and emotional state.

Case study questions

1. What do you think are the key difficulties for SIEs, and how do contextual and individual circumstances change the specific challenges SIEs face?
2. After reading this case study, what key factors do you think affect an individual's decision to migrate?

■ The context of self-initiation

In this section, we introduce a second case study (12.2), drawn from the direct care (in-home) sector in the United States. People from immigrant communities move to the United States for a range of reasons and often learn of the availability of direct care jobs from family, friends and others within their communities (Leutz, 2010). Political, social and legal factors converge to influence both the relatively high representation of SIEs as direct care workers (home health aides and others paid to provide hands-on care for the elderly or people with disabilities) and the persistence of low pay for these jobs. We begin with an overview of the trends and contextual factors influencing the self-initiated migration of these workers to the United States.

According to the International Organization for Migration (IOM), as of 2011 there were more than 57 million international migrants in the Americas, 50 million of them in the United States (IOM, 2012). A number of trends in self-initiation are associated with the context in which the movement occurs both in home and host countries. Among these trends are the trafficking of humans for labour and sexual exploitation and movement related to the Global Financial Crisis (2007–2008) and associated economic crises in developed countries that contributed to reductions in the numbers of available jobs. The economic crisis has also fuelled anti-immigrant sentiment, as fear of 'the other' becoming more acute and SIEs have increasingly become targets of intolerant attitudes (Al Nasser, 2011), causing some SIEs have returned to their home countries. However, there are still large numbers of people from Latin America and the Caribbean living in North America (and Europe) and who send money home (totalling in the tens of billions of dollars) to support people in their home countries (IOM, 2010). The Institute for Women's Policy Research notes a general lack of civic and political institutional support for immigrant populations in the US in response to immigration growth (Hess, 2009). Conversely, SIEs of colour have been the recipients of anti-immigration sentiment in the US for some time. In the 21st century, people from Latin America are often presumed to be undocumented and so often become targets of local efforts by law-makers (e.g. *Illegal Immigration Reform and Immigrant Responsibility Act, 1996*), law enforcement and sometimes vigilantes who seek to reduce immigration (Bell, Kwesiga & Berry, 2010; Esses et al., 2001).

The US Government categorises immigrants into four main groups:
1. lawful permanent residents form the largest legally admitted group and includes those who enter as part of family reunion and employment
2. humanitarian migrants
3. unauthorised immigrants
4. legal temporary residents who come as students or temporary workers (DHS, 2012).

Economic and labour market conditions affect migration flows in various ways. For instance, some jobs are seasonal. Others are for jobs labelled 'speciality' in areas related to technology and healthcare. Some of these are highly sought after and highly paid; others, while highly sought, are not highly paid relative to US pay standards. Work in the in-home care industry, performed by direct care workers such as home health aides, fits the latter description. Although US unemployment has accompanied an extended economic recession and may steer workers toward industries where many jobs are available, some workers are unwilling to fill jobs that they find unattractive from economic, social or other viewpoints (Leutz, 2010). Consequently, SIEs in the US can readily find work in categories that are low wage and seen as undesirable. The care work industry is one in which SIEs have helped to alleviate labour shortages. Despite problems related to language, culture and low compensation, this industry is expected to remain a magnet for some SIEs (Leutz, 2010; Lewin Group, 2008). For that reason, in the next section we examine in more detail SIE experiences in the in-home care sector.

■ Care work and self-initiated migration to the United States

In the United States, home health aide and similar jobs are readily available to SIEs, and overall, SIEs fill 20–25 per cent of positions (Lewin Group, 2008). Just as there are observed trends in migration flows between North America and the rest of the Americas, there are also trends regarding the heavy presence of female SIEs in the care work industries. A large proportion of the people who immigrate to the region are women (49 per cent of migrants overall) who work in the rapidly growing care industries in the US. Since many immigrants live in urban areas, the percentage of direct care workers who are SIEs is often even higher in cities. For example, in the Miami area, more than 70 per cent of workers are foreign-born, and SIEs account for approximately 66 per cent of care workers in the New York City and north-eastern New Jersey area and 63 per cent in the Los Angeles area.

Case study 12.2 examines the experiences of female SIEs in the US care industry (excerpts adapted from Berry, 2011). Roles in this sector include certified nursing assistants, home health aides, personal care assistants, direct support professionals and a range of other positions. Care workers provide support for people who are ill, injured, disabled, elderly or infirm. Those who work in clients' homes allow people who might otherwise be institutionalised to be able to stay in their homes. While this type of long-term care (in the home setting) is utilised more in Canada than it is in the US (IOM, 2010), the relative number of elderly (and those with disabilities) receiving in-home care is growing due to client preferences in the US and cost savings realised by supporting institutions. A number of contextual trends shape SIE experiences in the home care industry, as we will identify here.

While the economic crisis contributed to fewer jobs not only for immigrants but also for native-born workers, the home health aide industry has grown rapidly and so experienced a labour shortage. In the period 2006–2030, the number of elderly people in the US is projected to nearly double (Leutz, 2011), while the number of women in the age group from which these types of care workers are usually drawn will increase by less than 10 per cent (PHI, 2011). Because the numbers of ageing people in comparison to the native-born number of people who normally perform paid care work is so skewed for the US (IOM, 2010), those responsible for care of the elderly are increasingly relying on female SIEs to fill the gaps.

Many problems in the care work industry affect employees, employers and care recipients. The industry is characterised by low wages and poor working conditions: according to the US Bureau of Labor Statistics (BLS), this type of care work attracts low wages (at poverty level in some cases), is physically and emotionally exhausting and earns minimal benefits such as health insurance and paid earned leave (BLS, 2012; IOM, 2010). The low skill levels of the women who perform care work are often used to explain the low wages and poor working conditions. However, there are variations in the skill and education levels of the workers: 54–58 per cent have a high school education or less, while others have a college degree and some even have nursing or medical practitioner credentials from their native countries and work as home health aides or other direct care workers while they seek US credentials (Berry, 2011; Lewin Group, 2008). Other explanations include the constrained budgets of governments who often fund this care for those in society who cannot and the fact that women have traditionally performed care work, either without or for very low financial remuneration (Dresser, 2008; Folbre, 1995; IOM, 2010). Employers cite the great work ethic of immigrant women as a reason why employers are willing to hire them, but from the perspective of female SIEs, they are willing to work in such poor conditions mainly because they do not perceive alternatives for other work and because the environment does not support them in making complaints about these conditions. Such conditions may well contribute to growth in the number of female SIEs and to the shortage of home-country workers willing to work in the industry.

To summarise, the labour of female SIEs is sorely needed by the rapidly ageing societies in the US (IOM, 2010). Large and increasing numbers of self-initiated women perform care work, due to a combination of poverty in SIEs' home countries; a lack of alternative work options in the US; the care industry's readily available jobs; and a lack of institutional supports. Some in the US have recognised the need to address the labour shortage in the industry and the lack of adequate compensation and other supports both for the women who perform this work and for their families. Case study 12.2 presents real-life experiences of three migrant in-home care workers in the US (Berry, 2011).

CASE STUDY 12.2   FEMALE SIEs AND IN-HOME CARE IN THE UNITED STATES *

A nurse moved to the United States from Jamaica. After first trying to find work as a nurse, she applied for a job in New York City as a home health aide. She worked as an aide for three years while she retrained as a nurse, since her home-country nursing credentials were not acceptable for this work in the US Government regulations also require that home health aides receive a certain amount of training per year, delivered by a certified medical professional. The nurse then became a trainer for a home health aide organisation. Since qualified nurses are often required to perform home health aide training, one route out of the in-home care job for self-initiated women is as a nurse-trainer. This nurse commented on her experience and expertise as a SIE as follows:

I was an aide so I understand what these aides are experiencing working in people's homes. That's why I do so well at it. They know that I understand . . . Because of my prior education, I thought that I could do this and

found out what more was required for me to be a nurse-trainer here.

A doctor from a Latin American country moved to the US with her spouse. This former medical doctor and nurse-trainer also worked as a home health aide before becoming a US-credentialed nurse who provides training to home health aides. Her training in her home country did not qualify her to practice in the US but it did allow her to become easily certified as a trainer of care workers. She is bilingual, a great asset for administrators and educators in this industry, as many workers are from Latin American countries. On career experience as a home care worker, she said:

I was afraid of going into clients' home in some of the neighbourhoods but I had to go until I could get this job. Because some of the other aides also live in the neighbourhoods, I don't think they were as afraid as I was or at least they had to go. I was happy to have this job instead.

* Excerpted and adapted from Berry (2011).

A nursing assistant from an Asian country moved to the US and found work in a long-term-care institutional setting. She narrates the difficulties she has experienced as a self-initiated home care worker and as an immigrant trying to fit in:

My job is so difficult. The elderly people are mean sometimes and don't like people of colour. They call names and even hit you ... There [are] not enough staff on our floor and sometimes we are not allowed to take breaks. If someone calls in sick, it is worse for the rest of us ... I am going to school at night to try to get an associate's degree so I can do something else. I'm taking English-as-a-Second-Language classes ... Sometimes I have to miss [work] because of my family but I can't quit because my husband doesn't always have work.

Case study questions

1. How do contextual factors influence the experiences of SIEs in the care sector? In discussing this question, consider the context across multiple dimensions including the sociopolitical environment, economic context and sector- and industry-specific needs and demands.
2. What do you think are the potential challenges SIEs may experience in their new work context, based on the information in this case study?
3. How can organisations and policy-makers help to improve the experiences of SIEs, to ensure their full contribution to society and the economy?

■ The challenges of self-initiated careers

In this section, we introduce our third and final case study (12.3), about a career journey in South Africa. The international migration literature explores the difficulties SIEs often experience when they enter the labour market of a new country. These difficulties include joining the economically active labour force and finding suitable and rewarding jobs. The challenges in establishing a career in a new organisational and social setting may stem from restricted access to information, limited knowledge of the labour market context of the host country or inadequate or inappropriate human capital resources, such as language proficiency and cultural orientation (Raijman & Semyonov, 1997). However, the self-initiated labour force is made up of diverse groups with diverse career experiences and challenges. The extant migration literature focuses on economic migration from non-Western to Western countries, including exploration of gendered experiences and consequences of migration (Phizacklea, 1983; Basavarajappa & Verma, 1990). Yet matters of ethnic and class difference, and the experiences of skilled migrants (SMs), are often neglected. Aranda (2007) found that the kinds of capital SIEs bring with them from their home countries influence their social outcomes in the host country. For example, the experiences of middle-class Puerto Ricans on the US mainland showed that this group represented the colonial migrants from privileged economic and citizenship backgrounds. Consequently, the self-initiation experiences of such groups while they are in process of moving to, and settling in, a new country are likely to be substantially different from the experiences of migrants from less privileged social classes.

In general, SIE careers are an underexplored area of the migration literature. As we pointed out earlier, this literature focuses on obstacles that low-skilled SIEs face, and yet the self-initiated careers of SMs also need to be understood if organisations are to utilise their human resource potential. The corporate expatriation literature considers a career to be an organisational process in which the organisation and individual share responsibility (Seak & Enderwick, 2008). The self-initiation literature, on the other hand, takes an individual centred approach to careers (Altman & Baruch, 2012). As such, the notion of self-initiation fits well with the neoliberal framing of workplace relations as individualised, in which national and international careers are seen as a consideration for individuals rather than for organisations. As a result, individual workers are deemed to have the predominant responsibility for managing their careers and welfare (Al Ariss et al., 2012). The individualisation of responsibility has important implications for the career experiences of SIEs, as it may lead to lack of the kind of organisational and state-that would support their integration into the labour market and work context of the receiving country.

SIEs arguably operate in a **boundaryless career paradigm** more than any other group of employees. In comparison to corporate expatriation, where the company takes an active role in managing the process of an employee's movement to the new social, organisational and career context (Baruch, Steele & Quantrill, 2002), the burden and responsibility of career management in self-initiation heavily falls onto the individual expatriate. Whether an SIE is moving short-term or long-term, the traditional **organisational career paradigm** does not apply because self-initiation requires active career management in the host-country context, without the benefit of organisational support, at least during the early stages. In the traditional career paradigm, individuals are expected to be employed in the same organisation until they achieve seniority in terms of time and age (Arthur, 1994). On the other hand, in the case of boundaryless careers, individuals are seen as having full responsibility for successful performance in their career (Becker & Haunschild, 2003), and they typically move outside the company or to another country for career development reasons (Arthur, Khapova & Wilderom, 2005; Defillippi & Arthur, 1994). Sullivan and Arthur (2006) highlight the interdependence of physical and psychological changes in work arrangements, arguing that varying levels of physical and psychological mobility characterise the boundaryless career. Studies on the boundaryless career tend to reflect individual's independence of the traditional career arrangements and traditional organisation of migration.

However, the concept of the boundaryless career fails to address the complexity of self-initiated careers. SIEs' career development choices are made in the context of, for example, organisational structures (Schein, 1971); the varied resources at their

boundaryless career paradigm A model that sees individual careers as independent of organisational career structures and systems and that places sole responsibility for active career management on individuals.

organisational career paradigm A traditional model that sees individual careers as dependent on organisational career structures and systems and that places shared responsibility for active career management on the employer and employee.

disposal (Inkson, 2006); and their past employment history (Rodrigues & Guest, 2010). Oikelome and Healy's (2007) research into the experiences of overseas qualified doctors in the UK demonstrates that organisational and sectoral structures significantly influence individual career outcomes for SIEs in a wide range of issues related to reward, workload, autonomy and morale. As the authors conclude, organisational and sectoral boundaries may create career structures that systematically disadvantage some portions of the workforce, such as SIEs. Further, SIEs' family and broader community attachments, their links to the home country, and their demographic characteristics – such as gender, age, ethnicity, sexual orientation, nationality, occupation, disability and social class – are important in drawing the very boundaries of their presumably boundaryless careers (Parker, Arthur & Inkson, 2004). Organisations that employ an international workforce must look beyond boundaryless and individualistic career approaches to understand SIEs and to acknowledge their own positive and supportive role in engaging this group of workers. To ensure the full contribution of their international workforce, organisations need to equip themselves with tools and support structures to respond to the unique experiences of SIEs. In this sense, the scope of IHRM approaches to expatriate management needs to be widened to include SIEs (Altman & Baruch, 2012).

CASE STUDY 12.3   A CAREER JOURNEY IN SOUTH AFRICA

SIEs encounter a number of challenges, ranging from bureaucratic and financial obstacles (e.g. visa requirements, expenses, accreditation of qualifications) to difficulties related to culture and social relations (e.g. adapting to a new culture, lack of networks, being away from family and friends). This case study draws on a written account by a SIE to Africa provided to us, in which he explains the key challenges he faced before, during and after his migration to South Africa. The following is an excerpt from his account.

Typical challenges I faced:

- Visas (obvious, and can be expensive).
- Sense of belonging – you need to know who you are, what your roots are, etc. In my new city anything goes, while it offers immense opportunities, it is also essential to understand that many of these opportunities are dangerous if you're not strongly grounded. I've seen pretty normal people going off the radar and ending up in very dark places.
- Networking – very important, especially if the plan is to stay for several years. This is useful for work opportunities, but also for socialising and travelling. I found the churches useful in instilling a sense of community and [for] general assistance in networking.
- Appreciation of cultures – being from a small town in the countryside, moving to a cosmopolitan city introduced so many new cultures, religions and languages. You cannot isolate yourself, especially in the workplace. I used this as an educational opportunity to enrich my knowledge of people and their values, which was an amazing experience.

- Being challenged about intentions of leaving my home country (e.g. many of my new country colleagues assumed that I left South Africa because of my dissatisfaction with the new post-apartheid government [. . .], that I'm a racist). These talks often surface in a professional environment, and it is useful to be prepared in whatever your opinions are. The challenge lies in the fact that those challenging you are actually very racially orientated anyway.
- Comfort zones and sacrifices – you are bound to move outside several boundaries of comfort, be it family, friends, and simple logistical issues such as location-driven securities (ease of shopping, doctors, schools, gyms, safe walking/cycling routes). Also, sacrificing things like scenery and surroundings, weather, car (I [was] without a car for the first five years; it is not the end of the world, but it does restrict you in some luxuries).
- Keeping in touch with friends and family back home – while internet tools such as Facebook and Skype [are] great for keeping in contact, these facilities can be somewhat virtual, and require both ends committing equally. My biggest challenge came after several years when great friends had moved on (married, [had] kids, etc.) and gradually our reference frameworks started deviating and we lost common ground.
- Being independent – no more support and care offered through friends [or] financial support through parents.
- Starting from scratch (depending on the timing of your move) – I had to start a professional and social life from scratch, prove myself, had no reputation to fall back on and mostly no introduction when putting myself out in the market.

Case study questions

1. What challenges may self-initiated migrants face in their career journeys?
2. How should these challenges be addressed?

◼ Conclusion

In this chapter, we used discussion and examples to demonstrate the complexity of the process of self-initiation and the diversity of the experiences of SIEs. Earlier in the chapter (table 12.2), we provided a summary of the key trends that affect the self-initiation process at multiple levels. In this conclusion, we will briefly discuss possible policy and practice solutions to address the issues we have identified. In table 12.3, we identify policy and practice recommendations for self-initiation, adopting the multilevel framework that has been used through-out this book.

Important policy solutions at macro-level may help to improve the experiences of SIEs. To start with, supranational bodies have a role to play in regulating the international movement of workers as well as the treatment of SIEs in the host country. Further, international and national legislation can be used to tackle discrimination against self-initiated workers. The receiving country should have policies, regulation and support structures in place to ensure that SIEs feel

Table 12.3 A multilevel frame of self-initiation

Level	Trends and issues	Policy or practice recommendations
Macro	Globalisation; regional and national immigration policies or legislation; macro-economic, social and cultural conditions in the home and host countries; labour market policies; anti-discriminatory policies.	Supranational bodies have a role to play in regulating the international movement of workers as well as treatment of SIEs in the host country. Host countries receiving migrant labour need to have policies, regulation and support structures that enable inclusion of the SIEs in the new society and the labour market. International and national legislation should tackle discrimination against SIEs. Positive discourse that emphasises the contribution of SIEs to the society and economy needs to be developed.
Meso	Sectoral level: supply and demand for labour and specific skills; practices and policies of responding to self-initiation; traditions of anti-discriminatory policies and practices. Organisational level: demand for international workforce; workforce demographics; HR policies, strategies and practices in talent utilisation, inclusion and integration of diverse workforce; equality and diversity policies and programs.	Sectoral good practices and guidelines can be developed to ensure full utilisation of SIE labour. Organisations need to develop strategies to prevent underemployment of SIEs due to false conceptions and assumptions. Equality and diversity programs are important in raising awareness among employees on the contribution of SIEs and the benefits of internationally diverse workforce. HR policies need to ensure full utilisation of self-initiated worker's talent, their full inclusion in the organisation and their fair treatment.
Micro	Human capital; social networks and support structures; career expectations, aspirations and outcomes; strategies to overcome structural barriers; demographic and cultural diversity.	SIEs need to familiarise themselves with the host-country context and get their education and skills converted or recognised. They need to develop strategies to overcome structural barriers in the host country. These barriers may reside at macro–social, sectoral or organisational levels. Support networks are important in solving bureaucratic issues; in overcoming day-to-day and domestic challenges; gaining awareness of workplace rights; and sharing experience in general.

included and welcome in the new society instead of feeling disempowered, marginalised, excluded and unwanted. Finally, it is crucial to tackle anti-immigrant sentiments in the society, which often arise during the times of economic stagnation or recession. Therefore, it is important that the government and other stakeholders (including employers and trade unions) develop positive discourses that emphasise the contribution of SIEs to the society and economy.

The meso-level of self-initiation includes two sub-levels, within sectors and organisations. Representative bodies and umbrella organisations at the sectoral level have a significant role to play. They may be instrumental in spreading good practice across the sector and in developing guidelines and codes of conduct to ensure that companies use the skills and talent of SIEs to the full. At the organisational level, international HR managers, as the people responsible for the effective management of organisation's human resources, have responsibility in effective management and utilisation of the skills and talent of SIEs. In that context, the international HR managers need to develop strategies to ensure that SIEs are not underemployed because of false conceptions and assumptions. HR policies also need to ensure that SIEs' talents are appropriately used and that the organisation includes SIEs fully and treats them fairly. Equality and diversity programs are particularly important in raising awareness among employees about the contribution of SIEs and the benefits of an internationally diverse workforce.

As we have seen through the discussions and case examples in the chapter, SIEs are a very diverse group in terms of their background, individual circumstances and resources. As a result, SIEs display great diversity in terms of both their career expectations, aspirations and outcomes and their strategies for overcoming barriers they face in the receiving country. Some individual-level practices may also help SIEs to improve their experience of assignments, including the development of strategies for overcoming structural barriers in the host country. These barriers may reside at macro–social, sectoral or organisational levels. For instance, one of the key challenge SIEs face is that their qualifications and skills are not recognised in the new country, which leads them to be underemployed. Before they relocate, SIEs need to familiarise themselves with the host-country context and have their education and skills recognised, or converted to equivalents, in the destination country. Further, support networks are essential in solving bureaucratic issues; overcoming day-to-day and domestic challenges; gaining awareness of workplace rights; and sharing the expatriate experience in general.

■ Take-home messages

- SIEs decide to migrate for a wide range of reasons, including perceived opportunities and constraints in the home and host countries, individual and domestic circumstances and career aspirations.
- An understanding of the context is key to handling the process of self-initiation successfully. The national, sectoral and organisational contexts, and responses to and demands for self-initiation within them, frame the experiences of SIEs.
- Career issues in self-initiation can be complex. SIEs have diverse career experiences and they are also a diverse group, in terms of human capital, age, gender, ethnicity, social class and so on.

■ Closing the learning loop

1. What are the key self-initiation issues and trends at macro-, meso- and micro-levels? Explain with reference to the case studies presented in this chapter.
2. Why do you think people choose to migrate across national borders?
3. In what ways does context affect the experiences of SIEs, considering sectoral, national and international contexts?

4. To what extent can the careers of SIEs be described as 'boundaryless'? Explain your answer.
5. What policy and practice actions may governments and organisations take to improve the process of self-initiation?
6. What kinds of strategy may SIEs employ to overcome potential career obstacles in the host-country context?

›› *ACTIVITIES*

Group discussion

Break into small groups and debate this statement:

Differences between migrants, expatriates and self-expatriates are rarely significant.

Present arguments for and against this proposition.

Small group role-play

SIEs can contribute significantly to both national economic and organisational success. However, there are some barriers to effective and full utilisation of the self-initiated workforce. Below is a list of key actors who may influence the self-initiation process.

Break into small groups and choose an actor to represent from the list below. Each group should discuss effective policy and practice solutions that the actor they represent may put into action to improve the self-initiation process.

- Company owner or shareholder
- Employers' association (e.g. Britain's Confederation of British Industry [CBI])
- Government immigration department
- International HR manager
- Sectoral representative body or umbrella organisation
- SIE interest group
- Supranational or international body (e.g. EU, International Labour Organization, North American Free Trade Agreement, United Nations)
- Trade union

▪ **Online resources**

- For instructors: answers to activities; long media article with questions; additional questions and answers.
- For students: further reading; answers to case studies; IHRM in practice.

References

Acker, J. (2006). Inequality regimes gender, class and race in organizations, *Gender and Society*, 20(4): 441–64.

Al Ariss, A. (2010). Modes of engagement: Migration, self-initiated expatriation and career development, *Career Development International*, 15: 338–58.

Al Ariss, A. and Özbilgin, M. F. (2010). Understanding self-initiated expatriates: Career experiences of Lebanese self-initiated expatriates in France, *Thunderbird International Business Review*, 52: 275–85.

Al Ariss, A., Koall, I., Özbilgin, M. F. and Suutari, V. (2012). Careers of skilled migrants: Towards a theoretical and methodological expansion, *Journal of Management Development*, 31: 92–101.

Al-Nasser, N. A. (2011). Observations about migration in the global economy, International Organization for Migration, 100th Session of the Council meeting, December.

Altman, Y. and Baruch, Y. (2012). Global self-initiated corporate expatriate careers: A new era in international assignments?, *Personnel Review*, 41(2): 233–55.

Aranda, E. (2007). Struggles of incorporation among the Puerto Rican middle class, *Sociological Quarterly*, 48: 199–228.

Arthur, M. B. (1994). The boundaryless career: A new perspective for organizational inquiry, *Journal of Organizational Behavior*, 15: 295–306.

Arthur, M. B., Khapova, S. N. and Wilderom, C. P. M. (2005). Career success in a boundaryless career world, *Journal of Organizational Behavior*, 26: 177–202.

Baruch, Y., Steele, D. J., and Quantrill, G. A. (2002). Management of expatriation and repatriation for novice global player, *International Journal of Manpower*, 23(7): 659–71.

Basavarajappa, K. and Verma, R. B. P. (1990). Occupational composition of immigrant women. In Halli, S. S., Trovato, F. and Driedger, L. (eds), *Ethnic demography: Canadian immigrant, racial and cultural variations*, 297–314. Ottawa: McGill-Queen's University Press.

Becker, K. H. and Haunschild, A. (2003). The impact of boundaryless careers on organizational decision making: An analysis from the perspective of Luhmann's theory of social systems, *International Journal of Human Resource Management*, 14: 713–27.

Bell, M. P., Kwesiga, E. N. and Berry, D. P. (2010). Immigrants: The new 'invisible men and women' in diversity research, *Journal of Managerial Psychology*, 25(2): 177–88.

Berry, D. P. (2011). Organizational form and quality of care in the home health aide industry, doctoral thesis, University of Massachusetts Amherst.

Berry, D. P. and Bell, M. P. (2012). Expatriates: Gender, race and class distinctions in international management, *Gender, Work and Organization*, 19: 10–28.

Brewster, C. and Scullion, H. (2007). A review and agenda for expatriate HRM, *Human Resource Management Journal*, 7(3): 32–41.

Bureau of Labor Statistics (2012). Home health and personal care aides, *Occupational outlook handbook*, 2012–13 edition. United States Department of Labor, www.bls.gov/ooh/healthcare/home-health-and-personal-care-aides.htm. Retrieved 11 November 2012.

Defillippi, R. J. and Arthur, M. B. (1994). The boundaryless career: A competency based perspective, *Journal of Organizational Behavior*, 15: 307–24.

Department of Homeland Security, 2012. *2011 Yearbook of Immigration Statistics*. US Homeland Security Office of Immigration Statistics. www.dhs.gov/sites/default/files/publications/immigration-statistics/yearbook/2011/ois_yb_2011.pdf.

Dresser, L. (2008). Cleaning and caring in the home: shared problems? Shared possibilities? In Bernhardt, A., Boushey, H., Dresser, L. and Tilly, C. (eds), *The gloves-off economy: Workplace standards at the bottom of America's labor market*, 111–35. Champaign, IL: Labor and Employment Relations Association.

Espenshade, T. J. (1995). Unauthorized immigration to the United States, *Annual Review of Sociology*, 21: 195–216.

Esses, V. M., Dovidio, J. F., Jackson, L. M. and Armstrong, T. L. (2001). The immigration dilemma: The role of perceived group competition, ethnic prejudice and national identity, *Journal of Social Issues*, 57: 389–412.

Folbre, N. (1995). 'Holding hands at midnight': The paradox of caring labor, *Feminist Economics*, 1(1): 73–92.

Hardy, B. (1975). *Tellers and listeners: The narrative imagination*. London: Athlone Press.

Hess, C. (2009). IWPR launches new study of women and immigration, *Institute for Women's Policy Research Newsletter*, Winter/Spring, www.iwpr.org/publications/pubs/iwpr-newsletter-winter-spring-2009. Retrieved 11 November 2012.

Inkson, K. (2006). Protean and boundaryless careers as metaphors, *Journal of Vocational Behavior*, 69: 48–63.

International Organization for Migration (IOM) (2010). The role of migrant care workers in aging societies: Report on research findings in the United Kingdom, Ireland, Canada and the United States, MRS 41.

International Organization for Migration (IOM) (2012). Where we work: Americas – regional overview, www.iom.int/cms/en/sites/iom/home/where-we-work/americas.html. Retrieved 12 November 2012.

Jokinen, T., Brewster, C. and Suutari, V. (2008). Career capital during international work experiences: Contrasting self-initiated expatriate experiences and assigned expatriation, *International Journal of Human Resource Management*, 19: 979–98.

Lawler, S. (2008). *Identity: Sociological perspectives*. Cambridge: Polity Press.

Leutz, W. N. (2010). The changing face of long-term care and how a new immigrant workforce will shape its future, *Generations*, 34(4): 89–96.

Lewin Group. (2008). *A synthesis of direct-care service workforce demographics and challenges across intellectual/developmental disabilities, aging, physical disabilities and behavioral health*. Washington, DC: Author.

Oikelome, F. and Healy, G. (2007). Second-class doctors? The impact of a professional career structure on the employment conditions of overseas- and UK-qualified doctors, *Human Resource Management Journal*, 17: 134–54.

Paraprofessional Healthcare Institute (PHI) (2011). *Caring in America: A comprehensive analysis of the nation's fastest-growing jobs – Home health and personal care aides*, http://phinational.org/research-reports/caring-america-comprehensive-analysis-nations-fastest-growing-jobs-home-health-and. Retrieved 12 November 2012.

Parker, P., Arthur, M. B. and Inkson, K. (2004). Career communities: A preliminary exploration of member defined career support structures, *Journal of Organizational Behavior*, 25: 489–514.

Phizacklea, A. (ed.) (1983). *One way ticket: Migration and female labour*. London: Routledge & Kegan Paul Books.

Raijman, R. and Semyonov, M. (1997). Gender, ethnicity and immigration double disadvantage and triple disadvantage among recent immigrant women in the Israeli labor market, *Gender and Society*, 11: 108–25.

Rodrigues, R. A. and Guest, D. (2010). Have careers become boundaryless?, *Human Relations*, 63: 1157.

Schein, E. H. (1971). The individual, the organization and the career: A conceptual scheme, *Journal of Applied Behavioral Science*, 7: 401.

Seak, N. and Enderwick P. (2008). The management of New Zealand expatriates in China, *International Journal of Human Resource Management*, 19: 1298–313.

Sullivan, S. E. and Arthur, M. B. (2006). The evolution of the boundaryless career concept: Examining physical and psychological mobility, *Journal of Vocational Behavior*, 69: 19–29.

Suutari, V. and Brewster, C. (2001). Making their own way: International experience through self-initiated foreign assignments, *Journal of World Business*, 35: 417–36.

Conclusion

*Mustafa F. Özbilgin,
Dimitria Groutsis and William S. Harvey*

The international business context is changing rapidly, driven by international mergers, cross-border alliances and joint ventures, with consequent demands and increased competition for readily available, skilled and qualified labour to staff emergent global business needs. In such a dynamic context, the role of IHRM has grown more important and complex and yet arguably remains undervalued. This book has set out a multilevel framework for recognising, explaining and understanding the important role of HR in an international context, forming an introduction to IHRM for those new to the field.

The contributors have shown how multiple scales of analysis are connected, through the lenses of macro-, meso- and micro-level contexts, and in doing so they have challenged the dominant approaches of the academic literature on IHRM, with its tendency to silo work into a focus on country, region, city, industry, organisation, group or individual. The bulk of the scholarship has largely neglected the role of multiple stakeholder arrangements, with the focus placed almost exclusively on IHRM processes. For example, there has been much emphasis on the context of particular countries and on the perspective of employing organisations, but this has largely neglected prominent literatures around key concepts such as 'boundaryless careers', the 'war for talent', the importance of 'reputation' and new labour market 'intermediaries'. Equally, the electorates of national governments and supranational organisations continue to debate IHRM issues and, accordingly, we find their legislation surrounding the attraction and retention of foreign talent alters through changing immigration and citizenship policies. Such policies affect what types of worker can move into a country and therefore the types of worker international HR managers can access. The examples depicted throughout this book highlight that while it is valuable to understand IHRM in the context of organisations, there are other significant actors who affect and are affected by the attraction, recruitment, retention and development, performance management and reward of international assignees. Finally, the book has also demonstrated the unique regional challenges and opportunities by presenting dedicated discussions of regions and countries, particularly the Asia–Pacific, Europe, Africa and the United States.

To aid readers' navigation through the important and complex role of IHRM in today's era of economic globalisation, we have developed a unique approach which has encouraged consideration of multiple levels of analysis and recognition of how different actors are interconnected. Figure 13.1 demonstrates our emphasis on the significance of, and relationships between, multiple levels of analysis, all of which can make important contributions to our understanding of the multiple dimensions of IHRM.

Every chapter has drawn on this multilevel framework to provide an introduction to the opportunities and challenges associated with managing people in an international and cross-cultural context. Here, we review the contribution of each chapter.

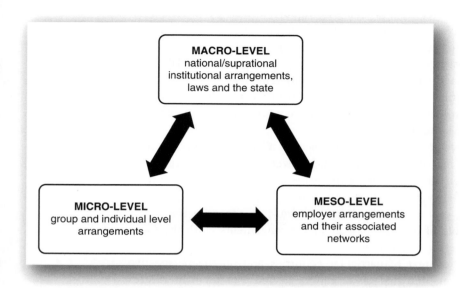

Figure 13.1 The relationships between macro-, meso- and micro-levels

■ Chapter review

■ *Global trends in IHRM*

Chapter 1 provided valuable context to IHRM, including the challenges and opportunities for organisations of managing global and domestic talent. Rofcanin and Zingoni argued that greater international competition, major technological advances, shifts in demographic trends, ebbs and flows in financial circumstances, the growth and decline of organisations, the different stages of international development and greater sensitivity towards workforce diversity, are just a few of the many factors which have heightened the importance of sound HR policies for countries and organisations as a means by which to operationalise and achieve competitive strategy. The authors also argued that talented employees are becoming more proactive in adapting to changing economic circumstances through job crafting, employer negotiations, voicing concerns with their employers and investing in their personal development. Finally, Rofcanin, Imer and Zingoni argued that talented workers are now becoming more engaged with ethical, social and environmentally sustainable issues within their organisations, which relates to Harvey's argument in Chapter 9 concerning the heightened importance of reputation in the context of IHRM.

■ Cross-cultural management and managing cultural diversity

Chapter 2 introduced the well-trodden but poorly understood areas of cross-cultural management, cultural diversity and diversity management strategies and initiatives. Groutsis, Ng and Ozturk argued that understanding these areas is important in the context of attracting and retaining workers from different ethno-cultural and linguistic backgrounds. They also argued that cross-cultural management and the management of cultural diversity are vital for countries and organisations seeking to integrate these internationally mobile stocks of workers. They rightly argued that a 'one size fits all' approach to managing diversity is not appropriate and what may prove effective in one regional setting may be inappropriate in another setting. The authors claimed that current approaches to cross-cultural management and cultural diversity in the context of IHRM have largely been dealt with separately. The result is that scholars of IHRM are given a one-dimensional and at best partial understanding of the challenges of managing, attracting and retaining internationally mobile stocks of skilled workers. They emphasised the need to appreciate the connection between cross-cultural management and diversity management initiatives.

■ Key players in IHRM

Chapter 3 outlined the main actors in the IHRM space. Hollinshead, Forson, Rocha-Lawton and Calveley claimed that many accounts have assumed that individuals within Western institutions have dominated the practice of global organisations. However, they found that individuals from diverse regions are now holding a growing influence with global organisations. As larger pools of talent emerge from countries such as China and India, so have the philosophies, policies and practices of home and host countries as well as multinational companies (MNCs). The authors went beyond the dominant categories of the IHRM literature, including expatriates, host-country nationals (HCNs) and third-country nationals (TCNs). The authors concluded by arguing that the key players in IHRM are diverse in terms of their identities and there is no orderly structure to current trends, but rather contestation, power struggle and misunderstandings. They argued that global organisations will do better if their policies diverge from old-fashioned Western practices and embrace today's more diverse workforce.

■ Recruitment and selection in the international context

Chapter 4 discussed the role of recruitment and selection in the international context. Potočnik, Latorre, Dereli and Tacer extended the analysis set out in chapter 3 by drawing our attention to the breadth of potential employees in the international space. The authors argued that greater analysis of job specifications is needed for organisations to establish exactly what type of workers and skills they need. They contended that a single organisational policy for promoting worker adjustment may not be as effective as a tailored approach, highlighting that international HR managers must go beyond a 'one size fits all' approach to managing international stocks of mobile workers. The authors showed what organisations can do to enable the integration of employees and their families to the new cultural environment, including socialisation programs and HCN mentoring. The authors concluded by arguing that a company incurs high social and economic costs when it does not recruit and select effectively – so, greater investment in sound practices is warranted.

■ *Cross-cultural training and development for overseas assignments*

Chapter 5 argued that the nature of international career management, such as employee orientation, training and development, has altered significantly in recent years. Berber, Rofcanin and Fried stated that employees expect greater levels of flexibility with their work as well as individualised work arrangements and career plans. Employee orientation and training has focused on increasing the task effectiveness and skills of workers, whereas employee development programs are focused on the individual development needs of workers and not necessarily on increasing levels of job efficiency. The authors argued that conducting training and development programs for international assignees should be sensitive to the cultural context. They further claimed that career planning, management and development programs are geared towards enabling employees to make the best career choices in different country and cultural contexts, matching the skills of employees with the requirements of the company.

■ *International reward*

Chapter 6 built on the foundations of international rewards and demonstrated the diversity and complexity of international reward practices in MNCs. Jenkins argued that a number of effective approaches can be applied and it is important to consider the value for organisations of international assignees working abroad, and hence the potential consequences if they are not rewarded appropriately to their expectations. Cross-country reward practices are valuable for practitioners and students of international reward to reflect on what constitutes good practice in particular contexts; value and recognise international assignees; and evaluate the challenges involved in the process of reward, including coordinating financial and non-financial components and international tax arrangements. Organisations can use this to help them critically reflect on the nature and meaning of their reward practices and amend their reward systems accordingly.

■ *Employee retention*

Chapter 7 focused on the value for organisations of retaining workers. Balta argued that organisations are able to retain workers through various strategies including job satisfaction, motivation, competitive remuneration packages as well as the provision of training and development opportunities. Job satisfaction and motivation can be promoted through providing employees with autonomy, clear task requirements and organisational policies, professional interaction as well as a positive status associated with their role. Competitive remuneration is important for attracting talented workers in the first place as well as retaining them, and it is an important means of satisfying and motivating local and global talent. Good working conditions as well as training and development opportunities are other important methods for retaining talent because they enable workers to feel satisfied with their physical surroundings and content with the level of opportunities to invest in new skills. This is particularly important in the international context because some skills which are relevant in certain contexts may not be relevant in other contexts. The increasing global and national surveys on employers of choice means that organisations need to ensure that they keep up to date with the needs of their existing and future employees to both attract and retain them.

■ *International labour relations*

Chapter 8 argued that international labour relations operate through multi-actor and multilevel arrangements. Özbilgin found that there has been a historical transformation of labour relations in the international context, with examples of increases and decreases in labour activity. There are clear demonstrations of growing struggles for power and influence over standards of labour as well as the terms and conditions of work. Although labour standards are often defined at a global level, they are interpreted and enacted at a local level, meaning that such global standards continue to be aspirational and highly contested. This reinforces the role of the macro-, meso- and micro-levels of analysis in international labour relations, with respect to how different actors create, change, implement and monitor particular standards. Özbilgin concluded by arguing that there are three different approaches to adopting international standards: principled, solidaristic and voluntary.

■ *Reputation in the context of IHRM*

Chapter 9 introduced the important emerging field of reputation, which is a collective assessment of an institution, organisation, group or individual compared to its competitors. Harvey argued that reputation is significant for different stakeholders because, while it is an intangible asset, it can also provide tangible results, both positive and negative. For example, an organisation with a positive reputation compared to its competitors will better enable it to attract and retain workers compared to its less reputable competitors. Potential and existing employees are becoming increasingly concerned with the reputation of organisations, including its leaders, hence reputation is an important HR domain for organisations to focus their attention, particularly at a time when there is an international 'war for talent'. Finally, Harvey argued that because so much talent is moving across international borders, it is not only the reputation of organisations and their leaders, but also the reputation of countries, regions and cities, which may determine where they decide to move.

In short, reputation is a multifaceted phenomenon that is becoming more widespread and significant for individuals, organisations, cities and countries. As such, the chapter provided scholars of IHRM with a new and important consideration in facilitating the attraction and retention of a talented workforce, who are increasingly aware of and influenced by reputation.

■ *Expatriation and repatriation in the Asia–Pacific region*

Chapter 10 focused on the theoretical and empirical issues related to the mobility of talent to, from and within the Asia–Pacific region. Caven, Kirk and Wang-Cowham argued that macro-, meso- and micro-level push/pull factors affect the management of globally mobile talent within and between Asia–Pacific countries. They raised the major issues that affect expatriation and repatriation across the region, including various contextual factors that constrain and enable mobility. The chapter summarised the various approaches to global mobility from the perspective of talented individuals as well as employers. Finally, the authors provided valuable insights for the IHRM scholar by focusing on mobility in the region and emphasising the value of understanding various cultural, economic, political and social contexts.

■ *Balancing inflows and outflows in the European context*

Chapter 11 argued that understanding international migration has been understood differently across academic disciplines and through the use of many theoretical approaches, frameworks and levels of analysis. Vassilopoulou, Samaluk and Seierstad argued that there are many types of migrant, some of whom move permanently while others move temporarily. The rights of migrants also vary depending on the country, historical and labour market context as well as the category of migrant moving to a host country. In contrast to the EU, the authors highlight that national policies are often guided by international guidelines, but this does not necessarily translate into consistent policies across countries. The experiences of migrants therefore will vary according to these policies, which will vary over different time periods. The authors argued that IHRM practices need to account for the varying experiences of migrants to ensure that the needs of talented workers are addressed.

■ *Self-initiated repatriation: case study lessons from Africa and the United States*

Chapter 12 began by defining and critically assessing what is meant by self-initiated expatriation, particularly compared to other groups such as migrants and expatriates. Tatli, Berry, Ipek and April identified multiple factors that determine whether and why people migrate, examining points such as global economic needs, employment opportunities, the functional requirements of MNCs, professional and social interests and the wishes of individuals. The authors presented two case studies from Africa and one from the United States to demonstrate the broad range of factors that can affect international mobility, and emphasised some of the major challenges that people can experience when moving across international borders, including the sociopolitical environment, economic context and sector- and industry- specific needs and demands.

▪ Closing words

Throughout this book, the authors have deliberately developed the discussion beyond the traditional and well-trodden sources of staff in IHRM, including: expatriate, HCNs and TCNs, extending the categories to also consider the importance of the skilled migrant and/or self-initiated expatriate. While the latter have not been a traditional source of labour for organisations, they have increasingly come to play a significant role in staffing international business concerns as organisations continue to expand their customer base, operations and supply chains internationally. In addition, countries and companies around the world are caught in an international tussle to attract and retain skilled and qualified workers, at the same time that these individuals are seeking to move abroad for work and lifestyle reasons, often independently of organisational secondments and intra-firm transfers. While in the past many skilled workers were moving from Western countries such as the US and the UK, we are experiencing a much greater diversity of international mobility from a broader range of countries, including emerging economies, as well as a growing number of women, dual career couples and younger workers moving for work purposes. In short, there has been a rise in the diversity of international mobility which has opened-up opportunities and challenges for host and home countries, institutions, organisations as well as for those individuals who are moving.

■ Index

Accession 2 (A2) countries 202
Accession 8 (A8) countries
    inclusion in EU 195
    and UK immigration policy 201–3
achievement 133
agency
    and career development of highly skilled
        migrants 206
    defining of social spaces 57
    definition 57, 205
    and individuals' migratory experiences
        205–6
Aglionby, case study 181, 189
alignment 114
Apple 168
Asia–Pacific region
    challenge of labour management 180
    definition 180
    factors influencing global talent flows
        182–3
    push/pull factors 183–6
    repatriation 186–7
    staffing 186
    talent flows 181
assertiveness 33
assessment centres (ACs) 79, 80
autonomy 132

Bangalore, information technology cluster
    173
basic pay 110–11
BBC 173
benefits
    definition 137
    and employee retention 137–8
    for overseas assignees 111–12
bicultural engagement 52–3
biculturals 52
Boots, case study 141–2
boundary spanning 49
boundaryless career paradigm 227
boundaryless careers 13–14, 171
brain circulation 181
brain drain 181, 200–1
brain gain 181, 201
Branson, Richard 169
British Petroleum (BP) 168
business case for diversity 29

career development 138–9
case studies
    Aglionby expands in the Asia–Pacific 189
    Boots 141–2
    career journey in South Africa 228–9
    career in textile design 102–3
    Chengdu Construction Industry 189
    death of Ahmet Yildiz 161
    Digifor faces labour shortages 206, 207–8
    expatriate adjustment in India 38–40
    female SIEs and in-home care in US
        225–6
    international labour standards 161–2
    Krewe Marketing 17
    Marikana massacre 161–2
    Mercator Group 85–6
    mineral mining in a developing country 175
    R & D Discovery China 59
    reluctance to relocation 122–3
    self-initiation in Africa 220–2
celebrity CEOs 169
celebrity firms 169
Chengdu Construction Industry, case study
    189
Chile, technology talent 172
Civil Society Organisations (CSOs) 155
coercive comparisons 57, 58
competitive advantage, and corporate
    reputation 168
completion 132
conformance 114
contract expatriates 51
corporate expatriation 215
corporate mandates 49
corporate reputation
    as an intangible asset 167
    and celebrity CEOs 169
    celebrity firms 169
    and competitive advantage 168
    consequences of positive and negative
        reputations 168
    consistency over time 169
    context 166
    definition and nature of 166
    importance of 167–9
    international assignees and skilled migrants
        171–3
    and labour market reputation 170–1
    multilevel approach to 166–7
    negative reputations 168
    role among employees 170–1
    role of employees 171
    role of intermediaries 173
    and status 169
corporate strategy
    adaptive orientation 116
    alignment of reward system 114
    exportive orientation 115
cross-cultural adjustment 36
    see also cultural adjustment

cross-cultural diversity management
  cultural dimensions 30–4
  macro-level dimensions 29
  meso- and micro-level dimensions 34–6
  multilevel approach 29
cross-cultural management
  business case 26–8
  definition 24
  overview 24–6
cross-cultural models 29
cross-cultural socialisation 96
cross-cultural training, definition 94
cross-cultural training and development
    97–100
cross-cultural training and development
    programs
  differing needs of inpatriates and
    expatriates 95–6
  during early arrival period 99–100
  in latter stages of arrival phase 100
  need for 94
  in pre-departure period 98–9
cultural adaptation, definition 77, 95
cultural adjustment
  capacity for 76–7
  conformist stage 100
  cross-cultural adjustment phase 100
  culture shock phase 99–100
  ethnocentric phase 98–9
  expatriate adjustment in India 38–40
  facilitation by HR practices and policies
    71–4
  individual factors 83
  phases of 98
cultural carriers 49–50
cultural dimensions
  country clusters 33
  criticisms of Hofstede and GLOBE Project
    32–4
  cross-cultural diversity management 30–4
  GLOBE Project 31–2
  Hofstede's six cultural dimensions 30–1
  Japan compared to US 31
  ranking of national cultures 33
  UK compared to Malaysia 32
cultural distance 25
cultural and linguistic diversity, and diversity
    management 35–6
cultural values 11
culture, defining 28–9
culture shock
  definition 95
  management of 99–100

demography, changes in workforce
    demographics 11–12

diversity, and international mobility 53–6
diversity management
  at workplace level 36
  cultural and linguistic diversity 35–6
  definition 27
diversity management policy 27
domestic migration 199
Domino's Pizza 171
dragon companies, definition 9
dual-career perspective 77

economic environment, trends in 8–9
economic migration 199, 215
emerging multinational companies (EMNCs)
  definition 10
  and FDI flow 9
emic model 29
emigration 199, 200
employee proactivity 14–15
employee retention
  Boots case study 141–2
  causal model for turnover 134
  and cross-cultural adjustment 36
  definition 25, 129
  importance 130
  and inpatriation 139
  and job satisfaction 132–6
  as major issue for organisations 129
  management 130–1
  and nationalisation 139
  nature of 129–30
  as a priority for organisations 129
  recruiting and training valuable staff 131–2
  and remuneration and benefits 137–8
  and repatriation 139
  strategies 136–40
  and teamwork 130
  training and development interventions
    138–9
  and working environment and conditions
    136–7
employee turnover
  causal model 134
  and job satisfaction 135–6
employment agencies, and A8 labour in UK
    206, 207–8
employment contracts, changing nature
    14–15
ethnocentric companies 10
ethnocentric organisations
  definition 115
  reward system 115
ethnocentrism, definition 8, 48
etic model 29
European Union (EU)
  Accession 2 (A2) countries 202

European Union (EU) (cont.)
Accession 8 (A8) countries 195
'four freedoms' 202
internal migration 196–7
labour standards 157
regulations covering A8 workers 202
expatriates ('expats')
characterisation 48
contract expatriates 51
as cultural carriers 49–50
definition 49, 95
differences from inpatriates 95
from less developed countries 205
reward systems 118–20
expatriation
alternatives to 50–3
corporate expatriation 215
definition 11, 180
female participation 53–5
increase in 10–11, 49
major purposes 50
strategic significance 50
experience, as selection criterion 78
exportive strategic orientation 115
external equity, reward systems 113–14
external recruitment
definition 75
of parent-country nationals 75–6
extrinsic rewards 109, 137, 138

family and couple adjustment 82
family situation, as selection criterion 77
financial benefits 138
see also benefits
financial environment, trends in 8–9
flexipatriates
advantages and disadvantages of 70
definition 71
tasks 70
floor of rights 112
focal firms 8
foreign direct investment (FDI)
definition 9, 10
and emerging multinational companies 9
foreign postings 48
franchising 9
fringe benefits 111–12
future orientation 33

gender egalitarianism 33
Generation X, definition 12
Generation Y, definition 12
geocentric organisations, reward systems 117
geocentrism 8, 49
Germany, recognition of qualifications of
skilled migrants 198

global commodity changes (GCCs) 56
global companies, definition 9
global compensation strategy 117
global financial crises 9
global mindset 24
global reward strategy 117
Global Unions 154
global value chains (GVCs) 56–7
global virtual team members
advantages and disadvantages of 71
definition 71
tasks 71
globalisation, definition 7
GLOBE Project
country clusters 33
criticisms of 32–4
cultural dimensions 31–2
glopatriates ('glo-pats') 187
Goldman Sachs 171
Google 169

Hofstede's six cultural dimensions 30–1
comparison of Japan and US 31
comparison of Malaysia and UK 32
criticisms of 32–4
ranking of national cultures 33
home country 7
host country 7
host-country nationals (HCNs)
advantages and disadvantages 51–2, 69,
186
in Asia–Pacific region 186
definition 8
international recruitment 76
support for parent-country nationals
(PCNs) 82
human agency *see* agency
human capital theory 198
human resource consultancies, cooperation
with 80
human resource management (HRM)
definition 7
differences from IHRM 7
human resource professionals, competencies
for international recruitment and
selection 71–4
humane orientation 33

idiosyncratic deals (i-deals) 15
immigrants *see* migrants
immigration 199, 200
in-group collectivism 33
India, case studies of expatriate adjustment
38–40
individualism (IDV) 30
indulgence orientation (IO) 31

inpatriates ('inpats')
  as biculturals 52
  definition 52, 95
  differences from expatriates 95
  socialisation process 97
inpatriation, and employee retention 139
institutional collectivism 33
intermediaries, and corporate
    reputation 173
internal equity, reward systems 113
internal migration, in European Union
    196–7
internal recruitment
  definition 75
  of parent-country nationals 75–6
international assignees
  attraction to and influence on reputation
    171–3
  definition 172
  and international labour standards 158–9
  phases of cultural adjustment 98
  reward systems for expatriates 118–20
  training following arrival 99–100
  training in pre-departure period 98–9
  types 51
international assignments
  expatriates and inpatriates 95–6
  socialisation process for 97
international business travellers
  advantages and disadvantages of 71
  definition 71
  tasks 71
international careers, nature of 13–14
international commuters 51
international companies
  nature of 7
  staffing 10–11
international division of labour 56–7
international employees
  alternative contemporary types 70–1
  categories of 69–71
international human resource management
    (IHMR)
  definition 2
  differences from HRM 7
  interplay of levels 3
  macro-level concerns 2
  meso-level concerns 2
  micro-level concerns 3
  multilevel approach 2
  nature of 7
  study of 2
international human resource management
    (IHMR) process
  key aspects 7–8
  use of technology 12–13

international human resource managers,
    implications of international labour
    standards 159
International Labour and Employment
    Relations Association (ILERA) 154
International Labour Organization (ILO)
  conventions on labour standards 113, 153
  establishment, aims and functions 153
international labour relations (ILR)
  definition 149
  historical context 149–50
  macro-level stakeholders 153–4
  micro-level stakeholders 155
  multilevel model 152–6
  multilevel model, stakeholders and focus
    156
  study of 149
international labour standards (ILS)
  case studies 161–2
  compliance issues 151–2
  definition and nature of 151
  enforcement of compliance 156–7
  implications for international assignees
    158–9
  implications for international HR managers
    159
  key actors in debates 151
  meso-level stakeholders 154–5
  principled approach 156–7
  rational institutional approach 152
  reasons for adoption 152, 156–8
  sociological institutional approach 152
  solidarity approach 157
  voluntary approach 158
International Lesbian, Gay, Bisexual, Trans
    and Intersex Association (ILGA) 155
international migration 198, 199, 215
international mobility
  and diversity 53–6
  self-initiated expatriation, migration and
    ethnicity 55–6
  skill levels of individuals 56
  women 53–5
international organisations, key actors 49–50
international recruitment and selection
  advantages and disadvantages of using
    categories of employees 69
  approaches 69–71
  challenges 68
  competence profile for recruitment and
    selection managers 73–4
  and corporate reputation 170–1
  costs of failure 83, 94
  determining competencies of HR
    professionals 71–4
  ethnocentric approach 69

international recruitment and selection (cont.)
  evaluation of process 81–3
  four-stage process model 72
  geocentric approach 69
  indicators of success 82–3
  planning 68
  polycentric approach 69
  process model 71–83
  recruitment 74–6
  regiocentric approach 69
  selection 76–81
  and stage of internationalisation 72–3
international selection
  final selection decision and job offer 81
  issues in selection methods 80–1
  selection criteria 76–9, 94
  selection methods 79–80
  self-selection tools 80–1
International Trade Union Confederation (ITUC) 153–4
international transferrees 51
internationalised companies, growth of 9–10
interviews 79
intrinsic rewards 109, 138

Japan, cultural dimensions compared to US 31
Job Descriptive Index (JDI) 133–4
job satisfaction
  defining 133–4
  definition 130
  and employee retention 132–6
  and employee turnover intention 135–6
  measuring 133–4
  and organisational commitment 134–5
  and pay 133
  and promotion 133
job status and recognition 132
jobs, changing nature 14
joint ventures 9

Krewe Marketing, case study 17

labour market reputation 170–1
labour market transformation, and migration 203–5
labour relations
  differences in laws and practices 13
  see also international labour relations
labour shortages, Digifor case study 206, 207–8
labour standards, international context 151
Lee Hsien Loong 172
legal environment, migration laws 201–2
licensing 9

linguistic ability, as selection criteria 77
long-term orientation (LTO) 31
low-skilled migrants 202

McKinsey & Company 168
macro-level migration theories 195
Malaysia, cultural dimensions compared to UK 32
mandates 49
Marikana massacre 161–2
masculine cultures 81
masculinity (MAS), cultural dimension 30
Mercator Group, case study 85–6
meso-level migration theories 195
micro-level migration theories 195
micro-politics 57, 58
migrant labour, and skills shortages 203–4
migrants
  agency in migratory experiences 205–6
  definition 51, 55
  nature of migratory experience 204–5
  use of term 205
migration
  definitions 215–16
  economic migration 199, 215
  internal migration 196–7
  and labour market transformation 203–5
  macro-level causes 196–7
  push/pull factors 172–3, 182–3
  push/pull model 185
  push/pull process 196–7
  spatial dimensions 199
  transnational migration 198–9
  types and implications for IHRM 199–201
migration law, national and international requirements 201–2
migration theory
  approaches 196
  human capital theory 198
  levels 195–6
  macro-level 195–6, 197–8
  meso-level 195, 196, 198
  micro-level 195, 196
  micro-level analysis of push/pull process 197, 198
  and neoclassical economic theory 197, 198
  overview 196–9
  segmented labour market theory 197
  social capital theory 198
  world systems theory 197–8
migratory experiences
  and agency of migrants 205–6
  understanding nature of 204–5
mining, case study in developing country 175

multinational companies (MNCs)
conceptual departures and notions of social spaces 56–7
governance systems 57
nature of 7, 48

nationalisation, and employee retention 139
neoclassical economic theory, and migration theory 197, 198
net migration 199
North American Free Trade Agreement (NAFTA) 158

offshoring 11
Olympus 171
organisational career paradigm 227
organisational commitment
definition 134
and job satisfaction 134–5
organisational cultures
components 34–5
and nature of business arrangement 35
overseas assignees *see* international assignees
overseas assignments *see* international assignments

parent-country nationals (PCNs)
advantages and disadvantages 69, 186
in Asia–Pacific region 186
definition 8
external recruitment 75–6
international recruitment 75–6
performance orientation 33
person–organisation fit 79
personal growth 132
personality traits, as selection criterion 78
Poland, brain drain 200
polycentric companies 10
polycentrism 8, 49
power distance 33
power distance index (PDI) 30
proactive employee efforts 15
promotion, and job satisfaction 133
psychometric tests 79
push/pull factors
in Asia–Pacific region 183–6
operation of 172–3
push/pull model, organisational perspective 185
push/pull process, micro-level analysis of 197

R & D Discovery China, case study 59
Ravenstein, Ernest 196, 197
recruitment
definition 68

see also external recruitment, internal recruitment, international recruitment and selection
recruitment practices 74–6
recruitment and training 129
regiocentric companies 10
regiocentric organisations, reward systems 117
regiocentrism 8
relational job design 14
relational rewards 109, 110
relocation, case study of reluctance 122–3
remuneration
definition 137
employee retention 137–8
repatriation
in Asia–Pacific region 186–7
definition 14, 180
and employee retention 139
reputation *see* corporate reputation
retention *see* employee retention
returnees 52
reverse brain drain 52
reward system design
alignment with corporate strategy 114
approaches reflecting alignment and conformance 115–18
balance-sheet approach to expatriate rewards 119–20
expatriate role and international assignments 118–20
external equity 113–14
federal approach 116–17
global reward strategy 117
going-rate approach to expatriate rewards 120
hybrid approaches 117–18
imperial approach 115–16
internal equity 113
legal compliance 112–13
macro-level implications and concerns 112–13
meso-level implications and concerns 113–18
micro-level implications and concerns 118–20
reward systems
basic pay 110–11
benefits 111–12
classification of rewards 109
and employee retention 137–8
goals 109
key elements 110
'new pay' approach 109
variable pay 109, 111

salary and wages 130
  basic pay 110–11
  and employee retention 137–8
  and job satisfaction 133
  'new pay' 109
  variable pay 109, 111
segmented labour market theory 197
selection
  definition 68
  see also international recruitment and
    selection, international selection
self-initiated careers
  boundaryless career paradigm 227
  challenges of 226–9
  complexity of 227–8
self-initiated expatriates (SIEs)
  advantages and disadvantages 69
  careers 215, 226–9
  definition 11, 26, 55, 68, 199
  management of diversity 26
  reasons for migration 215, 218–22
self-initiated expatriation
  in Africa 220–2
  contextual influences 215, 222–6
  definition 215–16
  focus of studies 55–6
  migration and ethnicity 55–6
  multilevel framework 217
  as multilevel phenomenon 216–18
  policy and practice recommendations 230
self-initiated migration, and care work in US
    223–6
Shea, Nicholás 172
short-term assignees
  advantages and disadvantages of 70
  definition 11, 71
  tasks 70
Silicon Valley 173, 181
Singapore, foreign workers 172
skilled migrants (SMs)
  advantages and disadvantages of
    recruiting 69
  attraction to and influence on reputation
    171–3
  definition 26, 68, 172
  management of diversity 26
  push/pull factors 172–3
  recognition of qualifications 198
skills shortages, and migrant labour 203–4
Smith, Greg 171
Social Accountability International 158
social capital theory 198
social spaces 57
soft skills 78
South Africa, case study of career journey
    228–9

South Korea, Indian workers 172
spatial dimensions of migration 199
staffing
  international organisations 10–11
  strategies in Asia–Pacific region 186
Start-Up Chile 172
status 169
strategic human resource management 7
subcontracting 9

talent flows
  in Asia–Pacific region 181
  definition 181
  triangular talent flows 181
teamwork, and employee retention 130
technical competencies, as selection criterion
    79
technological improvements, impact of
    12–13
temporary migration 200
tests, as selection method 79
textile design career, case study 102–3
third country, definition 7
third-country nationals (TCNs)
  advantages and disadvantages of recruiting
    52, 69, 186
  in Asia–Pacific region 186
  definition 8
  international recruitment 76
Toyota 169
trade sanctions 156–7
trade unions 153–4
trailing spouses 54
training and development, and employee
    retention 138–9
transactional rewards 109, 110
transnational companies (TNCs) 9
transnational migrants 198–9
transnational migration 198–9
transnationalism 198–9
transpatriates 120

uncertainty avoidance 33
uncertainty avoidance index (UAI) 30
United Kingdom
  cultural dimensions compared to Malaysia
    32
  employment agencies and A8 labour 206,
    207–8
  inclusion of A8 labour in migration policy
    195, 201–3
  stereotyping of A8 workers 203
United States
  care work and self-initiated migration
    223–6
  categorisation of immigrants 223

contextual influences on self-initiation
222–6
cultural dimensions compared to
Japan 31

variable pay 109, 111
virtual international employees 51

Welch, Jack 169
Woodford, Michael 171
work design, changing nature 14
Worker Registration Scheme (WRS) 202

workforce diversity
definition 12
impact of 12
working environment and conditions, and
employee retention 136–7
world systems theory 197–8
World Trade Organization (WTO) 153

Yildaz, Ahmet, death of 161

Zhongguancun high-technology region
(Beijing) 173